P. F. M. FONTAINE

THE LIGHT
AND
THE DARK

A CULTURAL HISTORY OF DUALISM
VOLUME III

J.C. GIEBEN, PUBLISHER
AMSTERDAM

THE LIGHT AND THE DARK

P.F.M. FONTAINE

THE LIGHT AND THE DARK

A CULTURAL HISTORY OF DUALISM

VOLUME III

DUALISM IN GREEK LITERATURE AND PHILOSOPHY
IN THE FIFTH AND FOURTH CENTURIES B.C.

J.C. GIEBEN, PUBLISHER
AMSTERDAM 1988

To my daughter Resianne,
philosopher and semitologist,
and her husband, my son-in-law Meinard,
bookseller and lover of books

No part of this book may be translated or reproduced in any form, by print, photoprint, microfilm, or any other means, without written permission from the publisher.

© by P.F.M. Fontaine / ISBN 90 5063 020 0 / Printed in The Netherlands

"For all things are called light and darkness"

Parmenides

CONTENTS

Preface	xi
I TRAGICA AND COMICA	1
1. The two bloodlines	1
2. The 'Thebes'-group of tragedies	2
3. The 'Troy'-group of tragedies	4
a. A curse on the House of Atreus	4
b. Iphigeneia's sad fate	5
c. Odysseus' wiles	5
d. The last days of Troy	6
e. Helen phantom or reality?	7
f. Family life	8
4. How difficult it is to live	10
5. How difficult it is to live with the gods	12
a. Euripides the 'atheist'	12
b. Euripides and the soothsayers' lore	14
c. Ridiculing the gods	16
d. The wrath of the gods	17
e. The immorality of the gods	18
f. Religion irrational?	20
g. Doubts in Sophocles	24
h. Aeschylus and his 'Prometheus'	25
i. Prometheus the rebel	26
j. Interpretations	29
k. Prometheus' foresight	31
6. How difficult it is to live en famille	32
a. The conflict between the sexes	32
b. Death as a partner	35
c. The wild force of sexuality	37
d. The real 'blood-guilt'	39
e. A case of pseudo-incest	41
f. Brothers and sisters	41
g. 'Why women?'	43
7. Women in comedy	47
a. Aristophanes: the man and his work	47

b. A man in a female assembly	49
c. The reversal of the sex-roles	50
d. The rebellion of the women	52
8. The tragical phenomenon	54
a. The three great tragedians	54
b. An exceptional cultural phenomenon	55
c. The Athenian theatre public	56
d. The origination of tragedy	57
e. Why only in Greece?	59
f. Hellas' 'Day of Atonement'	61
g. Aristotle on tragedy	62
h. Oppositions in tragedy	64
i. Tragedy the last word?	66
j. Two contradictory versions of life	68
k. Tragedy and Olympian religion	69
l. A question of guilt	71
m. Victorious necessity	73
n. Tragedy and Gnostic dualism	74
Notes to Chapter I	76
II SOPHISTICA AND SOCRATICA	84
1. Sophism	84
a. What is Sophism?	84
b. Some famous Sophists	86
2. The attack on the gods	88
a. Protagoras' agnosticism	88
b. Prodicus' atheism	88
c. Critias and the invention of religion	89
d. Diagoras	91
3. General relativism	91
a. Gorgias on non being	92
b. Protagoras' phenomenalism	95
c. Radicalization	97
d. The bankruptcy of philosophy	97
4. Greek nominalism	98
5. The dualism of nomos and physis	100
6. Socrates: the man	104
a. His life and death	104
b. Which Socrates was the historic one?	106
7. Socrates' 'daimonion'	108

8. Socratic knowledge	110
9. The right word for the right concept	112
a. The Socratic doctrine of definitions	112
b. The 'basic aspect'	113
Notes to Chapter II	115
III PLATONICA AND ARISTOTELICA	119
1. Plato: the man and his work	119
a. His life	119
b. The 'Corpus Platonicum'	120
c. Why the dialogue form?	122
2. From Socrates to Plato	124
3. The open and the closed society	125
4. Philosophy and knowledge	128
5. Can excellence be learned?	129
6. The doctrine of the soul	130
7. The first blossoming of Plato's great ideas	132
8. The doctrine of the soul further developed	132
9. The parts of the soul	135
a. The parable of the two horses	135
b. The threepartite soul	136
c. Platonic love	137
10. The rebirth of the soul	138
11. The doctrine of Forms	140
a. The essence of things	140
b. The Good and the godhead	142
c. Between being and non-being	143
12. Plato's terms for knowledge	145
13. Plato's dualistic scheme of knowledge	147
14. Plato's threedimensional state	149
a. Plato's threepartite society	150
b. Women in Platonic society	151
c. The rulers	153
d. The great mass of the people	153
e. Philosophers and non-philosophers	155
15. Plato's later works	156
16. Criticism of the doctrine of the Forms	156
17. The One and the Many	158
a. Can the Many exist without the One?	158
b. A personal problem for Plato	160

18. Plato's criticism of his ideal state 161
   a. The second-best state 161
   b. The 'guardians of the law' 162
   c. How free are Plato's 'free people'? 164
   d. Dualistic distinctions 165
19. One world or two? 167
   a. A 'vitium originis' in the cosmos 167
   b. The world-soul and the human soul 169
   c. The dualism of Demiurge and cosmos 171
20. Was Plato a dualist? 173
   a. Plato's concept of God 173
   b. Guthrie on Plato's 'archai' 175
   c. De Vogel on Plato's dualism 176
   d. De Vogel on Plato's 'archai' 177
21. Plato's dualistic oppositions 180
22. Plato's dualistic mentality 181
23. Aristotle: the man and his work 182
24. Aristotle and the oppositions in social life 184
   a. Woman as an incomplete being 184
   b. The superiority of the male 186
   c. Aristotle on barbarians and slaves 187
25. A dualistic element in Aristotle's psychology 189
   a. The composite soul 189
   b. Aristotle drifting towards dualism 190
   c. The pre-existent nous 192
26. The question of the first principles 194
   a. Form and matter, the great 'archai' of Aristotle 194
   b. What is Being? 196
27. The Unmoved Mover 198
   a. The bipartition of the cosmos 198
   b. The separation of god and world 199
Notes to Chapter III 201

Bibliography 213
General Index 221

PREFACE

In this country the summer of 1987 was cool, windy and exasperatingly wet. As a consequence my wife and I could not go as often as usual on our beloved bicycle tours. Instead I sat at my writing-desk and typed. In thirty-nine working-days between July 20 and September 5 I translated the whole of the original Dutch version of this volume into English. Then I sent instalment after instalment to my incomparable corrector, Dr. J.R.Dove, who was busy disclosing the secrets of English and American literature to bright young students at the University of Oulu in Finland. He worked more rapidly than ever; hardly had I typed a corrected instalment in the definitive camera-ready version, or another batch arrived. Dr. Dove modestly dubs his corrections 'suggestions' but I need not say expressly that I worked them carefully into my text. As always I feel deeply indebted to him. As a result of his speed the bulk of the book - the three chapters with their notes - was completed before Christmas. The rest was added between Christmas and New Year's Day.

Looking back to January 1986, when I started to translate Volume I, I don't comprehend where I found the courage to tackle that enormous pile of pages A-4 containing the Dutch typescript of Volumes I, II and III. One of my devices was not to count all those pages but simply to begin at the top. By dint of persevering I finally reached the bottom - with a deep sigh of relief. Henceforward I intend to write directly in English, in order to avoid the long detour over my beloved but to this end clearly unusable vernacular. For although Dutch is spoken by twenty million people in the Netherlands and Belgium, and read and understood by millions of South Africans, this is not sufficient to satisfy the commercial instincts of Dutch publishers.

This book is, in fact, the continuation of Volume II. It comprises the same period, the great classical age of Greece, but its preoccupations are different. These are Greek literature, mainly tragedy, and philosophy, mainly Plato, in the fifth and fourth centuries B.C. Volume III may be read independently of Volumes I and II without problems, but I think the reader would profit more if he or she read Volume II first. The definition of dualism employed throughout this work is the same as that used in the foregoing volumes. Dualism denotes the existence of two utterly opposed conceptions, systems, principles, groups of people, or even worlds, without any intermediate link between them. They cannot be reduced to one another; in some cases they are not even dependent on each other. The opposites are considered to be of a different quality - so much so that one of them is seen as distinctly inferior and hence must be repudiated or even destroyed.

Dualism is a rather intricate concept; it is possible to define it more subtly by creating a number of subdivisions. For this I may refer the interested reader to the afterword of Volume I. One of these subdivisions occurs in this volume too, that of radical (or absolute) and relative dualism. In radical dualism the two principles or worlds are absolutely coeval, they are both from eternity, and there is no interdependence whatsoever between them. In relative dualism the two systems or groups of people are dependent on each other. However strongly opposed they may be, they can, nevertheless, not do without each other. (I am quoting myself verbatim from the preface of Volume II.)

A considerable time ago already my wife Anneke had already corrected the typescript of the original Dutch version. Patiently as ever she did the same for the definitive English version. Or not exactly the same, for this being a camera-ready typescript, she had to paste little slips of paper with the correction of typing errors very precisely into the text. Since she likes literature she got on very well with Chapter I but having 'no head for philosophy', as she says herself, she had to plod her way through Chapters II and III. This she did bravely; it is an additional reason to be very grateful to her.

Besides Dr. Dove (who is not only a corrector but also a valuable adviser), there are two other 'general readers' of the text. The first is my daughter Resianne who supplied me with useful comment, in spite of the fact that she was busy enough with husband, children, and the preparation of a doctoral thesis of her own. The second was, as usual, Dr. A.Budé, a classical scholar, to whom I owe a great number of important criticisms. Both of them deserve my deep gratitude.

The three chapters of this book, in the Dutch version, were read and commented upon by two experts in these fields. Chapter I was perused by Dr. J.Nuchelmans, emeritus professor of Greek literature at the Catholic University of Nijmegen; Chapters II and III were read by Dr. M.F.Fresco, professor of philosophical anthropology and the foundations of humanism at Leyden State University. Both of them complied readily with my wish, although they have no lack of work. I owe much to their critical comments; I feel thankful to them too. Finally, the collaboration with Mr. Gieben, the publisher, went as smoothly as ever.

I wish to stress that the sole responsibility for this work rests with me, not only with respect to its contents but also regarding the translation and the typography. Chapter I was written in the second half year of 1984, Chapters II and III in the first months of 1985. This series will be continued with a volume on dualism in the Ancient Near East.

Piet F.M.Fontaine
Amsterdam NL

CHAPTER I

TRAGICA AND COMICA

1. The two bloodlines

Of the thirty-two tragedies of the three great Attic playwrights, Aeschylus, Sophocles, and Euripides, twenty-three may be grouped under two headings : Thebes and Troy. The other nine do not come under these heads, although they may include related subject matter. Eight plays come under the heading 'Thebes', one by Aeschylus, three by Sophocles, and four by Euripides; fifteen must be classified under 'Troy', three by Aeschylus, three by Sophocles, and nine by Euripides. We must, of course, be mindful of the fact that only a small part of all the tragedies has been handed down to us; the greatest number of the surviving plays are those by Euripides. I do not intend to pay attention to problems of authenticity and I shall leave on one side questions relating to the different narrative traditions.

I shall call these two groups of tragedies the 'two bloodlines', because, nearly without exception, they contain the most bloodcurdling stories about hate, murder and revenge. The wife kills her husband, the son his mother, the father his children, the brothers each other. All human relationships seem to have been frozen, set aflame, turned upside down or switched into the reverse, so that a father sacrifices his daughter and a son sleeps with his mother. This is not to say that the other nine plays are very much milder : here too a mother kills her own children. But along the two bloodlines, bloodstreams rather, fate moves on inexorably; this horrifying urge to murder passes from one person to the other, and generation after generation is drenched in the smell of blood. If ever that old palace of the Atrides in

Mycenae were peopled again, how many screams of terror and hatred and agony would rise from it!

2. The 'Thebes'-group of tragedies

Six of the eight plays of the Thebes-group are interconnected very closely for they contain the fortunes of King Oedipus and his family. The others have, indeed, something to do with Thebes but not with Oedipus; they are Euripides' tragedies 'Bacchae' and 'Heracles' Madness'. In Volume I, Chapter IV, Section 9 I wrote about the Bacchae because of its connection with the cult of Dionysus. The action takes place in the earliest days of Greek history, when Cadmus, the legendary founder of the Cadmeia, the citadel of Thebes, was living in this city of which he was the first king. His grandson Pentheus succeeded Cadmus when he vacated the throne on account of age. At that time the cult of Dionysus found acceptance in Boeotia; the women of Thebes too used to go to the mountains to venerate the god ecstatically. Pentheus revealed himself as an opponent of the new cult which he forbade. When, however, he went to spy on the women during their strange excesses he was discovered and killed by them in an atrocious way. I shall come back to this later.

The scene of 'Heracles' Madness' is laid in Thebes in the time of a certain King Creon but it is not a typical 'Theban' tragedy. When Heracles decides to make his voyage to the nether world, he puts his father Amphitryon, his wife Megara and his three sons under the care of Creon. This king, however, is killed by some conspirators; Lycus then becomes king. The new king tries to kill Heracles' progeny but in the end it is not he but Heracles himself who perpetrates the deed in a fit of insanity brought down upon him by Hera.

All six plays which have Oedipus and his family as their subject are based on Sophocles' 'King Oedipus'. An oracle has revealed to Laius, king of Thebes, that his son will first kill him and afterwards marry his mother Iocaste. In order to prevent such atrocities he exposes his little son in the wilderness where his feet were riveted together - hence the name 'Oidipous' (with swollen feet). However, the child is discovered and educated at Corinth. During a quarrel with a passer-by he kills the man - not knowing that it is his father Laius. He then frees the Thebans from their terror of the Sphinx, a monster. Because of this he is proclaimed king of Thebes and marries the widowed queen-mother - not suspecting that she is his mother, Iocaste. With her he has four children, Eteocles and Polynices, Antigone and Ismene. Many years later a plague rages in Thebes. The oracle then reveals that the cause of this is an incestuous marriage. When Oedipus finally is forced to recognize that this marriage is his own, he cuts out his own eyes, and Iocaste commits suicide (in other versions than that of Sophocles she does not kill herself).

Led by his daughter Antigone Oedipus arrives at Colonus, in Attica. This is where Sophocles' 'Oedipus in Colonus' begins (the poet himself came from that town). Having discovered his identity the inhabitants want to drive away the undesirable stranger who slept with his own mother; King Theseus of Athens, however, allows the unhappy man to stay. When Creon, Oedipus' brother-in-law, appears to conduct Antigone back to Thebes, it is Theseus who liberates her and her sister Ismene from the hands of Creon. Oedipus considers both his sons as his enemies, not without reason since in this version they have chased him away from Thebes and eventually succeed him. He predicts a fatal end for them. Oedipus then is taken away from the earth by the gods.

Not according to the chronology of the plays but rather according to their general subject the narrative continues with Aeschylus' 'Seven against Thebes'. After the departure of Oedipus his sons Eteocles and Polynices agree to rule Thebes in rotation. When Eteocles becomes king he does not adhere to these terms and refuses to cede the throne to his brother. Polynices who in the meantime has become son-in-law of the king of Argos then marches with an Argive army on Thebes in order to drive away Eteocles. Both brothers fall in a single combat; thus Oedipus' curse is realized. More or less the same story is told by Euripides in his 'Phoenician Maidens', although in this play Iocaste is presumed to be still living. A dramatic dialogue between both brothers has an important place in it.

The last tragedy in this thematic sequence is Sophocles' 'Antigone'. I treated this play at some length in my Volume II, Chapter IV, Section f-h. In this play Creon, king of Thebes, as successor to Oedipus, decrees that Eteocles shall be given a state burial, while the corpse of Polynices will remain on the spot where he fell. Polynices' sister Antigone opposes the king fiercely; she wants to bury her brother with her own hands. In consequence Creon has her immured in a subterranean dungeon. When he at last repents his decisions, as a result of the admonitions of the blind seer Tiresias, it is already too late : Antigone has committed suicide, and not only she but also her betrothed, Creon's son Haemon, and the queen, Creon's wife Eurydice.

3. The Troy-group of tragedies

a. A curse on the House of Atreus

The other bloodline conducts us from the Troian War to the downfall of the House of Atreus. This series of plays begins - if we concentrate on the narrative sequence rather than the chronology - in the palace of the Atrides at Mycenae long before there is talk of a fight for distant Troy. In the family of the Atrides too an old curse comes to fulfilment. The story begins in mythical times, incredibly long ago, with Tantalus who wanted to put the gods to a test. There exist varying versions of the way he did this but one of these is important with respect to our theme. He cuts his son Pelops into pieces and offers him as a meal to the gods. However, they see through him and revive Pelops. Later Pelops marries Hippodamia, daughter of the king of Elis. He does not fulfil the promises he made in order to marry her; therefore, he and his progeny are cursed.

Pelops who is also the legendary founder of the Olympic Games, had many children, among them Atreus and Thyestes. Having become king of Mycenae Atreus discovers that his wife Aerope has had an affair with his brother Thyestes. In order to revenge himself he invites his brother to his table and as a meal dishes up the children that had been born from this relation. When Thyestes discovers this he curses

Atreus and his whole progeny. In some versions Thyestes' son Aegisthus escapes death by Atreus' hand.

b. Iphigeneia's sad fate

The sons of Atreus on whom the curse now rests are Agamemnon and Menelaus. Menelaus, the younger one, becomes king of Sparta. He marries the famous Helen, the most beautiful woman of Greece, the daughter of Leda who also gave birth to Clytaemnestra and to the two Dioscuri, Castor and Pollux. About the father there are varying opinions. Helen may have been the daughter of Leda's legitimate husband Tyndareus, king of Sparta, or she may have been the child of Zeus himself who approached Leda in the shape of a swan. Her sister, Clytaemnestra, becomes the wife of Agamemnon. Paris, however, (also called Alexander), son of Priamus, king of Troy, and of Queen Hecabe, now arrives at Sparta. He seduces Helen, who has been allotted to him by Aphrodite, as a reward for proclaiming her the most beautiful of the goddesses, and abducts her to Troy. There is uproar in Hellas. All the princes, with their retinues, set off in pursuit.

When, however, they lie at anchor in Aulis - and this is the theme of Euripides' 'Iphigeneia in Aulis' - an adverse wind prevents them from continuing their journey. Calchas, the seer, reveals that the wind will turn if only Agamemnon, commander-in-chief, will sacrifice his daughter Iphigeneia to the goddess Artemis. On a deceitful pretext Agamemnon invites the girl to travel to Aulis; this she does accompanied by her mother. In the nick of time Iphigeneia is saved by Artemis (and brought to Tauris); nevertheless, fresh trouble is brooding since Clytaemnestra conceives an unquenchable hatred for Agamemnon.

c. Odysseus' wiles

The action of three plays takes place during the battle for Troy. Euripides' 'Rhesus' [1] links up with the tenth book of the Iliad. Achilles has withdrawn from the battlefield, the Greeks have been driven back to their ships, and the Troians are camping out in the plain in front of the town. They expect help from Rhesus, king of Thrace, and his excellent cavalry. The Troian Dolon goes out to reconnoitre whether the Greeks may be on the point of departure. He is, however, taken prisoner by Diomedes and Odysseus (the cunning of Odysseus is a recurring theme in many tragedies). Dolon reveals what is going on at the Troian side; as a result Odysseus is able to surprise Rhesus in his sleep and kill him.

Sophocles' 'Aias' is the great Ajax, one of the most powerful fighters of the Greek army. He hopes to get the weapons of Achilles after the death of this hero but instead they are allotted to Odysseus. Mad with rage he 'defeats' a herd of sheep and cows; perceiving what he has done he commits suicide to expunge his disgrace. Calchas succeeds only with difficulty in persuading Agamemnon and Menelaus to grant him a honourable burial.

'Philoctetes', another play by Sophocles, is only loosely connected with the Trojan theme. Philoctetes is a Greek hero who, during the voyage to Troy, has contracted an extremely painful disease as the result of a snakebite; the Greeks pitilessly abandon him on the island of Lemnos. However, he has Heracles' bow in his possession. The Greeks hear from a seer that they will not be able to capture Troy without this weapon - later it is to kill Paris, amongst others. They then send Odysseus and Neoptolemus to get hold of it. The subject of this play is, in fact, the moral struggle between young Neoptolemus and the wily Odysseus who wants to make use of Neoptolemus' innocence in an extremely base manner in order to deceive Philoctetes. Only because of a heavenly injunction Philoctetes consents in being taken to Troy.

d. The last days of Troy

Two plays, both by Euripides, have their scenes laid in the last days of Troy. The city has been captured by means of the wooden horse. Priamus, the king, is cut down at the altar by Neoptolemus, the vindictive son of Achilles. Astyanax, the little son of Hector and Andromache, is ruthlessly flung down from a tower - this on the advice of Odysseus who deems it imprudent to let a pretender live. Andromache becomes the booty of Neoptolemus, whereas Cassandra, the prophetess, a daughter of Priamus and Hecabe, is allotted to Agamemnon.

Thus it is told in 'Women of Troy'. In 'Hecabe' the initial situation is repeated. On the way from Troy the Greek fleet is held up in Thrace by contrary winds. This is ascribed to the fact that the spirit of Achilles is not yet conciliated; therefore, Polyxena, another daughter of Priamus and Hecabe, is sacrificed to his memory.

As if this is not calamity enough for Hecabe, who has become a slave herself, her son Polydorus is found dead on the beach. While Troy still stood, Priamus has sent him, for reasons of safety, to the king of Thrace, Polymestor; on hearing that Troy had fallen the king murdered the boy for his money, and threw his body into the sea. Thus the ill-fated Hecabe in this war lost her husband, her children Hector, Paris, Polyxena, Polydorus and still others, while she herself, her daughter Cassandra and her daughter-in-law Andromache, were carried off into slavery. When King Polymestor makes his appearance in the Greek army camp, he is blinded by Hecabe with the help of the Trojan women.

e. Helen phantom or reality?

'Helen', another play by Euripides, reflects the view of the Greeks of the classical period that it was incredible that the Hellenes should have incurred so many difficulties for the sake of a woman. There is a version of the story by the poet Stesichorus that the actual Helen, through the intervention of a god, was abducted to Egypt, whereas Paris, who of course did not notice the exchange, was fobbed off with a 'phantom'. In his own 'Helen' Euripides borrowed this version. As a consequence of this artifice the Trojan War became a highly abortive affair for, in the absence of the real Helen, it had been conducted 'all for nothing'; in the play itself this is stated with as many words more than once.

The idea was that in Egypt Helen would marry the king but Menelaus, her lawful husband, arrives just in time to prevent this. A shipwreck during the homeward journey from Troy throws him on the Egyptian coast; he then recognizes his wife and, by means of all kinds of tricks and devices in which Helen too takes part, he succeeds in getting a ship that brings them back to Sparta. Just as in 'Medea' the stupidity of the barbarians is exposed by the wily Greeks; the story, in fact, would make a fine screenplay for an opera, it reminds us of one with a similar theme, Rossini's 'L'Italiana in Algieri'.

f. Family life

If in this play our sympathies are enlisted on behalf of the brave Menelaus, the case is entirely reversed in Euripides' 'Andromache'. In this tragedy we are confronted with a thoroughly brutal Menelaus. 'Andromache', indeed, introduces us to a cycle of eight tragedies of which the first is not 'Andromache' but Aeschylus' 'Agamemnon'. When this king was absent in Troy his wife Clytaemnestra took Aegisthus, son of Thyestes and nephew of Agamemnon, as her lover. We have seen how fiercely this woman hated her husband since the sacrifice of Iphigeneia. When he returns from Troy he brings Cassandra with him as his concubine, and this circumstance decides his fate. Clytaemnestra kills him and his paramour with her own hands in the palace at Mycenae. Their little son Orestes escapes from the carnage because an old slave carries him to safety in Phocis.

Electra, the daughter of Clytaemnestra and Agamemnon, grows up in a blind hatred against her mother and against Aegisthus who now reigns over Mycenae. Out of fear Aegisthus wants to put her to death but even for Clytaemnestra this goes too far. Therefore, the girl is given in marriage to a poor peasant who, however, does not touch her out of respect for her royal blood. This is Euripides' version in his 'Electra'. In two other plays, the 'Choephoroi' by Aeschylus, and 'Electra' by Sophocles, Electra remains in the royal palace, albeit despised as much as a slave-girl. The events that then follow are brought on the stage by all three tragedians, in a highly dramatic, even ghastly manner. We find these events in the three tragedies I mentioned already. Orestes, now grown up, arrives in Mycenae with his friend Pylades and makes himself known to their sister Electra. For her the hour of revenge has now come; she persuades Orestes to kill their mother Clytaemnestra and to murder her second husband, Aegisthus. Orestes indeed performs these gruesome deeds [2].

The story is continued in Euripides' 'Orestes' and in Aeschylus' 'Eumenides' (although these two plays do not link up seamlessly). After the murder of his mother Orestes is persecuted by the avenging goddesses, the Eumenides or Furies; mentally deranged and accompanied by Electra he arrives in Argos [3]. There nobody is ready to extend hospitality to the matricide. King Menelaus hardly lifts a finger to save his nephew, and the Assembly condemns Orestes to death. He then plans to kill Helen, Menelaus' wife, for he hopes to win freedom by murdering the femme fatale of Hellas 'who killed so many men' [4]. After the murder, Orestes plans to take Hermione, the daughter of the king and Helen, hostage and to secure his retreat with his sword on her throat.

So once again Orestes breaks into a palace in order to kill a woman. Helen, however, is saved by Apollo himself who conducts her to heaven on the command of Zeus, her father. Let Menelaus, says the god, marry another woman. The divine mouth utters no word of censure to Orestes. On the contrary, he is to be permitted to marry Hermione (who, at the moment of the god's appearance, is still kneeling before him with his sword across her throat), as soon as the Aeropage in Athens clears him of his blood-guilt. This is according to the Euripidean version; in Aeschylus' tragedy, on the other hand, Orestes is referred to the Athenian tribunal by the oracle of Delphi. During the session of the court Apollo himself pleads strongly in favour of Orestes and finally succeeds in having him acquitted. It is, however, thoroughly typical of Euripides to handle legendary material in his own specific way.

This is equally the case in his 'Iphigeneia in Taurica'. Here the Aeropage has ordered Orestes to steal the statue of Artemis from her temple in Tauris (on the Crimea) and to bring it to Athens. If he were to succeed, the blood-guilt would be wiped out, and the curse would be exorcized. The temple in question, however, is precisely the sanctuary where Iphigeneia has been brought by Artemis from Aulis. She is a priestess of Artemis, and she has been ordered by Thoas, the king of this county, to sacrifice to the goddess those Greeks who are cast ashore there. Such is the fate in store for Orestes and Pylades when they arrive in Tauris. However, brother and sister recognize each other. They hatch a cunning plot that will enable them to escape along the sea road, and, to add insult to injury, they purloin the statue of the goddess. Once again we meet the theme of the fooled barbarian. Apart from that, this is one of the very few plays in which nobody is killed.

The reverse is the case in the last tragedy of the Troy-series, 'Andromache' by Euripides. As we saw already, Hector's widow Andromache has become the wife of Achilles' son Neoptolemus and the mother of their son Molossus. Ten years later Neoptolemus takes another wife, Hermione, the daughter of Menelaus and Helen. However, she proves barren, and, in her jealousy, she lays the blame on Andromache for this. When Neoptolemus is away in Delphi to consult the oracle, Menelaus arrives. Together with his daughter he contrives a plan to kill Andromache and her little son. They are, however, saved by the courageous intervention of old Peleus, Achilles' father, and Menelaus slinks off. Neoptolemus is killed in Delphi by a street crowd on the instigation of Orestes. The reader will remember that Hermione had been promised to him, and this is his revenge.

4. How difficult it is to live

This complex of stories, atrocious as it is, stands at right angles to the idea of the Greeks that we, as heirs of Renaissance and Neohumanism, have of them. But it does not square either with the idea the Greeks had of themselves. They did not see themselves as patricides and matricides, as condoners of incest, as rebels against the gods. What happened on the stage must have seemed to the audience wild and unnatural, but then it was the intention of the playwrights to horrify and to shock. In great numbers the spectators witnessed Antigone defying the polis, Prometheus cursing Zeus, Orestes absenting himself offstage to kill his mother, and Medea to slaughter her offspring. Nothing could go more against their own laws and their own feelings; but nevertheless they sat there, for the course of a whole long day, in order to see three of these tragedies. The polis whose laws and authority were trampled underfoot in them refunded the admission prices, and in this way encouraged its citizens to expose themselves to these harrowing spectacles. But what were they looking for, those Greeks of the great classical period?

The phenomenon that we call 'Greek tragedy' can be - and has been - interpreted in many ways. In connection with our theme the following explanation may be brought forward. What the spectators looked for was a representation of their own existence that would be at the same time concrete and mythical; they hoped to find in it an explanation of the fundamental oppositions in their own life, public and domestic, of its difficulties, even of its impossibilities. In Volume I and also here and there in Volume II we saw that the Greeks found it difficult to live with their gods. Sometimes, again, they felt themselves trapped in the polis. Another great problem was that the poleis were utterly unable to associate with each other in peaceful ways. But their greatest difficulty was that their own personal and intimate existence, their lives as husbands and wives, was full of fractures, was, indeed, a field of craters which nobody could cross without hurting himself. What the Greeks saw on the stage was exactly this. Once, after a presentation of Edward Albee's 'Who is afraid of Virginia Woolf?' I heard a spectator say : "I saw my own marriage"; likewise the Greeks saw, in the dramas, their own world, their own life.

Naturally enough the drama did not reflect that world in a literal or realistic way. This was not at all the case. In fact, it would have been out of the question. In evaluating themselves the Greeks, like the peoples of every other nation, had an almost infinite capacity of self-deception. Tragedy, however, does not start from this surface of make-belief and self-deceit; it breaks right through it and finally reaches those deep layers of dissatisfaction, frustration and resentment which, in the foregoing volumes, have been laid bare so often. Tragedy reflects an 'Unbehagen in der Kultur', it is extremely 'uncultural', uncivilized, even anticultural, although it is one of the most treasured legacies of Hellenic civilization. It is anticultural because it drives the norms and conventions of a well-regulated society into a corner. And this is its essential task.

The Greeks flocked into their theatres because they understood this. They wanted to see there, enacted on the stage, the crisis of their existence. At the same time, however, they wanted some sort of resolution. The tragic writers, obviously enough, did not cater to this desire by applying happy endings; there are few happy endings in tragedy. No, the resolution of the tension is achieved by situating the action in a mythical past. In this mythical shape it is no longer directly aimed 'ad hominem', at the individual spectator, but it assumes, rather, a timeless, universally human dimension in which even the gods get their place. However violently the Greeks suffered from their own problems, tragedy taught them that their ills were not specifically Greek (although they were more conversant with them than others) but natural to all humanity. It is for this reason that Greek tragedy is still 'contemporary', so much so that I vividly remember a presentation of 'King Oedipus' by the pupils of the secondary school where I then taught, so convincing and so deeply felt that the youthful audience, usually so restless, watched in the deepest silence the terrible story of the man who married his mother.

5. How difficult it is to live with the gods

a. Euripides the 'atheist'

A certain Aristodemus, a very small person, does not sacrifice to the gods, he does not pray either and does not make use of the fortune-teller's art [5]. Such an attitude of atheism or rather agnosticism, in any case of practical irreligiosity, was probably not uncommon in the last decades of the fifth century B.C. We know of clubs in which the gods were ridiculed; in Volume II it was shown that in Thucydides' great work the supernatural no longer occurs; we are also aware of the existence of a free-thinking circle around Pericles. Euripides who celebrated his greatest triumphs in this period was one of them; already during his life he was, therefore, accused of atheism. "He says that there are no gods", according to a saleswoman in Aristophanes; the result of this was a drop in the sale of religious articles [6]!

That Euripides was an atheist is a charge that was repeated more than once in Antiquity [7] and is re-echoed in our own days [8]. "His stories assume that 'the gods' do not exist; if we do not keep this in mind, we shall miss the very essence of Euripides", says Verrall [9]. In Verrall's quotation, however, the words 'the gods' are put between brackets. We ought to understand that Euripides was fighting against a traditional idea of the gods still prevalent in his age, an idea that was, at times, forcefully defended by means, for instance, of the so-called 'aseby-lawsuits' against persons who were accused of irreligiosity. "Euripides was a soldier of rationalism, ... a resolute consistent enemy of anthropomorphic theology, a hater of embodied mystery", this is how Verrall concludes his book on this author [10].

We need not, however, infer from these words that Euripides was an atheist on principle. Several passages give evidence of at least some belief in the gods. "O Earth's Upbearer ... Whoever you are, O past our finding out, Zeus, be you Nature's law, or Mind of Man, You I invoke", prays Hecabe, and Menelaus answers : "What strange prayer this unto the gods?" [11]. Zeus is not seen here as the highest of all the gods, as the godhead par excellence, such as Aeschylus sees him, for example; he is regarded, rather, as the projection of a human idea. Euripides does not seem averse from the assumption that it is the Mind of Man that keeps the world going.

In a first and superficial reading of Euripides we do not get the impression that we have to do with a rebel against the Olympians, not even with an impious man. In his plays people sacrifice and pray; the gods are present in them, even as 'dramatis personae', since they intervene in the action, sometimes decisively. There are even eulogies : "I praise the god who set our life in order, lifting it out of savagery and confusion. First he put wit in us, and then gave language, envoy of words, to understand the voice; and fruits of earth to eat, and for this food watery drops from heaven, to quench our thirst and nourish the yield of land". The poet condemns those, moreover, who dream that they are wiser than the gods [12]. The soothsayer's art is one of the divine gifts, and it is a fool who dares to ridicule it [13].

b. Euripides and the soothsayers' lore

A more careful reading of Euripides brings to light contrary opinions. "The lore of seers, how vain it is, how full of lies" [14]. Is this the opinion of Euripides himself? A great many words have been written on this subject. We must keep in mind, nevertheless, that Euripides writes dramas whose essence consists of the fierce oppositions we find in them. One of these is the conflict between the ancient belief in the Olympian gods and the new modernistic trend of thought. As a good artist the poet presents every kind of opinion, even those which he does not adhere to, in a convincing way. We find a fine example of this in 'Suppliants' where Theseus, king of Athens, fights a verbal duel with a herald from Thebes over the advantages and disadvantages of democracy and tyranny; here the Theban defends tyranny with such a fervour that the reader might easily conclude that Euripides was an opponent of democracy [15]. However, the whole context of his life and work proves that this cannot be true. Furthermore, it must be borne in mind that all three tragedians borrow their subjects nearly exclusively from Greek mythology. If Euripides was out to destroy the Olympian religion, he would at the same time have robbed the myths of the force that is proper to them and in doing this made his own work impossible.

It is well worth noting that the seers intimate several times that the gods want a human sacrifice. We have already alluded to the fate of Iphigeneia who, for that matter, was saved from the sacrificial altar by the goddess herself. Other sacrifices, however, are a feature in the plays. I mentioned already how Polyxena, youngest daughter of Hecabe, queen of Troy, was sacrificed in Thrace by the Greeks in order to obtain a favourable wind [16]. Another instance is that of Menoeceus, son of Creon, king of Thebes, who, according to the seer Tiresias, had to be sacrificed to bring about the deliverance of the town from the Argive army that was ready to storm it; when his father shies away from this deed, the son kills himself [17].

Human sacrifice was not unknown to Greek religion. In historical times there were still a few sanctuaries where such sacrifices were regularly performed; even in Athens human sacrifices occurred in exceptional circumstances. Just before the Battle of Salamis, in 480 B.C., in order to obtain a favourable outcome, Themistocles had three young Persians sacrificed, nephews of King Xerxes - this again at the instigation of a seer. Plutarch says that Themistocles recoiled from this deed but that the populace forced him to it [18]. It seems to me that although Euripides presents such sacrifices without explicit disapproval, he goes along, nevertheless, with the repugnance many educated people must have felt against them. The theatre public must have been moved by the presentation of a young girl like Polyxena who is dedicated to death, and by the grief of her mother. It must have sympathized with Creon who recoils from the killing of his own son : "Never such depth of misery will I seek ... for love of children fills all men's life, and none to death would yield up his own child" [19]. But Euripides' strongest, albeit built-in argument (for he could not, of course, change the traditional version), seems to me his presentation of the consequences of the sacrifice of Iphigeneia, the never-ending blood-feud leading up to all those horrifying events in the family of the Atrides.

Outbursts against the 'Unwesen' of the seers are so frequent that they clearly evince an inner repulsion on the part of the dramatist. But this is equally true with regard to other religious phenomena : the endless utterances against them finally amount to a complete condemnation. As Nilsson says : "The number of such utterances is highly important, that is to say, their frequency, and, one must add, the intensity with which this or that question, this or that insight, is brought forward; for they show what was on the mind of the poet himself, and what moved the progressive minds of his time" [20]. Doubts with respect to the old myths are repeatedly formulated. Heracles presents the 'Leitmotiv' : "These are the minstrel's sorry tales" [21]. Helen herself tells the old story how Zeus, in the shape of a swan, visited her mother and how she, as a result of this connection, was born from a swan's egg; she then adds laconically : "if the tale be true" [22]. In another play the chorus sings : "if credence-worthy the story be" [23]. In order to gauge the effect on the public the reader may imagine a passion play in which, from time to time, he is confronted with the following interjection : "if all this is but true".

c. Ridiculing the gods

In an interesting passage Euripides retells the legend of how Zeus once ordered the sun and the stars to revolve in the opposite direction and here too the chorus is critical : "This is what the poets say but I can hardly believe it. Why should Helios turn backward his sun chariot only to repay mortals for their deeds?". Then follows a shattering sentence : "Such tales are useful to scare human beings into obedience of the gods" [24]. The opinion that the gods resorted to absurd tales to bolster their cultus could not have been conducive to religious devotion.

Sometimes one gets the impression that the gods are ridiculed. If this impression is correct, then Euripides too has his place in what the Germans call the 'Götterburleske'. I detect this in particular in the story of Paris and Helen. Everybody knows the famous tale of the three Olympian goddesses, Hera, Athena and Aphrodite, who fell out amongst themselves because of the question which of them was the most beautiful. It is already ridiculous that they ask a mortal to act as their arbiter, and still more ridiculous that this mortal has to be a notorious playboy. Hecabe, the tragic victim of what started so innocently as a beauty-contest, has some questions to raise about this : "why does Hera want to be the most beautiful? Does she wish to have a husband mightier than Zeus? And Athena? Does she expressly wish to remain a virgin? Doesn't this make the goddesses into fools?" [25]. And so it is indeed. Decharme is right in saying that this representation is incompatible with the traditional character of the goddesses [26].

When Paris abducted Helen from Sparta, the jealous Hera intervened and brought the woman to Egypt. Into the loving arms of Paris she put a precise counterpart of Helen, and till his death he was never aware of this [27]. As I mentioned already, in the seventh year of the homeward voyage from Troy Menelaus comes to Egypt, recognizes his wife and is reunited in love with her. Is it any wonder that a veteran should exclaim : "and all this misery for a phantom?!" [28]. On the spectator too it must have had a peculiar, destabilizing effect that the whole of the Trojan War was the result of a divine hoax; even Homer was obviously a victim of it.

d. The wrath of the gods

We do not only know the 'Götterburleske', we also know the 'wrath of the gods'. In Greek religion the distance between gods and men is great, the gods are cold and disinterested; therefore, human beings do not understand why they should love the gods with all their heart. On the contrary, on the surface there may be veneration but underneath glimmers wrath that not infrequently flares up. We find this also in Euripides. When it dawns upon the veteran to whom I alluded a moment ago that he and all his comrades have been made fools of by Hera, he shows himself embittered : "The ways of the godhead are past finding out! Lightly he turns and sways us to and fro" [29]. Still harder is Helen's opinion that Zeus drove Greeks and Trojans into the war in order to disburden mother-earth of a good number of men [30]. It may be mentioned in passing that the image of Zeus is shifting here in the direction of a blind and impersonal force of nature or a historical fatum.

In 'Phoenician Maidens' Polynices, son of Oedipus, says that one of the gods is maliciously ruining the race of Oedipus [31]. Or take this spiteful remark by Orestes : "We are enslaved to the gods - whatever the gods may be" [32]. "All things the gods confound, hurl this way and that, turmoiling all, that we, in our ignorance, may venerate them" [33]. The following exclamation seems only too relevant : "O gods! - to sorry helpers I appeal" [34]. Venomously Hecabe remarks that not every (sic) folly must be called Aphrodite's work, although her name is derived from 'aphrosunê', that is 'unwisdom' [35]. Orestes expresses himself as follows : "Not even gods, whom men call wise, are less deceitful than the fleeting dreams. Utter confusion is in things divine and human" [36] - a sentence that amounts almost to a liquidation of the world of the Olympian gods.

It will, therefore, not surprise us that mortals occasionally deem themselves better than the gods. In 'Madness of Heracles' Heracles' father states this plainly : "Zeus, ... as a mortal I outdo your godhead in worth. I have not abandoned Heracles' sons. But you have come cunningly to steal unto my marriage-bed, to steal another's right that does not belong to you. Yet you are unable to save your own dear ones! You are unwise or else you are unjust" [37]. Somewhat later Heracles says to his father : "I count you a truer father than Zeus" [38].

e. The immorality of the gods

With remarks such as these we have arrived at another topic of great importance, that of the immorality of the gods. In Volume I, Chapter IV, Section 3 I have already pointed out that this is a charge that can be found in a great number of Greek writings. It seems to me that this is very evident in Euripides too. Nestle quotes a line by Sophocles : "Whatever the gods may do, it never is wrong" [39], and contrasts this with a verse by Euripides : "When the gods commit evil they are no gods" [40]. According to Nestle the meaning is the same : 'divinity and sin exclude each other', but the conclusion is different. In Sophocles the gods do not commit evil, in Euripides they do - and very frequently too! - and therefore they are not gods [41].

In Euripides' dramatical work the list of Olympian villains is extremely long indeed. Point-blank Orestes blames the murder of his mother Clytaemnestra on Apollo : "It was Phoebus who ordered the matricide" [42]. In another context it is the goddess Iris who states that it was Hera's idea that Heracles in his madness would kill his own children [43]. Therefore Heracles curses her : "Now let her dance, that glorious bride of Zeus, beating with sandalled foot Olympus' floor; she has compassed her desire ... To such a goddess shall we pray now?" [44]. It was Hera too, says Eurystheus, who inspired him to prosecute the children of Heracles, "would I or no" [45]. Did not, in the Scamander plain, Greeks and Trojans fall in dense rows, fighting for a Helen who was not even in Troy, only 'by Hera's whiles' [46]?

Another time it is Athena who urges the Athenians to destroy Thebes [47]. Aphrodite in particular has a very bad press, 'insatiate of wrong as she is' [48]. For she is to be found at the very origin of the

Trojan War and of all the disasters that came from it. It was she who was at fault when Paris abducted Helen promised to him as the prize of the beauty-contest [49], 'by the treacherous malice of Cypris (= Aphrodite), the bringer of death's desolation' [50]. Confronted with Paris' mother Hecabe Helen defends herself by saying that she had lost her reason, when she followed Paris : "Punish her (Aphrodite)!" [51]. In yet another passage Aphrodite rages against Hippolytus because he venerates Artemis and spurns the love goddess; inspired by revenge she makes the stepmother of Hippolytus, Phaedra, fall in love with her stepson. The reader will be familiar with the sad consequences of this infatuation, if not from Euripides' 'Hippolytus' then from Racine's 'Phèdre'. Nor is Zeus spared : "If there really is a god in heaven he must always make the same people unhappy" [52]. In this case the suspicion of divine injustice leads inevitably to doubts of the very existence of the supreme god.

Euripides reserves his sharpest shafts for Apollo wo, in 'Ion', plays a very sorry role. In this play the sun-god violates Creusa, the daughter of King Erechtheus of Athens and then leaves the girl to her fate. When she has given birth to a child she tries to cover her shame by leaving it behind in a cave. But, without telling the mother anything about this, Apollo orders Hermes to bring the baby to Delphi, where it may be reared by the Pythia (who is not informed either). Nobody has any further news from the god with the nearly disastrous result that mother and son, utterly in the dark respecting their relation to one another, are within an inch of killing each other when, at a later stage, they meet. All ends well, but during the rest of the play Apollo remains safely at a safe distance; it is, finally, Athena who has to act as a 'dea ex machina'. Although the play ends with a song of praise for Apollo, the harm has been done. It cannot be otherwise but the spectators must have received a dubious impression of this capricious divinity.

The 'dramatis personae' themselves express their opinions bluntly enough : "No shame made the lover-god quail", thus Creusa, Apollo's victim, accuses the god [53]. The old paidagogos who straightforwardly calls Apollo 'bad' [54], even advises Creusa to put the Apollo-temple on fire [55]. But the fiercest indictment comes from Ion himself, Apollo' and Creusa's son : "Phoebus, what ails him? He ravishes maids and then forsakes them ... How can it be just that you should enact laws for men and that you yourself are lawless? ... It were unjust to call men vile, if we but imitate what gods deem good. They are vile who teach us this" [56]. In my opinion the following conclusion in 'Bellerophon' is that of Euripides himself : "Does someone say that there are gods in heaven? By no means! There are no gods! This is only so for fools who still believe the old fairy-tales" [57].

f. Religion irrational?

On reading the dramas consecutively one gets the irresistible impression that for Euripides religion was something irrational. The gods are governed by their passions - Hera by her jealousy, Apollo by his infatuation, Aphrodite, who is senselessness par excellence, by her erotic impulses to which even Zeus is subject, 'who rules all the gods, yet is her slave' [58]. Perhaps this basic idea of the great tragedian may help us to explain his play 'The Bacchanals'. The problem with this play, as its commentators know only too well, is that it, although being a drama by the 'atheistic' Euripides, nevertheless exalts a god, Dionysus, praises his cult and shows how a scoffer comes to grief. Yet I cannot help asking myself whether, in fact, the real theme of the play is madness, far more than is the case in 'The Madness of Heracles' in which the hero is temporarily insane.

The reader must try to imagine how an Athenian (male) public may have reacted to 'The Bacchanals'. In their eyes the Dionysus-cult was probably a kind of cultic feminism from which they were practically excluded. In this cult the women, perhaps even their own wives, as 'Bacchae' indulged in excesses, somewhere in the wilderness or in the mountains in the middle of the night. The stories that circulated about this must have aroused insatiable curiosity - women who danced naked, hung with snakes, who tore a sacrificial animal to pieces and gorged its meat raw. It was perilous to meddle with them in this state. Whether all this was true is another question but what Euripides showed them on the stage must have confirmed the suspicions of the public.

In Thebes the women depart to celebrate the wild feast. Pentheus, the king, fiercely opposes this. "They call it the service of Bacchus but what they mean is Aphrodite" [59], that is to say, sexual excess. "It is not your Thebes that has power over us but Dionysus" [60], the women scream at him. What this means is a rejection not only of the polis but of the whole structure of (male) rationality of which the polis is the highest form. In his own person, although in unrecognizable disguise, Dionysus visits the king and persuades him to go and spy on the female festival. Under the influence of the god the king too loses his senses and is clad in female attire; Dionysus himself acts as his 'lady's maid'.

As a maenad he now hurries to the spot where the women have gathered. In order to see better he climbs up a tree. But the women discover him, they shake the tree till Pentheus falls down; then he is literally torn to pieces. The women are so frenzied that Pentheus' own mother Agave takes the lead in the attack upon her son. And although he keeps wailing : "Mother, I am your son!", she is 'full of Bacchus' and does not listen, she even calls him a 'beast' [61]. Then Agave descends the mountain with the head of her son on her thyrsos-stave, and thus she enters Thebes [62]. In her frenzy she has laid her hands on 'the head of the polis', the seat of rationality. Could a symbol be more clear?

Verrall, who saw Euripides above all as a rationalist, thought that, with 'The Bacchanals', the poet wanted to deal the Olympian religion a crushing blow : Euripides is exclaiming in this drama, see, this is where religion leads [63]. Another view, however, is a completely different one. Euripides, old and tired, and disappointed in science, returns, it is argued, to the beliefs of his youth, a kind of late conversion that is [64]. Others look for a middle course : the poet, although he is no adherent at all of Dionysus, shows, nevertheless, a secret longing for mysticism [65].

What is easily lost sight of in such speculations is the will of a great playwright to produce the strongest possible dramatic effect. This does not mean that he was after a cheap success. His approach to his subject matter is serious and considered and the plays demand a similar attitude of audiences and critics [66]. Nevertheless, the first principle of drama is conflict, and in this drama the basic conflict is that between the forces of reason and frenzy. It could, of course, be argued that Euripides chooses the side of frenzy in this tragedy. He is a great psychologist, his power of projecting himself into a situation is unequalled, his talent as a dramatist is exceptional. It is no wonder that the bacchantic orgy overwhelms us with an incredible force, even seems to convince us temporarily. Thus it must be in really great dramatic art. Euripides never underestimated the depths of the psyche, neither in his spectators nor in himself. He knew the dark side of life only too well. Nilsson pointed out that Euripides' sympathy for mystical and orgiastic cults - which is evinced in several passages in other plays too - coincides with his fascination for demoniacal women [67].

In the end, however, Euripides chooses the side of reason. When Agave comes to herself again and then, of course, deeply repents what she has done, she promptly lays the blame at the door of the god and comments : "It fits not that in wrath gods be as men" [68]. I share the opinion of Decharme that this represents Euripides' own view : the gods resemble men much too closely, they are senseless and unreasonable [69]. Yet while it is true that in the last resort Euripides tips the scales in favour of reason, in the play as a whole there is a fairly equal counterpoise between reason and insanity. In doing so Euripides fulfils the most essential function of drama : to reconnoitre what is beyond the frontiers of civilization and to show what lies beyond those frontiers. The frenzy, that is shown here, as also the frenzy in 'The Madness of Heracles', is a religious frenzy for which the Olympian gods are responsible. Its consequences are both catastrophic and saddening.

Yet, in my opinion, Euripides does not dismiss religion entirely. He accords it a modest utility. It has its value for the common people. The chorus of Maenads delivers themselves as follows : "Wisely you must hold you apart from the over-wise. But the faith of the heart of the people ... shall suffice for me too" [70]. The seer Tiresias (a

Bacchant himself) adds the following : "It is not for us to reason about the gods. We hold the traditions, old as time, of our fathers, no reasoning shall cast them down, not even if we climbed the highest tops of wisdom" [71]. Although this would seem to represent an attack on philosophy from the standpoint of undiluted philosophy, I cannot believe that this is the voice of Euripides himself. Even if he may have recognized the limited utility of religious tradition, in the last resort he saw religion as a threat. In its ecstatical, chaotic and irrational form it was the total antithesis to all that was represented by the ordered existence of agora and polis.

It is a common notion of all Greek literature, of Euripides too, that fate plays its capricious game with men. Nobody is safe from it [72]. But, and this is the important point, not even the gods are safe from it : "No mortal has escaped misfortune's taint, nor god - if minstrel-legends be not false" [73]. Let us listen to a prayer by Talthybius, the herald of the Greek army, and, therefore, so to speak, an official spokesman : "What shall I say, Zeus? - that you look on men? Or is this a fancy that we falsely hold for nothing, when we believe there is a race of gods, while chance controls all things among men?" [74]. Euripides was aware of this impossible contradiction : "Either there is fate and then there are no gods or there are gods and then there is no fate" [75]. This is a neat little piece of theology that has strayed into Euripides' work.

Generally, says Nilsson, in speaking of the gods Euripides does not seem to mean the Olympians but rather something abstract and irrational, for instance, the Moira. "He need not bother himself with the relationship between the gods and fate in earnest, to him they are identical" [76]. If this is correct, then Euripides takes a stride in the direction of later gnostic-dualistic conceptions, to wit, that the conditio humana should not be ascribed to the will of a rationally acting godhead nor to man's personal guilt but to something fatal and inexplicable in the nature of the cosmos itself [77].

The work of Euripides was an important factor in the destabilization of the Olympian religion. What he brought up was not new; we also find his ideas in philosophers and sophists. The poet was no theologian and no propagandist; what he had to say he put into the mouth of his stage-figures. It seems evident to me that he himself no longer believed in the Olympian gods. However, this does not mean that his aim was to subvert established religion. He registers the facts as he perceives them. New forces are threatening the old gods; they are already tottering. At the same time he has an inkling of what is to come. This will not be religious nihilism or general agnosticism or the replacement of the Olympus by critical and philosophical thought. No, it will be what Nilsson terms 'the religious form that will dominate the world of Late Antiquity' [78]. In 'The Bacchanals' Euripides is already pointing to it : the coming of esoteric dualistic Gnosticism.

g. Doubts in Sophocles

Sophocles, a contemporary of Euripides, who died either in the same year, 406 B.C., or a year later, was, to all intents and purposes, a faithful adherent of Olympian religion; he was even a priest of Asclepius. But according to Nilsson, he was 'religious like a good citizen' [79]. What does this mean? That Sophocles fulfilled his religious duties faithfully, that he was devoutly present at cultic events, that he honoured the gods? Certainly he does not attack the gods, he does not undermine their authority, he does not make them ridiculous. If this is what Nilsson means, then Opstelten would seem to subscribe to it with his remark that this tragedian kept the jealousy of the gods 'consciously out of doors' [80] : it is the spite of their fellow-men that plunges people into misery, not that of the gods. On the other hand, the religiosity of the good citizen may equally imply that, all things considered, religion remains somewhat conventional; in personal life it does not get pride of place. In this connection it is interesting to note that in Sophocles' plays, while the gods are conspicuously present, they are always kept somewhat in the background; the limelight is reserved for mortals. Hardly ever the gods intervene in the action, with the exception of the prologue of 'Aias' where the goddess Athena carries on a conversation with Odysseus and Ajax.

At the same time Sophocles can write in the closing words of 'Trachiniae' that 'there was nothing that was not Zeus', or, in Storr's Loeb translation, that 'Zeus has wrought it all' [81]. The reference is to unusual deaths and calamities of every kind. Perhaps the name of 'Zeus' is used here in a more general sense for 'gods' or 'things divine'. Other texts confirm this : "the gods throw people into blindness" [82]. This is a step into the direction of abstraction [83]. The meaning that is attached to 'time' and 'fate' also, as Greene points out, contributes to this sense of abstraction [84]. 'Time', 'chronos', is far more than clock-time or 'lapse of time'; it is a power that overlooks everything [85]. Now, when time is called 'pankratis', ruling everything, one may very well ask : and what about Allfather Zeus? "Time in his endless course gives birth to endless days and nights" [86], "time in its slow, illitimable course brings all to light and buries all again" [87]. Where, again, is the providence and the justice of the gods in the following words of Iocaste, the wife of Oedipus : "Why should a mortal man, the sport of chance, with no assured foreknowledge, be afraid? Best live a careless life from hand to mouth" [88]. Oedipus calls himself 'child of fate' [89]. No wonder that even the pious Sophocles permits himself this fierce outburst : "The gods are completely indifferent" [90].

h. Aeschylus and his 'Prometheus'

"The gods, it seems, have long since ceased their care of us. The service they value at our hands is that we perish" [91]. Even in Aeschylus, the predecessor of Sophocles and Euripides, we encounter such utterances of rancour against the gods. Nevertheless this poet ranks as a truly religious man, somebody for whom religion was something vital, decisive and all-pervading. In his plays the gods stand fully in the limelight; they intervene directly in the action; they are real 'dramatis personae'. "He brought", says Nilsson, "the old religion to its highest and deepest development", but, this Swedish historian of religion adds, he came too late, since the old religion was beginning to crumble already [92]. The question, indeed, is whether or not the pious Aeschylus may not have furthered this process of decline somewhat. For there is his 'Prometheus'.

'Prometheus bound' is the story of somebody who, knowingly and willingly, opposes Zeus. The hero - whose name signifies something like 'foresight' - belongs to the cursed race of the Titans that was defeated by Zeus. Prometheus who dare not risk brute force against the supreme god, obstructs him, nevertheless, with a more subtle range of devices. His principal act of defiance is to give mortals, who can never count on the special sympathy of Zeus, every kind of assistance. The Titan teaches human beings all kinds of arts and skills; his crowning feat is to give them fire which he has stolen from heaven. This infuriates Zeus. He chains Prometheus to a rock at the edge of Oceanus, far away in an inhospitable country. Already at the first reading of this curious play two things are notable : it is full of bitter utterances against the gods in general and against Zeus in particular. And the sympathies of Aeschylus are evidently on the side of Prometheus.

This partiality of the author is so striking, 'Prometheus' is obviously situated at right angles with the rest of his work, that it has got many a commentator into very great trouble. Some have even gone so far as to deny the authorship to Aeschylus [93]; in that case 'Prometheus' would have been written by a later author. An important argument against this, however, is that in antiquity itself nobody doubted its authenticity. In her review of the status quaestionis, Irene Zawadka finally concludes that the most recent treatises plead in favour of Aeschylus' authorship; the papyrus finds too speak for it [94]. A solution has been sought in the circumstance that, after all, the poet was no theologian but a tragedian. In other words, he may be forgiven a certain inconsistency [95]. Although this idea could be a pointer it is, nevertheless, not really satisfying. Even then the disparity with the other dramas remains too great.

i. Prometheus the rebel

Prometheus himself says that his hard fate was imposed on him because he was a benefactor of mankind [96]. Zeus had even intended to destroy the human race but he, Prometheus, had saved it [97]. Here, once again, the jealousy of the gods is obvious; they cannot suffer mankind to prosper. "I hate all the gods", the chained Titan exclaims, "that requite me wrongfully with ill" [98]. And he adds that he rather would remain chained to his rock than to serve Zeus [99]. Somewhere else he even calls Zeus 'empty-headed' ('kenophroon') [100]. One should try to evoke the theatrical effect of such scenes. Such a denunciation of the highest of all the gods must have been awe-inspiring as the fine accoustics of the theatre carried it upward along all the rows.

Prometheus, however, is not the only victim of Zeus' arbitrariness. Io appears, Inachus' daughter, who once was the beloved of Zeus, but her lover had changed her into a cow when Hera objected against the umpteenth girl-friend of her husband. This did not help her at all for, in spite of her disguise, Hera found her out and sent a gad-fly to torment her. Io loudly complains of her sufferings : "Wherein, o son of Cronus, have you found offence in me that you have bound me to this yoke of misery?" [101]; somewhat further she calls herself the victim of Hera's vengeful purpose' [102]. Her father Inachus who had tried to save her is expressly ordered by Zeus to chase away his child to the outskirts of the earth. Should he not comply, then Zeus would destroy his whole race with his thunderbolts [103]. Here again a human being stands before us as the target of divine hatred and jealousy. It is not difficult to guess who enlisted the sympathy of the spectators.

It is of the greatest significance that Prometheus, 'gifted with foresight', continually prophesies the downfall of Zeus. Allfather himself is the third in the succession of supreme gods, and his reign too will end. This causes Io, a human being that is, to rejoice whole-heartedly [104]. Not even the supreme god will prove stronger than fate; even he will not be able to escape what is in store for him [105]. Zeus, Prometheus predicts, will contract a marriage from which a son will be born to him; this son will dethrone him [106] just as he himself drove his own father from the throne. "The day will come when Zeus ... shall be humbled" [107]. His rule will not last long [108] - "Have I not seen two sovereigns (Uranus and Cronus) cast out from these heights?" [109] -, and not one of the other gods will be able to help him except Prometheus [110]. It is a curious comment on the omniscience of Zeus that the supreme god now wishes to know what marriage Prometheus means. In order to obtain an answer he sends

Hermes to his victim [111]. But the chained Titan is not prepared to disclose the secret unless he is unbound [112]. Zeus then decides, in his powerless rage, to push Prometheus still deeper into Tartarus, and this is, indeed, what happens, "You see the wrongs I suffer", are the very last words of the unhappy Titan [113].

As in all tragedies the chorus, in this play the daughters of Oceanus, has a role of its own. The function of the chorus is to comment upon the events, more often than not in a reconciliating manner; it does not see it as its task to push matter to extremes. One might say that it represents the spectators in the theatre; the chorus articulates, so to speak, their emotions. What we should realize, before we even speak of inconsistencies, is that the chorus certainly does not support Prometheus in every respect. It pities him because it knows that Zeus is adamant [114]. It seems to the members of the chorus - they are Oceanides not human beings - that Prometheus favours mankind somewhat to much [115]. The chorus does not think highly of men : they are 'no better than a dream' [116]. The chorus itself would not dare to oppose the will of Zeus; it reproaches Prometheus that he does not fear the supreme god [117]. Later it advises the hero to follow the counsel of Hermes and to resign himself to Allfather's decrees for "it is shameful for the wise to persist in error" [118]. Even the 'father' of the chorus, Oceanus, appears in person in order to bring Prometheus to his senses; to that end he uses the maxim of Delphi 'know yourself', that is, don't think you are better than the gods [119]. In this way Oceanus and his daughters counterbalance utterances in the play which, otherwise, would seem too daring to the public as well as to the author himself.

On the other hand - it is not a simple play - the chorus does not say these things out of godliness or respect. Oceanus expresses this straightforwardly : there is no other course possible, Zeus is in total control, so adjust yourself to the situation; if you don't your present fate will be childplay compared to what will happen in the future [120]. New lords are ruling now on Olympus, the chorus says, "with new-fangled laws Zeus wields arbitrary power" [121]. The impact of the Greek word that is used here, 'athetoos' = arbitrary, irregular, is reinforced by the fact that the spectator has continually before his eyes the afflicted Prometheus and from time to time is confronted with that poor child of man, Io. When the chorus voices every now and then its pity for the unhappy Titan, the public can hardly do otherwise than sympathize with him. One must add, however, that the poet gives Prometheus every opportunity to formulate his rebellious insights.

j. Interpretations

'Prometheus bound' is a play that has always inspired interpretation in depth. Some - Roman - commentators saw Prometheus as the rebel against Zeus, as the symbol, therefore, of political rebellion against the tyranny of kings [122]. To early Christians Prometheus was the sufferer; Tertullian even called him 'the veritable Christ' and forgot that this Titan does not exactly evoke the image of the lamb that is led to the slaughter but does not open its mouth. Goethe and Romanticism, Shelley foremost, detected in Prometheus the symbol of the rebellious individualist, of man with his free will, in his tragic fight against the powers that be. What they forgot is that everyone, Zeus and Prometheus and all men, are dominated by fate and, therefore, are not really free [123].

Quite another kind of interpretation aims at bringing 'Prometheus' more into line with Aeschylus' other plays. Many scholars have ascribed a religion of a personal sort to this poet, a religion that exalts Zeus at the expense of the other gods; there are scholars who make Aeschylus into one who is more or less a monotheist [124]. The goal of this personal religion would be to purify man by suffering [125]. This interpretation is mainly based on 'The Suppliant Maidens' and 'Agamemnon'. This would mean that Aeschylus gradually drew away from the anthropomorphic conceptions of Homer and developed purer and more spiritual religious notions. In order to fit 'Prometheus' into this scheme it was assumed [126] that Aeschylus made Zeus go through a development from youthful tyrant to benevolent ruler. Others again suppose that there are two sides to Zeus : the god of justice, and this is the more 'theological' or speculative aspect, and the god of nature, that is the god of ungovernable and destructive forces; this is what Kitto calls the 'Hesiodic' aspect [127].

Perhaps Aeschylus has something to say about this himself. He said that his plays were pieces of Homer's great banquet [128]. He himself, therefore, does not repudiate Homeric mythology. Plato objects to this predilection of the poet. He attacks him fiercely because he tells myths and, in doing so, pictures the gods falsely. For instance, says the philosopher, Aeschylus says that the gods are unjust and that they are responsible for the existence of evil in the world [129]. The poet even says that they are deceivers. "We will not allow teachers to use him for the education of the young" (i.e. in Plato's ideal state) [130]. Plato in any case could not discover this purified conception in Aeschylus. Neither do many contemporary scholars. They are of the opinion that a Greek god whose character changes and who undergoes a development is impossible; there are no parallels in other gods [131]. However, to quote Nestle, the fact that the poet bases himself so firmly on Homeric religiosity does not mean that there are absolutely no changes. A new element, and this is fundamental for the whole tragic genre, is the introduction of suffering man, of a human being who is a victim of fate or of the gods or of himself or of his fellow-men; such a suffering man was almost unknown to Homer. Very probably we can detect here the influence of the Dionysus-cult, because this god is the personification of suffering, death and resurrection [132].

Present-day man is strongly inclined to choose, with all his sympathy, the side of the sufferers and the oppressed, in this case the side of Prometheus; if this were correct then Zeus would be a pitiless tyrant. The question, however, is whether the Greek public felt likewise. The Greeks of that time, as Lloyd-Jones very aptly remarks, simply did not know that special relationship between God and man, a relationship in which man is subject to the divine vigilance of the Jahve of the Old Testament and the Father-God of the New. When Zeus exercises justice, it is a hard and revengeful justice. We must not forget that Zeus defends his lawful rights against Prometheus; the spectator, although he may have sympathized with the Titan and abhorred the hard-handed action of the supreme god, will not have seen this in another light. Prometheus is Zeus' personal opponent, he rejects the Allfather's authority, so why should the god show mercy, why should he feel any scruples faced as he is with an assault on his power? If he had shown himself as lenient, it would have surpassed the comprehension of any Greek of the fifth century [133]. Like Sophocles in his 'Antigone' he does not aim at stirring up sympathy or antipathy nor is he interested in 'pro' and 'contra'. He is writing a drama, and this drama owes its force to contrasts. Zeus is hard but defends what belongs to him; Prometheus is, indeed, immoderately punished but his attitude is not realistic; therefore the chorus rebukes him [134].

k. Prometheus' foresight

If we wish to know what Aeschylus meant with this play we must pay attention to its title. It is called 'promêtheus', somebody with foresight. This name is, of course allegorical, the more so since there also exists an 'Epimetheus' (in Hesiod), somebody who is wise after the event. Let us consider the events that Prometheus foresaw. He is the great preceptor, the one who taught civilization to mankind; "every art possessed by man comes from Prometheus" [135]. 'Prometheus' as an idea or a program does in fact mean the capacity of man for cultural progress. This program is incorporated by the poet in a Titan; this means that human civilization contains an anti-Olympian element, something that the new gods do not like to see. This is expressed very pregnantly by the fact that Prometheus had to steal fire from heaven; the Olympian gods begrudged this primary source of energy to mankind and tried to hamper their progress in this way.

There is more. Prometheus also taught men 'many ways whereby they might read the future' [136]. This brings to light a truth that is far from pleasant to the gods but not less unpleasant to man. The rule of the Olympian gods is not eternal. They too will disappear. And what will come then? I believe that this is the real reason why this tragedy is called 'Prometheus', it is about foresight. Aeschylus fulfils here the crucial function of the tragedian : he indicates the frontiers of human existence, he dares to express what the public feels dimly and uneasily but what it represses. This is that their gods are 'historical'; they have an origin in time and will also find their end in time. Even for the Olympians there will be a 'Götterdämmerung'.

It was difficult for the Greeks to live with their gods, because these were wilful and arbitrary, because they were no models of moral behaviour, jealous and egocentric as they were, and, in particular, because they did not love human beings. Greek literature, from beginning to end, brims over with this. Aeschylus, however, indicates here the real reason to keep at a safe distance from these gods : their power-base is shaky. Who entrusts himself to them completely will be dragged down in their fall. Aeschylus surely was pious, the gods must be venerated, as gods they are entitled to this. But like none other he has gauged the limits of this religion. Thus even Aeschylus, by making this known to his spectators, contributed to the destabilization of the Olympian religion.

6. How difficult it is to live en famille

a. The conflict between the sexes

Generally spoken Greek tragedy does not excel in esteem of women. Most of the time woman is pictured in the same modest and retired role that she also occupied in society; female choruses do not voice feminist ideas [137]. In Aeschylus denigrating terms about women are far from rare. "Your task is to hold your peace and bide within the house", in this way Eteocles sums up general male sentiment [138]. Actually he does not even want the Theban women to implore the gods for a favourable result of the battle. For, he says, "matters abroad are man's affair - let no woman advise thereon" [139]. Eteocles, for that matter, reveals himself as a first-rate misogynist : "Neither in evil days nor in happy property may I have to house with womankind. Has she the upper hand, it is hard to live with such insolence; but, if she is seized with fear, she is still a greater bane to home and city" [140]. And at whose door is the blame laid? "O Zeus, what a breed have you given us in womankind!" [141].

This conspicuous contempt of woman is given a quasi-scientific background in 'Eumenides' where a genetic theory of a sort is formulated by nobody less than Apollo, the god of wisdom. "The mother of what is called her child is not his parent but only the nurse of the newly implanted germ. The begetter is the parent whereas she, as a stranger for a stranger, only preserves the sprout" [142]. This explosive theory [143] receives an exceptional weight here because its claim to divine authority exonerates Orestes from matricide; according to this theory the woman he has killed, Clytaemnestra, is not his mother. One must also pay attention to the words : "as a stranger for a stranger'; if they were consistently applied this doctrine would completely alienate the children from their mothers. But not only a god proclaims this absolute male superiority, a goddess, Athena, does the same. "In all things, save wedlock, I am for the male with all my soul, and am entirely on the father's side"; this she confirms with a personal argument : "For mother I have none that gave me birth". She too casts the ballot in favour of Orestes [144]. This clearly is the right order of things.

However, what we find in the world of tragedy is that certain women do not resign themselves to their role. "Lady, like a prudent man you speak wisely", say the old men, who think they know everything, to Clytaemnestra [145]. Clytaemnestra is the Lady Macbeth of antiquity; she takes the male role - from which Macbeth-Aegisthus shrinks away - unto herself. The chorus reproaches the man thus : "Why then, in the baseness of your soul, did you not kill him (Agamemnon) yourself, but leave this slaying to a woman?" [146].

The whole Trojan War started because of a woman. Helen is purloined from Menelaus, and in order to revenge the offended husband all the Greek princes hasten to Troy. When the voyage does not progress well, Agamemnon proves prepared to sacrifice his own daughter Iphigeneia : in order to win back a woman another woman is made into a sacrificial victim [147]. However, this deed is not presented as inherently justified but rather as a paroxysm of male self-sufficiency - the weighing of military success against the life of a woman, in which the father yields to the commander -, which, according to Aeschylus, does not redound to the credit of Agamemnon [148].

Clytaemnestra's revenge is carried out in 'Agamemnon'. I believe the initial question Aeschylus asked himself in constructing this blood-curdling drama was as follows : what would happen if a woman (a society woman) were to behave exactly like a man? Clytaemnestra is 'androboulos', she has a man's heart, thus it is stated in the very first lines [149]. She governs Argos during the absence of her husband, she issues orders, she effects arrangements. When Agamemnon returns from Troy, we witness a curious scene that makes it clear which of the two, the male or the female, is the strongest. Agamemnon arrives in his carriage at the door of his palace. Clytaemnestra comes to greet him and urges him to enter his house over the purple carpets which she has spread out before him. The king refuses to do this; he finds this barbaric or else an honour that is due only to the gods. But although he declares firmly : "This is my last word", Clytaemnestra finally has the best of the verbal duel that follows and Agamemnon falls in with her [150].

What she really wants is to be like a man. "Here lies the man", she says scornfully above the corpse of the king, "who did me wrong, minion of each Chryseïs at Troy". A moment ago she has also killed his last bedfellow, Cassandra, which, to quote her own words, meant 'an added relish of (erotic) delight' for her [151]. Pomeroy perceives this reversal of roles very sharply. She refers to an utterance of Clytaemnestra about her paramour Aegisthus : she will have no fear, 'so long as the fire upon my hearth is kindled by Aegisthus' [152]. This, says Pomeroy, is exceptionally shocking since it is the traditional task of a woman to tend the hearth [153].

Gagarin, who devoted some fascinating pages to the conflict between the sexes in the Oresty (the trilogy Agamenon - Choêphoroi - Eumenides), summarizes the plot of 'Agamemnon' as follows : the crime of male against female (i.e. the sacrifice of Iphigeneia) is counter-balanced by that of female against male, the deceitful (and therefore feminine) murder of Agamemnon, husband, ruler and commander-in-chief. The male side, that was originally wronged by the abduction of Helen, reached a high pitch of masculine military domination in order to revenge this injustice. Now the pendulum swings back to another extreme, the man dominated by a woman. The chastisement of Troy was only possible at the expense of the feminine forces in Argos (represented in particular by Iphigeia). Now these feminine forces arrive at such a complete domination that all the men, Agamemnon, Aegisthus, the chorus, become subjected to the power of Clytaemnestra [154].

In Sophocles' 'Antigone' the basic conflict is between ruler and subject but, at the same time, there is another conflict, that between man and woman [155]. Creon reacts nervously not only to attacks on his power but also to those on his male supremacy. Segal says correctly that these two factors are closely interconnected for Creon [156] : "No woman shall be master while I live" [157]. What the king fears in particular is the reversal of roles : "Now if she (Antigone) thus can flout authority unpunished (by wanting to bury Polynices against the express command of the king), I am the woman, she is the man" [158].

b. Death as a partner

In all the families that Greek tragedy presents to us basic relationships are severely disturbed. They have a hostile, even a bloody character. The son (Oedipus) kills the father (Laius), the son (Orestes) kills his mother (Clytaemnestra) on the instigation of his sister (Electra), the father (Heracles) kills his own children, the mother (Medea) kills her children, the mother (Agave) kills her son (Pentheus), the father (Agamemnon) sacrifices his daughter (Iphigeneia), the wife (Helen) flies her husband (Menelaus), the husband (Jason) repudiates his wife (Medea), the mother (Clytaemnestra) chases away her daughter (Electra), the brothers (Eteocles and Polynices) kill one another, the sisters (Antigone and Ismene) fly at each other, to say nothing of those who destroy themselves out of despair because their families are ruined, Iocaste, Haemon, Eurydice.

Once again the great tragedians fulfil their essential task : they reconnoitre the frontiers of human civizilation and society, they venture themselves into the wilderness beyond those frontiers. In human existence civilization and nature nowhere and never fit seamlessly. There are no political regulations, no moral prescriptions, no social taboos that are able to dominate effectively all that has to be dominated. Who or what can banish every aggression, all discord, all disharmony? Who or what is able to conciliate all oppositions and to settle all disputes? In every civilization the family is the prototype of society; it is in the family that man and woman consort together, it is here where children are born and educated and where people work jointly for their livelihood and care for each other. The family is also the primary institution in which human relationships are taught and experienced and valued. The parents pass down the values of society to the children; they are the first teachers who school the children as social beings. It is for these fundamental reasons that always and everywhere the family is fostered and protected, is praised and sung, is also glorified and idealized in terms of a peaceful and happy companionship in contrast to the cruel and violent society. Even to-day there are countless novels, movies, paintings that present the family in this light. This satisfies the desire of people to have, what Lionel Trilling calls, 'a noble vision of life' [159].

At the end of Woody Allen's great film 'Interiors' a woman, a mother, walks straight into the furious waves of an unleashed sea. There she drowns herself - in a scene worthy of Greek tragedy. This movie is called 'Interiors' because this woman is an interior designer. But however clever she may be in arranging interiors, she did not succeed in arranging her own 'interior' harmoniously, that is to say her own private family sphere. Allen's film - and he is not the only modern artist to succeed in this - runs parallel with the great traditions of tragedy. This tradition makes it abundantly clear that, although the family is the origin and the primary cell of society, nevertheless all the ills of society are to be found in it. The basic trouble with society is that it is not 'close-fitting' : society, which we may equate theoretically with civilization, is constantly assailed by 'nature in the sense of savage, ungovernable and irrational forces. The principal elements of wild nature are death and sexuality; they remain outside the control of codes of behaviour and rationality.

c. The wild force of sexuality

Death is one of the great partners in tragedy, so much will be clear. However, with regard to sexuality, at first sight this seems less evident. Had we not better turn for this to Aristophanes who, as an author of comedies, is much more direct and plain in this respect? Often he handles the man-woman problems and reflects realistically the marital situations of his age. One must, however, not lose sight of the fact that the scene of most tragedies is laid inside a family, in the house of Oedipus or in that of the Atrides; this means that they are built on the relationship of husband and wife. Not a few of the plays take this situation as their basic subject. I mention only 'Agamemnon' and 'Medea', two of the most impressive. The kind of reality that tragedians present to the spectators - this means also to us - is that of the family situation. They reduce and condense the general and historical reality that surrounds us to a microcosmic reality which they transpose into mythical terms.

The fact that in tragedy death is 'wild' and uncontrollable must necessarily lead to the conclusion that the same is the case with sexuality. People may wish to close their eyes to the interplay between them, but the testimony of art, even to-day, is unambiguous. The poets know that strong fluctuations in one sphere have their repercussions in the other. Hence an unbridled sexuality is intrinsic in tragedy. We must realize clearly that all human relationships have a sexual component; this means that they may easily be experienced sexually. All kinds of sexual combinations are not only possible but actual. Within the family this is doubly valid, even threefold. The origin of every family is the basic sexual relationship between the parents from which offspring are born. The family therefore originates in an erotic connection; all the relations within a family are coloured by it, much more, indeed, than in other human relationships.

The conclusion is obvious : from a biological or anthropological point of view the family is the particular domain of sexuality. This is not established by the very origin of the family but also by the intimacies, the daily intercourse, the shared communion of close family life. When, within the family, all primary things are taught and learnt such as eating and drinking, walking and toilet training, why then not also sexuality? Only a few years ago the French film-director Louis Malle made a movie in which a mother-son-incest occurs. Admittedly the mother (as interpreted by Léa Massari) actually provoked her son to this act but Malle's presentation of it implied that there was no reason to get excited over it. Those who did this and spoke of an immoral film forgot to pay attention to the title. For the movie was called 'Le souffle au coeur'; this is a medical term indicating a dysfunction of the heart, something abnormal that is; one has to be prudent with and must not let it get grow. In fact, both church and society oppose incest.

Nearly everywhere in the world and in most periods of history and civilizations - for there are some exceptions - incest is the object of severe prohibitions and is surrounded with strong taboos. In the penal law of my country, the Netherlands, even pseudo-incest is punishable, for instance sexual relations between stepfathers and step-daughters [160], although they are no blood-relations [161]. The reason for such severe stipulations is not so much that, in sexual relations between relatives, the chance of handicapped children (or of sterility) is greater than in other sexual relations. No, it is absolutely required for the existence and the continuity of human society that, with regard to sexuality, people should not restrict themselves to those in close proximity to them. They must even renounce this completely. They must be jotted out of the narrow circle of family life. Else there would only exist mini-societies, and because of the ensuing risk of sterility and physical retrogression of the offspring, these would constantly be threatened with extinction. "That is why man is destined to leave father and mother ..." [162].

The doorway to sexual relations inside the family, with those between the parents excepted - legalized because they are necessary -

has been nailed up very solidly. So solidly that all of us stand at the other side of the doorway, and want to stay there. We really find incestuous relationships not only inacceptable but also a subject unfit for discussion, perhaps even unthinkable. Nevertheless, our attitude respecting incest varies with the closeness of the relationship. Marriages between second cousins are rarely objected to and usually countenanced; marriages between first cousins are more problematical. A sexual relation between uncle and niece is deemed reprehensible but is not severely reprobated; one between an aunt and her nephew is thought a ridiculous thing, in particular on account of the great difference in age [163]. Incestuous intercourse between brother and sister is found repellent [164], that between father and daughter criminal.

d. The real 'blood-guilt'

However, incest between mother and son is thought of as horrifying and inconceivable. When, in the school where I was a teacher, 'King Oedipus' was going to be performed (I mentioned this already), the ignorant pupils of the non-classical streams had to be informed in advance of the meaning of Greek tragedy in general and of this drama in particular. The teacher who was asked to go over the contents of the play with two classes of seventeen and eighteen year olds resolutely refused to do this : incest, that was a subject about which he did not want to talk! And above all not to minors! And yet this was a man who could certainly not be dubbed 'prude'.

Mother-son incest is the real 'blood-guilt', indeed. For instead of turning outwards, away from the family, to find a sexual partner, the son returns to his origin, the maternal womb from which he issued. This shatters all that is seen as normal in human existence. Nevertheless, Sophocles chose this as the motif for 'King Oedipus'. He must have been conscious of what he was doing when he, on a date somewhere between 440 and 430, asked the citizens of Athens to come to the theatre to see this. The combination of Sophocles' artistic abilities, the exceptionally daring theme, and perhaps a certain apprehension on his part because of the expected effect on the public yielded a drama that is one of the two greatest in world-history, the other being 'King Lear', where the relation between Lear (who has no wife) and Cordelia, his beloved daughter, also shows incestuous traits.

Sophocles weakens the shock-effect somewhat, because Oedipus and Iocaste do not know that they are son and mother. On the other hand, Iocaste is in any case twice as old as her husband, and, therefore, if he were not her son, she 'might have been his mother'. I believe that something of an incestuous desire creeps into every sexual relationship in which the difference in age is great, for instance a generation. It is on account of this that the wretched Oedipus puts out his eyes. He has sinned unwittingly but this does not exonerate him in his own eyes.

The spectators take their seats in the theatre armed with the reality of their own exogamous relations. Then Sophocles confronts them (and us) with the reality of endogamous relations. But he does not present these as an alternative; no, he lets the two irreconcilable realities collide. The way in which the Athenians experienced the man-woman relationship was problematic enough but their family life was an idyll compared with what Sophocles showed them. He puts this on the stage to bring home to them that the first reality, that of an exogamous family life striving after harmony, is conditioned by the second reality, that of the primary, inwardly directed relations of exclusive family life. They saw before their eyes that this primary reality is 'unlivable'; the situation on the stage condemned itself vigorously.

At the same time the inevitable and necessary prohibition of incestuous relationships causes tensions in the family as it exists, since the sexual tendencies are forced to direct themselves outwards; the result is that the family loses its coherence because the children have to leave the home to find partners. Tensions such as these were probably felt deeper in Hellas, in the Athens of the fifth and fourth century B.C. than in any other period of human history. As deeply as man can gauge Sophocles showed the dualistic, that is the incurable opposition in the very heart of human existence, the difficulty of living together in a family. And there was no solution, no 'katharsis', for the spectator who saw Oedipus stumbling off the stage, with the blood streaming from his eye-sockets, could identify with him, but, notwithstanding, did not go home 'purified'. Oedipus, 'most powerful of men' in Thebes, 'who knew all the famous riddles' [165], succumbed to the greatest of all riddles, that of human origin.

e. A case of pseudo-incest

There is another case of incest in Euripides' 'Hippolytus'. Hippolytus is the son of Theseus, king of Athens, and of Antippe (or Hippolyte), daughter of Minos, king of Crete. Phaedra falls in love with her stepson Hippolytus, actually a case of pseudo-incest but, nevertheless, one of illicit love within the frame of the family. We have already seen earlier that the love-goddess Aphrodite was behind this : "(Hippolytus) rejects the couch; of marriage he will none" [166], for he serves Artemis. The goddess cannot endure this and makes Phaedra become enamoured of Hippolytus.

The woman is well aware that this is an illicit passion. Her 'âme damnée', however, is her old nurse who asks her : "You love, ... you are as many" [167]. Nobody is stronger than Aphrodite. Be careful! She knows how to track down those who scorn her. Why be so scrupulous? Do not the gods do themselves exactly what they like in this field? Those who are wise among the inhabitants of this earth throw the mantle of love over discreditable passions. It is really not possible to conduct our lives according to the norms. Is it not pure presumption to want to be stronger than the gods themselves [168]? Of course this ends fatally. Since Phaedra is not able to seduce her stepson, she vindictively slanders him to Theseus. The king is only too ready to believe her, and, in his rage, becomes the cause of Hippolytus' death.

f. Brothers and sisters

Shortly before I summed up all the disturbed family relationships in tragedy. Perhaps it has struck the reader that there is one notable exception : the relation between brother and sister. However, we may well ask whether the predicate 'normal' can be attached to it. We find in tragedy two famous pairs of brothers and sisters : Antigone and Polynices, and Orestes and Electra. It seems to me that there are incestuous undertones here. I cannot efface the impression that something more than sisterly and brotherly attachment comes into play here.

This is perhaps not very conspicuous in the relation between Electra and Orestes. Nevertheless, in the three plays in which they make their appearance the relation between brother and sister overshadows the bond of friendship between Orestes and Pylades completely [169]. Together brother and sister revenge their murdered father by killing their mother Clytaemnestra and her lover Aegisthus; in this way they form, so to speak, a new 'married couple' that repairs the breach in their parents' marriage by a new unity of acting and intention.

That there is an incestuous element in Sophocles' 'Antigone' seems evident to me. I know that many scholars vehemently reject this possibility; Waldock spends many pages on proving how normal Antigone finally is [170]. However, does it not strike us immediately that Antigone does not waste a word on the fallen Eteocles who, for that matter, is also her brother? She is the betrothed of Haemon but if only the Antigone-passages had been handed down to us we should hardly notice this. It is Polynices here and Polynices there. Even in the beginning of the play, Antigone says to her sister Ismene, in view of the possibility that she might perish when trying to bury her brother : "How sweet to die in such employ, to rest sister and brother linked in love's embrace" [171], as though it were the tomb of a married couple. She also curses the marriage that her brother has contracted, his bond with Argeia, the daughter of Adrastus, king of Argos. This marriage enabled him to march with an Argive army against Thebes, with the result that he undid himself as well as his sister [172].

At the same time Antigone is very well aware that she is the issue of an incestuous marriage and is, therefore, doomed to die unmarried [173]. It is as if she wishes to make it clear that destiny and the course of events drive her to Polynices. Then follow some revealing lines : "Had it been a husband dead I might have wed another, and have borne another child to take the dead child's place, but, now my father and my mother both are dead, no second brother can be borne for me" [174]. When Creon condemns her to a slow death in the rock-tomb, she calls this her 'bridal bower', her 'nympheion' [175]. There is no mention of Haemon in her long lament. Obviously she had rather be united in death with Polynices than on earth with Haemon.

g. 'Why women?'

For the commentators of antiquity Euripides was the only tragedian, says Pomeroy, who had the reputation of being a misogynist [176]. Aulus Gellius informs us that this poet thoroughly disliked women either because of his natural disposition or because he has had two wives who spoilt the pleasures of marriage for him [177]. However, this author was writing five centuries later. Perhaps Sophocles hit the mark more accurately when he, reacting to the assertion that Euripides was a misogynist in his plays, answered : "In his plays he hated them but in his bed he liked them" [178].

Whatever the nature of Euripides' personal inclinations may have been, it won't do, of course, to ascribe every anti-feminine expression of one of his heroes to his own personal opinion. Pomeroy even believes that a man like Euripides, who had a reputation to keep up as a critical mind and a freethinking man, cannot have been plainly anti-feministic [179]. Many of his heroines are strong self-conscious personalities, the reverse of subjected or oppressed. Apart from that, the reader will be able to note a number of passages that are friendly to women, and not a few expressions that show that this poet understood them.

In 'Medea', to start with, we find an incredible passage, voiced by a female chorus, in which a reversal of the normal order of things is announced. "Upward and backward to their fountains the sacred rivers are stealing; justice is turned in injustice, the order of old to confusion (this refers to the repudiation of Medea by Jason) : the thoughts of the hearts of men are treacherous wholly, and, reeling from its ancient foundations, the faith of the gods is become a delusion, ... for women the old-time story is ended, and bad fame will no longer have women in its grip" [180]. But these enthusiastic words follow on a vehement tirade by Medea herself that ends thus : "I will prove that I am a woman indeed! Men say we are most helpless for all good, but perfectly able of dark deeds" [181]. It is, therefore, the question whether the chorus really announces the victory of 'the soft forces', to quote the words of the Dutch poetess Henriette Roland Holst. For "when a woman suffers wrong in her marital rights, no spirit more bloodthirsty shall be found" [182].

What will all those male spectators, probably far from examples of conjugal fidelity, have made of a passage like the following? "We women are of all unhappiest, who, first, must buy, as buys the highest bidder (with this the dowry is meant), a master over our bodies ... Will the lord we gain be evil or good? Divorce is infamy to us, we may not even reject a suitor!" [183]. Here again fierce Medea sums up the whole misery of Athenian womanhood. Perhaps the reaction of the men is reflected in the answer of Creon to Medea's question, why do you banish me? : "I fear you" [184].

Yet however terrible her revenge was, would it not have dawned on the male public that Jason acted basely when he repudiated Medea, in spite of the fact that it was she who had obtained the Golden Fleece for him? Jason did not try to conceal that his real reason for divorcing Medea was that he could better himself. Having lived for ten years as an exile in Corinth, he suddenly gets a prospect of the throne of that city, if only he will repudiate Medea and marry Creon's daughter Creusa [185].

"Woman is but woman - born for tears", says Medea [186]; this is also the opinion of Creusa, Apollo's victim in 'Ion' : "Woman's lot as touching men is hard; and since the good are with the bad confused, hated we are" [187]. If only we had not married, sigh the suppliant women in the play of that title, for our children have fallen in battle [188], doubtless a complaint of many Greek mothers in those days.

Utterances like these testify to a certain understanding of women; this prompts Pomeroy to say : "My subjective estimate of Euripides is favorable" [189]. But if she had kept in view the rule of Nilsson that I have mentioned already, i.e. that one must pay attention to the frequency and intensity of the utterances, in this case about women, then she would have had reason enough to reconsider her opinion. First there is a reiteration of the theory that we have already found in Aeschylus, that the father is the unique origin of the child, and the mother no more than the field that receives the seed. When forced to choose between his parents Orestes takes the part of his father who begat him, rather than of her who was 'the field that from the sower received the seed' [190]. It is often said that Euripides had modern insights and was well acquainted with the science of his time, but here he does not show this. Current medical opinion is reflected in the 'Corpus Hippocraticum', a collection of texts dating from the fifth to the first century B.C.; they present the doctrine of the 'two seeds', a male and a female, so that both sexes have an equal part in the conception [191].

When Iocaste asks her son Polynices who has married in far away Argos, whether his marriage is happy or unhappy, he answers cautiously : "Unto this day I find no fault in her" [192]. This is the very minimum but could many Athenian husbands have said more? "Shame is this, when foremost in the home is wife, not husband", this is the opinion even of Electra [193]. "For a woman silence and discretion are fairest, and still tarrying in the home", thus Macaria, the well-educated daughter of Heracles [194]. Aethra, Theseus' mother, adds to this : "Seemly it is that women, who are wise, still act through men" [195]. In this way Euripides took care that conventional opinions about the role of women were proclaimed by the women themselves.

What men have to say about women is something quite different; utterances in an unfavourable vein are very frequent. "Womanfolk is scandal-loving", says the old paidagogos in 'The Phoenician Maidens' [196]. Sensible men do not permit their wives to receive visits of other women in their homes : "They are teachers of iniquity"; this again is put by the author into the mouth of a woman [197]. "For us the cloistered virtue is chastity" [198]; as long as there are no other men in the case the husbands have no problems with their wives [199]. This is all the more important since "all women are found burning with the slur of lust" [200]. How tender conjugal love must have been if Hecabe can say that it is the custom ('nomos') that women are not allowed to look at their husbands [201]! It is true, of course, that the whole Trojan War has been fought to protect the inviolability of marriage; it is also true that Agamemnon declares that he cannot allow Greek women to be abducted by barbarians [202]. Later, however, the offended husband, Menelaus, states coolly that he has come to Troy, not so much on behalf of Helen, but rather to revenge himself on Paris. He would kill his wife with pleasure in revenge for so many fallen friends [203]. In short, "women are born to mar the lives of men" [204].

In Euripides a question keeps recurring that is constantly repeated in tragedy as well as in comedy, a question called by Loraux 'typically Greek' : 'why women?' [205]. "Nor sea nor land nurture such a breed : whosoever has spoken ill of women or shall hereafter speak, all this in this one word I include", this is the opinion of Polymestor [206]. "Would that mortals in another way could get themselves children, and that womankind did not exist; then no curse had lighted upon men" [207]. One must pay attention here to the sharply dualistic terms : the mortals ('brotoi') and the men ('anthropoi') are exclusively the males; it is not 'the women' that are contrasted to them but 'womankind', the female sex, which is obviously no part of humanity. "If only no woman lived, a good thing would it be - not one on earth", says a satyr, but since he is a satyr, he quickly makes a 'reservatio mentalis' : "except a few for me" [208]. That woman is really 'nonexistent', is the tenor of a bitter word by Iphigeneia : "A man that dies from the house, leaves a void; a woman matters not" [209]. Earlier, when she was going to be sacrificed, she said : "Worthier than ten thousand women one man is to look on the light" [210].

If still somebody is not convinced that Euripides did not have a high regard of women, I might advise him - for her this is not necessary, I imagine - to read that long tirade of the misogynist par excellence, Hippolytus. Servant girls must not be permitted to converse with the mistress of the home; the only thing they do is to conspire against the men. No, the housewife should only have dumb animals for company. Still worse than stupid women are bright ones since, by means of these, Aphrodite causes the greatest evils. "I hate a woman with brains, in my home nobody may be smarter than is convenient". The best wife is a nullity, a simpleton who is completely useless. "Why have you given, Zeus, a home beneath the sun to woman, this specious curse to man (again 'anthropoi')? For, if you will raise a mortal seed, this ought not to be got of women but in your temples should they (the men) lay its prize, or gold, or iron, or a weight of bronze, and so buy seed of children ... and dwell free in free homes unvexed of womankind". And he concludes his outburst thus : "My woman-hate shall never be satiated ...., leave me free to trample on them for ever" [211].

7. Women in comedy

a. Aristophanes : the man and his work

In preparation for this chapter I read all the Greek tragedies. A long stay in this snakepit of emotions and passions is an unsettling experience. One is almost overcome by a sense of vertigo as one follows the desperate fortunes of tragic protagonists who, one after another, are brought down by an incomprehensible and uncomprehended destiny. It is almost as though one were taking a journey through the high mountains. The inhabited earth seems far away and one becomes overwhelmed by ever more terrifying vistas. The air is rarefied, the chest gets oppressed, one breathes with difficulty, there is a giddy feeling in the head. Then it is a considerable relief to descend to the valley where real people live and to surrender oneself to the guidance of Aristophanes, the grandmaster of Greek comedy. His plays are full of an unvarnished realism; even now, after some 2300 years, he is perfectly able to turn illusion into reality - which is the hallmark of great theatre -, not only when we see his comedies played but even when we read them. Spectators and readers feel that they are almost participants in the dramatic action. One might almost be an eye-witness, posted unobtrusively on the corner of the street, when Lysistrata, for instance, assembles her fellow fighters in the early dawn of an Athenian day.

The man who performs this miracle, the poet Aristophanes, is said to be the outstanding representative of what is dubbed 'the Old Comedy' [212]. He is, in fact, the only representative of fifth-century comedy; the plays of his contemporaries are lost with the exception of a number of fragments. On the other hand, we are still in the possession of eleven complete plays of the forty-four by Aristophanes, plus fragments of the others. We know pretty little of the poet himself; even the dates of his life are not certain. His plays had their first nights between 425 and 388. What we know is that he was reasonably well off, that he was married and that he had a son.

Aristophanes' comedies are still eminently readable for a modern public, and in great part they are still theatrically effective. As they are, however, replete with allusions to contemporary social and political situations, they need a lot of explanations for the spectator of the present day. Many times, certainly, Aristophanes is really brilliant and his scenes are still as irresistibly comical as they were then. But sometimes his 'vis comica' weakens; he then has recourse to farcical effects with stereotyped ingredients like a drunken old man etc. His plays teem with erotic double-meanings and obscenities. His allusions can be very gross; at times they are barely distinguishable from 'soft porno' [213].

With regard to our subject, Aristophanes is important because of what he has to say about women. They are one of his favourite themes; he even devoted three whole plays to their problems. In general Aristophanes is kindly disposed towards women, although at times he is unfriendly, in particular towards older women. Again and again he ridicules the feminine addiction to drink, and also, not rarely, their nymphomania. Another reproach goes as follows : "Weight a woman will bear, if a man imposes it on her; fight she won't and she can't :

in fight she has always a fright" [214]. In this virile and aggressive society this was one of the principal reasons for contempt of women.

b. A man in a female assembly

The three plays I mentioned are 'Thesmophoriazousai', 'Ekklesiazousai', and 'Lysistrata', summarized by Cedric Whitman as 'the war between the sexes' [215]. I start with 'Thesmophoriazousai' since this play links up with my earlier section on Euripides. Aristophanes disliked this tragedian immensely; in his eyes Euripides was much too progressive while he himself was safely on the conservative side. In a great number of places he gives the most forceful expression to his loathing. In this play Aristophanes is taking the well-known misogynism of the tragedian as his target. Euripides has to appear before the assembly of women in order to justify himself. He does not feel like going and persuades his cousin Mnesilochus to act as his substitute. This man is disguised as a woman by his friend, the poet Agathon, with the help of his well-assorted wardrobe. Agathon is an effeminate person, actually the prototype of that decadence of which Aristophanes only too frequently reproaches his contemporaries [216].

Well-disguised Mnesilochus ventures into the assembly of the women. Immediately after the opening of the proceedings a woman takes the floor and accuses 'that son of a greengrocer' - the favourite gibe against Euripides - of attributing every possible evil to women: they act surreptitiously, they lust after men, they are fond of wine, they are unreliable and talkative, in short, they are good for nothing and a catastrophe for men [217]. Another woman backs her up. But then - and this is going to be the comical effect - Mnesilochus stands up and suggests that Euripides - let us be honest, ladies! - might be right in one or two points. And now he, or 'she', indulges in the fancy that 'she' has made a fool of her husband in order to be able to receive her lover at night; he continues with the story of a woman who succeeded in saddling her husband with a supposititious child. He/she concludes in this way: "Then wherefore rail we at Euripides? We are not one bit more sinned against than sinning" [218]. Among the indignant shouts of the excited women Mnesilochus adds more samples of this kind. Furiously the women decide to scourge 'her'. They tear the clothes of 'her' body, and, lo, it is a man! Nothing daunted the evildoer snatches away the child of one of the women and threatens to kill it if he were to come to grief, only to discover, when he has unrolled the swaddling-clothes, that, instead of a child, he has a large wine-bottle in his hands.

The chorus then pays the men back for their accusations. We women, they say, are obliged to sing our own praises, the men never have a good word for us. And if we are really such an evil, why do you want to marry us at all costs? And why do you fly into such a rage, when you, on coming home, see that your dear little wife is not there? We are not like you, we do not have our pockets full of public money. Men! Pot-bellied robbers, altar-thieves, kidnappers! We are much better in managing a home than you are [219]. This shows us clearly how Aristophanes differs from Euripides : he offers the ladies a fair chance to defend themselves forcefully. But at the same time it is perfectly evident that a war is going on, the war of the sexes.

c. The reversal of the sex roles

The 'Ekklesiazousai' or 'the assembly of the women' is especially important since the poet reverses the sex roles completely in this play. He raises the question of what would happen if the women were in control of public affairs; in this way he develops what Danièle Auger calls 'a Utopian project' [220]. Praxagora, an Athenian lady, wrapped in man's attire, gathers a number of women for an assembly that will be the exact counterpart of the 'ekklesia', the Athenian (male) Assembly. Democracy will, therefore, be turned into a 'gynecracy'. "We women dare this daring deed to do, if we can seize upon the helm of state and trim the ship to weather through the storm" [221].

When the women have assembled according to the rules, Praxagora presents her social-political program [222]. There will be general equality (that is to say, of men and women), everyone will have an equal share of the riches of the state, such as agrarian products and the revenues of the silvermines. Everything will be paid out of the public purse; everyone will have to deliver all that he produces to the public store-houses.

Since no one need fear that he will be a loser there will be no deceitful keeping back of goods. Marriage will be abolished. Men and women will be free to choose their partners. In order to ensure that the beautiful will not always enjoy the preference, qualities other than good looks must determine the first choice. The children will not be the possession of the parents. And who, for that matter, will know who the father is? They will be the responsibility of the state. Old people and the disabled will be maintained by public funds. All work will be done by slaves, and everyone may have them at his or her command. In case of trespassing the guilty citizen will be punished by temporary denial of food and wine. Meals will be furnished in great public halls.

The second part of the play is on a considerably lower level and becomes more and more a farce. It aims at making the new women's program ridiculous. A citizen (Praxagora's husband) who comes to deliver his goods quarrels violently with another character who says that he is not mad enough to hand over his products. A young man who wants a girl and has the choice between a youthful wench and some old prostitutes is almost torn to pieces by the latter because he prefers the younger one. The intention of the author seems to be to show that the plan of the women is doomed to fail because of the inveterate egotism of mankind.

It is, therefore, highly questionable whether Aristophanes really wanted to tell us that women would do much better than men. True enough, he gives Praxagora every occasion to develop her ideas; the poet himself certainly had grave objections against the inequality and avarice prevailing in Athens. Suzanne Saïd rightly points out, however, that the women, in their role of social planners, have to revert to the male role. The title too is deceptive, for it is not a real women's assembly; in the beginning Praxagora states very clearly that they come together merely in order to rehearse [223]. I mentioned already that Praxagora, just like all the other women, wears men's clothes. And these vestments are those of their own husbands. They have even glued beards to their faces : "Come, fasten on a beard, and be a man" [224]. They no longer depilate themselves and they let their skins tan in the sun (a society woman who stays at home has a fair complexion). But in spite of all this nobody can forget for one moment that all of them are women : they simply speak and act like women. Saïd talks of an 'impossible change of roles' [225]. Her conclusion is that, according to this play, human nature is unchangeable [226].

It is exactly the Utopian program of Praxagora that proves this very clearly. For what is presented to us is the complete welfare state where everyone gets what his heart or his belly wishes for. The polis, once controlled by the heroes of Marathon and Salamis, now becomes a super-housewife. This is the victory of the oikos over the polis, of privare interests over the common good. "The whole system of Praxagora", Saïd says, "is meant to satisfy the material needs of the individuals". What Aristophanes wanted to show his fellow-citizens is where they were heading. His 'gynecracy' is the ultimate (albeit impossible) consequence of the decay of Athenian democracy. That - he often ridicules the politicians on the score of effeminacy - is, obviously, no compliment for the women, quite the contrary.

d. The rebellion of the women

'Lysistrata' is perhaps the most pleasant play of Aristophanes; it is just as much alive as on its first night in 411 B.C. Lysistrata is an Athenian lady who is more than tired of the never ending wars of the men. She succeeds in persuading her partners in misfortune to start a women's strike. They decide to refuse to the men the nuptial bed until they, the men, shall have concluded peace. But soon they do not stop at this. Lysistrata sticks at nothing and succeeds in getting the collaboration of a Spartan (female) delegation. The Spartan men too must be put under pressure. The Spartan women persuade Lysistrata that they must lay hands on the war-chest. Therefore they occupy the Acropolis, the domain of the virgin Athena who guards the federal treasure. Once on top of the hill they are the masters of the situation, and the war of the sexes is a fact. Barricading the rock suits Lysistrata very well because several women want to disappear stealthily homeward. In a drastic way the men show that they are lovesick but they are turned down. Finally the men promise to behave better in the future, and the play ends with a dance festival.

This comedy - just like other scenes in his work - makes it perfectly clear that Aristophanes hated war and that in his view the women are right. He evidently admires Lysistrata and does not make her ridiculous at all. He demonstrates with gusto how she is able to hit the men, her own husband not excepted, in their weak spot, their sexual desires. It is true that the occupation of the Acropolis turns the whole town upside down but then the author is of the opinion that Athens is ruled (by the men) in a catastrophic way. However, his aim is not to prove that the women are superior and would do so much better than the men; only too often he points to their typical failures, their addiction to drink and their nymphomania. He does not plead for equality of the sexes either [227]. At the end of the play power reverts to the men : they will go on to conduct the affairs of the polis.

Michèle Rosellini remarks that woman in this play presents two contrary characters : she is the curse of the men and the cause of all their misery, but at the same time she is the bearer of all domestic values [228]. Here we have the great dualistic antithesis from which Greek men never were able to liberate themselves; I treated this at length in Volume II, Chapter IV, Section 4. It may be summed up in this way : "We can't live with such tormentors, nor, by Zeus, do without you" [229]. Somewhere else Aristophanes refers to women as 'our household pests' [230]. Thus Rosellini is right in saying that the image of woman in this play is constantly determined by a certain ambivalence [231].

What was it that Aristophanes wanted to make clear? His reason for writing was surely not to offer once again an exhaust-valve for that old and ineradicable hate of women. Rosellini is of the opinion that it is 'a homoeopathic treatment' : Lysistrata applies a therapy to the degenerate city in which the ill is combated with something worse. "The illness itself becomes the remedy." The men who, by going to the war, deny their bodies to their wives, gain a new insight because the women deny their bodies to their husbands. Was this a solution? No, it was not, for the war went on as usual. Nevertheless, it was a demonstration [232], a demonstration of something that did not exist and would not exist : peace between all the Greeks, coupled with harmony between man and woman [233]. From this deepest desire of a great author this Utopian play was born.

8. The tragical phenomenon

a. The three great tragedians

The three great tragedians, Aeschylus, Sophocles, and Euripides, are more or less contemporaries; they partook in and, at the same time, caused the enormous and unique cultural movement of the fifth century B.C. Aeschylus' first (preserved) tragedy, 'The Persians', was performed for the first time in 472 B.C.; Sophocles and Euripides died shortly after one another in the years 407-405. In antiquity this synchronism was expressed in this way that Aeschylus fought in the Battle of Salamis in 480 B.C., Sophocles, as an ephebe, sang the 'paean' during the victory celebrations, and Euripides was born in that year.

Aeschylus was born in in 525/524 B.C. into a prominent family of Eleusis; he fought, as an Attic soldier, at Marathon and on the ships near Salamis, perhaps also in the sea battle of Artemisium and in the decisive Battle of Plataeae. Twice he travelled to Syracuse, probably in 470 B.C., to attend a performance of his 'The Persians' at the court of Hieron I. We do not know why he went there again in 456 B.C. He died in 456 at Gela in Sicily where he is also buried. We still have seven of his ca. eighty tragedies. Both his sons were tragedians too, but of their work we know next to nothing [234].

Sophocles too came from a prominent family at Colonus in Attica, where he was born in 497/496. He too participated in Athenian public life; he was a 'hellanotamias' (a high official of the Sea League) as well as a stratege. He performed also cultic functions. In his youth he was a beautiful young man, and he remained a fascinating person till far into his old age; he never lacked praise and honour. He died in 406 B.C. His son too was a tragedian. Of the 123 plays of Sophocles only seven have been preserved [235].

Euripides was probably not born in 480 B.C., as the legend has it, but in 485/484, on the island of Salamis. His father intended him for a career in sports but the son had other ideas. He studied with Anaxagoras and Protagoras, the philosophers, and perhaps he was a friend of Socrates. Although he did not fulfil public functions, he is said to have belonged to Pericles' 'cercle'. In my opinion he resembled Beethoven : he was grumpy and immersed in himself, self-contained and lonely. Nevertheless, he was married twice and he had three sons. When he was nearly eighty years old he travelled to the court of King Archelaus of Macedonia in Pella, where he died in 406 B.C. Of his 89 plays nineteen are known to us [236]. Of the total literary output of the great tragedians together, only thirty-three of the nearly three-hundred dramas written by them have been handed down to us.

b. An exceptional cultural phenomenon

The efflorescence of Greek tragedy in the fifth century B.C. was an exceptional cultural phenomenon. In his great book on 'the tragical and history' Alfred Weber is able to cite long periods of history, the Middle Ages for instance, and many peoples, the Chinese for example, that did not know the tragic genre at all. In the time of the Reformation and of the wars of religion tragedy experienced a second bloom - and this is no accident - from Shakespeare to Racine. In the nineteenth century we find tragic themes in the opera, in those of Verdi who borrowed many a subject from Shakespeare, and of Wagner, in particular in the tetralogy of the Ring des Nibelungen. In our days it is especially the film directors who continue this genre, from Eisenstein to Stanley Kubrick [237].

But nowhere and never did this phenomenon manifest itself with such an intensity as in the Athens of the fifth century. Of the tragedies that were performed a disconcertingly great number have disappeared and of many a tragedian we know hardly more than his name, but what we still have in our possession is astonishing enough. Thirty-three dramas of three great tragedians who were contemporaries in the same city, with some never excelled master-pieces like Antigone, King Oedipus and Medea, how can we explain such a sudden and grandiose outburst of creativity?

We do not overstate the case when we see the efflorescence of tragedy as closely connected with the greatness of the city of Athens, even as a powerful and decisive element of this splendour. Aristophanes saw it thus; to him the peace and happiness of his town were directly dependent on the success of tragedy. This success, this general acceptance of tragedy by the Athenian 'demos', was, in his eyes, dangerously threatened by Socrates who 'has robbed tragedy of everything that is great in it', and by Euripides who, according to him, was not capable of writing a good tragedy. At the end of his comedy 'The Frogs', he makes Dionysus, the 'patron' of tragedy, award the great prize, not to Euripides (who witnesses the scene furiously), but to Aeschylus. This poet is even allowed to leave the nether world in order 'to save our city with wise maxims'; in his seat down there Sophocles may take his place in the mean time but on no account Euripides [238].

c. The Athenian theatre public

Let us pay some attention to the theatre public of those days. Since the municipality refunded the costs of a visit to the theatre everyone was able to attend the great annual theatre festival. The core of this festival was the performance of nine tragedies by three different authors who contended for the first prize. On three successive days there were three tragedies, each series followed by a satyr play. Add to this that on the preceding day five comedies of as many different authors were performed, and it will be clear that the spectators saw seventeen plays in four days. With the accompanying religious ceremonies the whole festival lasted five days. Hour after hour the the public sat on the stone seats of the theatre, each day for at least seven or eight hours. The only occasion that somehow reminds us of an Athenian theatre festival is the performance of the Ring in the Festspielhaus at Bayreuth.

d. The origination of tragedy

The religious ceremonies I mentioned tell us something about the origin of tragedy. In this connection I consider myself absolved of the obligation to explain how tragedy may have developed from cultic plays. There is much difference of opinion on this point. But everyone agrees that there is a direct relation between the cult of Dionysus and the development of tragedy; since this is important for our subject I shall hark back to it.

It will be evident that, for the miraculous phenomenon of the sudden blossoming of tragedy, there exists no historical explanation that fully tallies, an explanation so convincing that everyone has to admit that it is the correct one. All creative acts are somehow a mystery; they defeat explanation. Nevertheless, it is possible to sketch an historical frame work in which the origin of this phenomenon becomes at least intelligible. In doing this one will detect long lines of communication throughout the whole of Greek history.

In his book Alfred Weber relates how, from the thirteenth century B.C., mounted tribes penetrated into a broad region of the world, from the Balkans and Asia Minor via Iran and the Indian subcontinent to China. In the period after 2000 B.C. they had already been preceded by a first wave that brought the Hyksos in Egypt and the Achaeans in Greece. These Achaeans conquered Crete; the stories about the Trojan War testify of their presence in Asia Minor too. However, the consequences of these invasions were not as sweeping as of those that started about 1200 B.C. [239].

Perhaps 'nomad tribes' would have been a more apt description of these peoples than 'mounted tribes', for Weber understood by this term wandering tribes that move about with great herds of horned cattle. This would make it possible to situate the inroads of the tribes of Israel (that were not mounted) into Canaan, ca. 1200 B.C., in the same historical context. At the same time Greece was invaded by the warlike Dorians. They not only subjected the ancient non-Greek population but also dislodged the Ionians and the Aeolians who were related to them. These began to resettle themselves in the islands of the Aegean and on the coasts of Asia Minor; here they were followed by part of the Dorians themselves [240].

This worldhistorical phenomenon that is also to be observed in India and China brought the local autochthonous populations into contact with peoples that held totally different conceptions of life. These local tribes were sedentary agrarians; they lived in villages and in small towns, and even in larger and sometimes highly developed political complexes, like states. The religious culture of these agrarian populations was everywhere one that originated with the veneration of mother earth, of the 'Great Mother'. It was, therefore, a religion of the soil, of the fertile womb, chthonic and feminine.

The wandering tribes that, from 1200 B.C. on, threw themselves on those civilizations, had no fixed domiciles; they were nomads and lived by their cattle. Veneration of the soil was, therefore, alien to them. Their nomad life was hard and full of privations; they had constantly to fight for new pastures. Weber says that tribes like these also easily turn to the sea, because they do not feel themselves bound to one particular corner of the earth. In the case of the Greeks this certainly proved true [241]. The attitude of the peoples we are speaking of is hard and masculine; they have a strong tendency to dominate and to rule [242]. The chapters of Volume II should have shown that, until far into historical times, a masculine attitude to life and the mentality of the ruler were preserved in Hellas - combined with contempt of all those who were considered weaker and inferior, like women, slaves and barbarians.

All mounted tribes, Weber goes on, have a tragic conception of life; one may also find this in the great Germanic heroic myths, in the sagas of Beowulf, Hildebrand and the Nibelungen [243]. The 'hero' is the central character in the stories of these peoples. The Book of Samuel enumerates all David's heroes, 37 in number, and refers to their deeds - for instance, "He (Abisai) it was that engaged three hundred men with his own spear, and slew them" [244]. David who, when still a boy, defeated Goliath, was, of course, the greatest hero of them all. Usually, however, this hero is a tragical hero; fate constantly puts him to the test, and he is used to living in a critical situation. In this way he becomes representative of an extra-dimension of human life, for through his sufferings the great question comes to the fore : what is the meaning of such sufferings in the cosmos [245]? And perhaps also : is it possible to reconcile the idea of an ordered cosmos with suffering, especially with unmerited and uncomprehended suffering? This is a question about the meaning of life; at the same time it lies at the origin of tragedy.

e. Why only in Greece?

Weber has some difficulty in explaining why the tragic genre originated only in Greece and nowhere else. He offers the explanation, however, that autochthonous populations always present us with a bureaucratic and hierocratic civilization of a highly conservative and clerical sort. Although the priestly and administrative caste of the new rulers possessed a more speculative mind, they nevertheless adopted this conservative and conserving attitude since they were to graft their own systems on this clerical culture. This meant that life went on in the same channels. As so often in history the victors were mentally subjugated by the vanquished. In this case, according to Weber, the mentality of the invading tribes was almost everywhere absorbed by the chthonic attitude of the autochthonous populations. The author calls this attitude 'ein grosses, seelisch-geistiges Gegenreich' [246]. In classical Greece, however, we are never confronted with a priestly caste and an officialdom; therefore, the new rulers of Hellas were not absorbed mentally by the 'Gegenreich' [247]. The most important consequence of this was that they preserved intact their heroic attitude and their tragic conception of life. The Iliad, although it had its origins in the Ionian urbanized and merchant civilization, testifies to this [248].

Mario Understeiner, in his investigation into the origins of tragedy, develops an opinion that broadly agrees with that of Weber. His vision is not world-wide, for he restricted himself to the Greek habitat on both sides of the Aegean. Here there took place, he tells us, a curious mixture of Hellenic and pre-Hellenic elements. The Hellenic masculine and patriarchical civilization, with its religion of Allfather Zeus, came upon a feminine culture, with the cult of the Magna Mater. Neither of these civilizations succeeded in absorbing the other completely; hence it is not surprising that this partial amalgamation did not lead to a harmonious culture. A unique situation came about, not to be found elsewhere, that of two distinct civilizations within one geographical orbit which were, nevertheless, to influence each other profoundly. It is highly probable that, by way of reaction, the hard, virile and aggressive attitude of the Hellenes was fortified and strengthened, which may explain certain tendencies in the social and political life of the Greeks. It could also be that, as a consequence of this ambivalence, they remained conscious of a breach in their existence. Because of this 'vitium originis' the Greeks, so we may surmise, never became the luminary people of which Neohumanism liked to dream.

According to Untersteiner, this ambiguity can be detected very clearly in the legend of the origin of Dionysus. Semele, an earthly woman, became pregnant by Zeus but Hera was jealous of her and ordered Zeus to kill her with his lightning. However, he tore the not yet fully developed child from her womb and hid it in his thigh till it was born. Now Dionysus is a vegetation godhead of the Mediterranean religion; his mother Semele is probably identical with the Phrygian earth goddess Zemelo. Therefore, Dionysus is actually the product of both religions. However, the older chthonic element is pushed back in favour of the dominating patriarchical religion. Thus precisely in Dionysus, the 'patron' of tragedy, the ambiguous situation of Greek civilization comes to the fore. In my opinion this is also evidenced by the curious attitude of tragedy respecting women. On the one hand, woman is assigned a very modest and humble place, she does not count, many a denigrating word is heard, even outbursts of violent hatred; on the other, impressive female characters appear who seem to be modelled on Magna Mater herself.

In this sphere of Mediterranean chthonic religion tragedy had its origin, says Untersteiner, but Greek genius added a new and yet unknown element to it that makes tragedy to what it really is. This element is 'theoria'. This 'theoria' is the contemplative and creative faculty that is typical of Greek civilization and that is lacking in other contemporary cultures. Untersteiner concludes his book with these words : "In this contrast between a masculine and a feminine world, conditioned by the collision of two civilizations, a serious problem arises, that of the rights of the one and the other, a conflict that will lead to a tragical situation. The world of women refuses to be brushed aside so easily; every time she will appear again with her claims. In the Greek myths that have been revised according to patriarchical spirituality, a kind of contradiction can be found therefore. The result of this was the irreconcilable coexistence of godheads belonging to either one of both worlds, the feminine Mediterranean and the masculine Indo-European ones" [249]. Tragedy recovers these oppositions from dumb unconsciousness and sets them in the full light of the day. At the same time it is made clear in this way that Greek existence was based on irreconcilable dualistic partitions.

f. Hellas' 'Day of Atonement'

With these speculations before us it becomes easier to explain the function of tragedy in Greek life of the fifth century B.C. One knows what the Athenians, out of their own free will, annually let themselves in for : for days on end they saw three series of three tragedies plus a number of comedies and satyr plays, together, as Weber has it, 'ein Bild der Lebensrealität' [250]. One may well ask oneself why the spectators subjected themselves to such a psychic burden [251]. The reader should be well aware by now of the sort of experience the Athenians underwent in the theatre : tragedy is a bark that sails on a stream of blood, says Gerhard Nebel [252]. It is of the greatest importance that this five-day event was no fashionable modern festival like the Holland Festival or the Maggio Musicale di Firenze but a religious ritual itself framed in a ritual, under the patronage of Dionysus. His statue stood in the theatre; it was solemnly carried to its place by ephebes, during a light-procession on the eve of the festival. It is no accident that Wagner wanted the first part of the

Ring, 'Das Rheingold', to be the 'Vorabend' of the tetralogy. Dionysus' altar, adorned with vine-tendrils, was placed in the orchestra; his high-priest sat on the first row in a marble seat. Originally the first prize for the winner was a he-goat ('tragos'), the pre-eminently Dionysian animal [253].

According to Weber, the proper social function of tragedy was of an apotropaeic character, this means that it averted evil. One must make a comparison with a passion-play here; Weber claims that a tragedy does not depict a mystery but performs a cultic-magical act [254]. Rightly this author says that the public could only stand such a concentration of horrors, distilled from the myths, because what they saw agreed with their own psychical condition. They saw the insoluble oppositions of their own existence they were more or less aware of presented to them in a highly intensified form and heightened into a paroxysm. It was, as it were, a magical substitution of their own existence.

At the same time, however, this tragical manner of presentation has an alienating effect; this is caused by moving the scene to long ago mythical times where the whole action is laid in a circle of kings and princes as well as by dramatical condensation which makes everything far worse than it is in every-day life. Artifices like these create some necessary distance between the spectator and the play. They remove the sorrow of an unbearable, even impossible existence from the spectator. The annual theatre festival was, so to speak, Hellas' 'Day of Atonement'. It carried Hellas' adversity away with it, just as Israel yearly loaded an animal with its impurities and trespasses and then chased it into the desert. And was this animal not also a he-goat [255]?

g. Aristotle on tragedy

It is time now to summarize. What we have to do still is to enumerate those oppositions that have their place in tragedy. This is necessary because the subject matter of dualism is (irreconcilable) oppositions. In order to be able to do this the reader who is conversant with Volume I must allow me to repeat (nearly) verbally a passage out of this book, one about Aristotle's ideas on tragedy [256]. "The first one to define the notion of the 'tragic' more exactly was Aristotle. The way he did this is considered inadequate by many, because he is supposed not to have hit the essence of what is tragic ... According to him, tragedy originates from the epic genre. Expressly he cites the Iliad and the Odyssey as the precursors of tragedy, for, he says, 'Homer was a supreme poet in the serious style, since he made his representations not only good but also dramatic' [257] ...

Epic poetry coincides with tragedy in this respect that it represents heroic action. But whereas the epic poem may embrace a larger span of time, tragedy 'tends to fall within a single revolution of the sun' [258] - one of the classical requirements for the unity of drama. A tragedy is 'not a representation of men but a piece of action, of life, of happiness or unhappiness'. So the soul of tragedy is its plot - the 'mythos', says Aristotle -, and 'character-study is included for the sake of the action' [259].

What makes a drama into a tragedy? ... When a thoroughly good man suffers a reversal of fortune our sense of justice is outraged; the fall of a thoroughly bad man satisfies our sense of justice but cannot be categorised as tragic. Thus the tragic hero should not neither be wholly good nor wholly bad - someone like you and me, a modern scholar comments. ... 'It is through no badness or villainy of his own, says Aristotle, that he falls into misfortune, but rather through some flaw in him' [260]. Of course one thinks here of Oedipus who married his own mother, not knowing that Iocaste was his mother. For 'flaw' Aristotle uses the Greek word 'hamartia' ".

Many scholars are of the opinion that the great philosopher was in the wrong with his theory that tragedy is about 'decent people' who are destroyed by some personal error [261]. And indeed, if one sticks to Goethe who, as a dramatic artist, knew better than Aristotle what is tragic, then the essential tragic element is not a human error that causes somebody's ruin but 'the unbridgeable opposition' between Fate and the human will. But even if Aristotle did not give us the whole truth about tragedy, neither was he completely wrong [262]. It seems to me that he hit the mark with his statement that tragedy is 'mythos'. The subject of the great tragedies is not the psychology of their characters; the actors wore masks that represented types. Not a few commentators are of the opinion that Euripides is already drawing away from tragedy proper by gradually introducing more shaded sketches of character. One must not overlook the fact that Aristotle brings to light one of the most essential oppositions in tragedy, that between the action and the persons. The action steadily grows more forceful; it overpowers the characters and finally destroys them.

h. Oppositions in tragedy

Turning away from Aristotle now I intend to present the oppositions in tragedy. First of all, there is the opposition between life and death. The point is not that so many persons meet an horrible end in these dramas, but that death is continually present. Ceaselessly one feels the mortal menace, ever again there is talk of the nether world, of finiteness and decay, of the tomb; some plays even have their actions laid around a tomb [263]. Often the dead execercise a terrible influence : the 'dead' Iphigeneia (of course she is still alive but nobody knows this), the murdered Agamemnon, Clytaemnestra whose murder unleashes the Furies against Orestes, Polynices whose corpse remains unburied on the battlefield. In this wrestle between life and death death ever again proves the strongest [264]. Therefore Gerhard Nebel, in one of his striking characterizations, calls death 'the sacrament of the tragic world - a sacrament that the tragic figures administer to one another or also to themselves' [265].

Another of these great oppositions is that between history (as it is rendered by historians) and myth. The only play with a more or less actual subject is 'The Persians' in which the Battle of Salamis is the pièce de résistance. But even in this play Aeschylus causes an effect of alienation by laying the scene far away in a barbarian country. All other plots without exception are borrowed from Greek mythology, in particular from the Mycenaean sagas. The 'mythos' meant by Aristotle is 'action' indeed, the plot that is, but it is another kind of action than that which is presented to us by historiography.

Myth is a timeless action that repeats itself, contrary to the discreet and irrepeatable facts of history. The Athenians who saw these tragedies did not feel in any way that they were attending a festival of historical dramas; what they undoubtedly felt was that the mythical content of the plays was closely bound up with their own existence.

The opposition between historical time and mythical time is closely related to that between history and myth. Historical time always goes forward, either lineally or in big cycles; mythical time, however, is not really time but a fixation on the past. "It is not a frame of events ... but energy ... Tragic time never goes on but makes things happen" [266]. A tragic story is always turned backwards; it runs from the present to the past [267]. In one of the tragedy lines, as I indicated before, everything is caused by the curse that remains festering in the family of the Atrides. 'King Oedipus' offers an excellent example. At first sight the story seems to proceed in a historical direction, in the sense that the action is addressed to the future. Thus Oedipus, as a responsible ruler, desires to take measures against the pestilence in his city. Tragic time, however, says Rosset, takes over when the servant reveals his origin to Oedipus. From then on the ball rolls back till the meaning of the Delphic oracle is fully understood; as soon as this moment is reached Oedipus' existence is destroyed in an instant. The essence of tragedy is, according to Rosset, the tension between these two kinds of time [268]. This invariably ends with the sweeping away of historical time by the mythical.

Furthermore there is the opposition between the cosmos (and its terrestrial image, the polis) and the anticosmical forces. Again and again the order of the world is made meaningless, scored off and disarranged by elementary forces of nature. In 'The Persians' the sea takes its revenge for the recklessness of King Xerxes who dared to bridge it and insulted it. When Antigone rebels against the polis she is invoking the forces of death. Everywhere Death is present, indomitable, elusive and supreme. It is the women who act by order of Death; one could almost say, in accordance with Nebel, that tragedy dominated by women : nearly all the males in it are weak and insignifificant [269]. In this way the light world of the polis is set against the dark one of woman and death.

Next there is insanity. Heracles is blinded by it. It also appears as love-sickness by which, for instance, Phaedra is overpowered. Fire too is such an elementary force; Prometheus steals it from heaven. As a Titan he belongs to the older, more elementary godheads; Zeus, on the contrary, as an Olympian ruler, dominates the elementary forces but he himself is not elementary [270]. However, he is not able to govern elementary nature. The fire is stolen from him by a Titan; this theft touches the cosmic god in his very being. It is sometimes said that Aeschylus hit upon the idea of the Prometheus-theme, when he had looked into the seething crater of the Etna : evidently this vulcano was to him the symbol of the subterranean forces that go their own way unimpededly.

Over against the beautiful harmony of the cosmos, the idea the Greeks cherished so much, over against 'eudaimonia', happiness, well-being, the highest goal of polis existence as well as of philosophy, is set the fornlornless of man, his absolute loneliness. Our fellowmen are at an enormous distance, utterly unable to help. Exactly this is the essence of the tragic situation : everyone is caught up in it. But the same applies to the gods : they retreat always further, they cannot give help or they do not wish to help. On the contrary, in so far as they are present, they act to the disadvantage of human beings. And they too have to obey a tragic fate. There is, says Nebel, in this way no longer a 'you' for human beings; there only rests a 'the'. And what will, in this situation, remain of the 'I'?

i. Tragedy the last word?

In tragedy regular and systematic existence, governed by clearly designed rules and laws, seem to be abolished and replaced by irreconcilable oppositions. The agora, once so accessible and well-ordered, is turned into something that resembles the no man's land between the trenches of World War I. Now the question arises whether tragedy was the last word for the Greeks. To Clément Rosset, following in the footsteps of Nietzsche and according to his neo-Nietzschean point of view, this certainly seems true. Therefore, his book is not called 'the philosophy of tragedy' but 'the tragic philosophy'. We shall have to return to this question.

For the moment we may well ask ourselves whether in tragedy man is still responsible. Rosset called tragedy 'the alliance between the ideas of irreconcilability and irresponsibility' [271]. What happens to man is insuperable, inevitable, he is swept away by it as though by a banjir. The tragic idea, says Rosset, signifies the downfall of all ethical values; the notion of merit loses all its force [272]. But the idea of human liberty becomes empty too : "Greek tragedy surely affirms human greatness. But it is impossible to admit that it proclaims the freedom of man" [273]. This impotence is found in the cases of Phaedra and Medea. Both women are perfectly aware what they are going to do; from time to time they want to step back in order to be free again but in spite of this they are heading straight for the abyss.

The Athenians of the fifth century B.C. were extremely fond of tragedy. But the pleasure they derived from it can never have been what Aristotle presents to us. "Through pity and fear it (= tragedy) effects relief (katharsis, purification) to these and similar emotions" [274]. But how is it possible that fear will banish fear? "I have never understood", Fontenelle (1657-1757) wrote, "how passions are purified by the passions themselves; neither do I understand why it is good to be cured from pity" [275]. And, considering that the philosopher is speaking in undeniably medical terms, F.L.Lucas adds to this : "The theatre is not a hospital" [276]. No, the pleasure the Greeks derived from tragedy must have been of another kind [277].

It is a fact that every interpretation conflicts with the essence of tragedy. The spectator, or reader, must not analyze it but undergo it; it must come over him [278]. Tragedy does not effect a purification but a transposition, from the individual to the general : our sufferings are worldwide and timeless, they are not only part of our own life but of all humanity. "Tragic humanity is grounded in the universality of death and sorrow, in the general feeling of impossibility and weakness ..." [279]. This applies in particular to the Greeks of the fifth century B.C. for they found on the stage a far-reaching concurrence between tragedy and themselves. But at this point we must return to the question whether this concurrence was complete. Had the Greeks of that time a tragic view of their existence, was life for them preeminently tragic, was tragedy their last word? If the answer were 'yes' then tragedy is a station on the road to Gnostic dualism from which station only one line proceeds. But I feel it is not as simple as that.

j. Two contradictory versions of life

I have already pointed out the effects of alienation that create a certain distance between spectator and play. We also realize that tragedy as a literary genre appeared and disappeared all of a sudden. Had tragedy really been the last word it would not have 'ceased into nothingness' at the death of Sophocles and Euripides. There were other possibilities left open to the Greeks, such as a religious and a philosophical view of existence. Human life, thinks Nebel, must be a mixture of the right doses of certainty and anxiety. But are not the Furies too powerful in tragedy, isn't the horror too great? The short duration of tragedy may explained by the simple consideration that the spectators could not stand more of it [280].

Perhaps this hangs together with the curious rule that the events of the drama had to be enacted 'within one revolution of the sun'. This caused strange distortions - only a few hours after the fall of Troy Agamemnon comes home already - but the spectator takes this in his stride. What must have been more difficult, however, was to cope with the enormous concentration of suffering that was at the heart of tragic action. I can only surmise that after this harrowing exposure to sorrow and pain, the Athenians returned to the more prosaic rythms of life with a sense of relief.

Speculations like these, however, tamper with tragedy from without; they belong to the kind of interpretations that actually harm it. But there is also an element in tragedy itself that shows that the drama is not absolute and not wholly without a way out. At last the curse is taken away from the house of the Atrides. Oedipus dies in peace and ascends to heaven (but only Theseus knows this). We have a sufficient number of fragments of Aeschylus' second Prometheus-drama 'Prometheus unchained' to know that there is finally a sort of reconciliation between the Titan and Zeus. Therefore Una Ellis-Fermor spoke of 'a possible resolution, of some reconciliation' [281]. One detects two contradictory versions of life but to neither of them does the tragedian commit himself completely [282]. One is 'a (religious) interpretation of suffering', the other 'an intense (but non-religious) awareness of pain and evil' [283]. "The tragic mood is balanced between the religious and non-religious interpretations of catastrophe and pain" [284]. Ellis-Fermor calls this 'balance' 'Manichaeistic'; what she really means is 'dualistic' since the tragedian does not offer a solution, and it is in this tension that tragedy has its source [285].

I believe this to be correct if only one realizes that the scale of evils that are not interpreted religiously is considerably heavier than those which are interpreted in a religious way. This is especially so in Sophocles. I for one would rather accept this opinion of I.A. Richards : "Tragedy is only possible to a mind which is for the moment agnostic or Manichean. The least touch of any theology which has a compensating Heaven to offer to the tragic hero is fatal" [286]. Thus one only suggests with considerable hesitation that there might be some sort of a happy ending for Oedipus, especially in view of the fact that the curse is only taken away when it has utterly spent its fury. Although there are indications of another 'version of life', the moments of a non-religious interpretation are only too numerous.

k. Tragedy and Olympian religion

Tragedy forms another stage in the retreat of Olympian religion. Although it is not primarily atheistic, it does seem to raise the question of what would happen if the gods left the world to itself or adopted an utterly inimical attitude towards mankind. In several sections of Volume I and II I tried to show how established Greek religion gradually lost ground. In the fifth century this process made itself already painfully felt. Natural philosophy had laid the foundations for criticizing the gods; this meant a philosophical line of thought that no longer was religious. Philosophy is basically 'Titanic', it challenges traditional beliefs, particularly with regard to the supernatural. It is nature that forms the focus of attention of the Ionian natural philosophers. They derive their notion of cyclical time from the course of the world stream around the earth or from the revolution of the starry skies [287]. "Every philosopher is the cousin of an atheist", was the conclusion of Alfred de Musset [288]. The Sophists, more about whom in Chapter II, declared natural philosophy bankrupt but they took over its criticism of religion; they even carried it to an unprecedented height.

Nebel suggests that Thales - and by 'Thales' he means Ionian natural philosophy and the criticism of religion that was one of its main aspects - that "Thales would already have meant the end of the gods, if Dionysus had not intervened and saved them" [289]. Dionysus revitalized Olympian religion for the last time. Now tragedy has its origin in the Dionysus cult. This cult, however, differed in emphasis from the older Olympian religion. In Dionysian religion the gods no longer descend to mankind but man must ascend to the godhead; he tries to take possession of it and become absorbed in it [290]. "Kommt der neue Gott gegangen, hingegeben sind wir stumm, stumm" [291]. Wordless abandonment had not been, up till then, however, a characteristic of Hellenic religious life.

Tragedy also seeks to bridge the gap that separates mankind from the lost gods. "The Greeks owe it to Dionysus that the 'seinsmächtige Wort" was not passed straight from the epos to philosophy; instead Hellas starts the tragic song" [292]. When tragedy is nearing its end, Socrates and Plato come to the fore, both of them avowed opponents of tragedy. Their endeavour will be to find an answer to natural philosophy and Sophism as well as to tragedy. Plato in particular seeks to realize this by means of a theosophical, we might perhaps even say, a mystical philosophy.

Yet it would be wrong to assume that tragedy erects new altars to old gods, on the contrary, it directed many bitter words against them; of this we have assembled sufficient evidence. But tragedy is 'religious' in the sense that there exists a kind of 'tragic piety' that dissociates itself from the rationalism that was steadily gaining ground [293]. This tragic piety reveals a void. In the period between Homer and Aeschylus man has lost shelter. He is seized by anxiety. The philosophers try to take refuge in infinity; tragedy, however, situates man in the midst of absolute finiteness [294]. There man stands unprotected looking at everything that goes wrong and turns itself against him. Nowhere is there a way out. The gods perhaps? But Olympus is empty. When the gods manifest themselves, they are malicious; they fall upon innocent people, abuse their innocence, overburden them with adversity and chase them to death. And nobody knows why.

1. A question of guilt

In tragedy the most horrible crimes are committed; therefore, here too there exists a question of guilt. Why does all this adversity come over the tragic heroes? Two centuries ago, says Von Fritz, there was a general opinion that in tragedy 'poetic justice' was prevalent [295]. Justice in these plays is punishment for sin and expiation of guilt. Even to-day this idea of poetic justice colours many a judgment on tragedy [296]. It is not difficult to see where this idea of 'poetic justice' originates and even why it is called so; it comes from Aristotle's 'Poetica'. There he says that the main character of a tragedy changes from a situation of happiness ('eutuchia') to one of unhappiness ('dustuchia'), not as a consequence of villainy ('mochtêria') but as the result of a great error ('di'hamartian megalên') [297].

With this divining rod in hand, numerous commentators seek out the errors of the characters in tragedy or of those that are intrinsic to them. It is, of course, no problem to discover these in abundance; the great tragedians never make any attempt to present their figures as innocent or even as likable. It is even the case that two of the oldest tragedies are built on human mistakes. In 'The Persians' Xerxes calls down disasters on himself and his country by his overboldness; Prometheus is punished because he deliberately stole fire from heaven [298]. It is impossible to allege that there is 'tragic guilt' here [299]. In other dramas also there is no lack of errors that are only too human. Antigone has been reproached for her pride; evidently it is wrong to defy the polis, and the person who does so will have to bear the consequences [300].

Oedipus has been charged with much more; he is an evil character, his errors are great and numerous. When, for instance, he hears from the oracle that he will kill his father and marry his mother, he does not return to Corinth (as far as he is concerned the Corinthian royal couple are his parents). This, indeed, is rebellion against the gods [301]. The moralist, however, overlooks the fact that Oedipus, by virtue of an oracle, will not have to do this but will do it, in spite of himself. The inevitability of tragic guilt presents itself here. For exactly because he wants to escape his destiny he runs straight into its arms. It is easily overlooked that the oldest saying that the son will kill his father and marry his mother, already dates from before Oedipus' birth. Many other personages of tragedy may also be disapproved of; Suzanne Saïd presents us with a list of such instances [302].

According to Von Fritz, some unclearness regarding the word 'guilt' becomes evident here. True enough, the tragic heroes are not perfect, they commit errors, they have their failings, often they are shortsighted, and not seldom they cannot be exculpated from moral guilt too. But all this is still something different from 'tragic guilt'. What happens to tragic heroes is more, much more, than what is their due from a moral point of view; they are not punished or expiating but persecuted people. "(It) is common to all Greek tragedies that suffering (of the tragic hero) in no way tallies with what may be imputed to him as a consequence of personal guiltiness" [303]. At this point even Aristotle steps back somewhat. Earlier he had said that tragic fate befalls somebody who is neither conspicuously good nor conspicuously bad; now he adds that such a character is rather good than bad [304]. This brings us somewhat nearer to the notion that tragic suffering is fundamentally unmerited, and that the concept of 'tragic guilt' must be kept free from moral connotations.

For the cause of tragic failure the English language prefers using the term 'tragic flaw' 305). This is a rather neutral word that only signifies that something went wrong. All things considered, this seems to me to be a better term than 'tragic guilt'; it is true that guilt points more to a great catastrophe than 'flaw'; at the same time, however, the first term is very easily charged with morality or even moralism 306). One thing must be made perfectly clear : when there is talk of tragic guilt, then the cause of it is not man, however imperfect he or she may be. The 'guilt' resides somewhere else, in a region that is above man, he has no share in what fatally happens, it is something outside his reach. It comes down on him.

The most apt word is, perhaps, 'inevitability'. Life is full of things that we are not able to avoid but usually they are of a trivial kind : a child suddenly develops measles, and, as a consequence, a holiday trip has to be cancelled; a speaker does not turn up, and the program of a whole evening becomes a blank. For this kind of things makeshift contrivances or compensations are found; therefore, we may not call them tragic. Even worse things are not tragic in the proper sense of the word, like the death of an husband or the burning down of a home; here too life rights itself again.

But "the inevitability of tragedy crushes man". He is unknowing, he does not understand what happens to him. Whatever way out he chooses, it is always the wrong one. If Antigone chooses for the polis she betrays her conscience; if she follows her conscience, then death awaits her. "Tragic freedom only offers a choice between one-sided options" 307). Exactly the greatest tragedians will hear nothing of conciliation in the most terrifying of their plays : King Oedipus, Electra, Antigone, all of them end in an absolutely hopeless way 308).

m. Victorious necessity

We have arrived now at the most essential of all the tragic oppositions, at the very fundament on which tragedy is built; it is an opposition that is perfectly dualistic since the opposing parts are inequal and at the same time irreconcilable. "Tragedy always offers a conflict ... between inevitable power, which we may call necessity, and the reaction to necessity of self-conscious effort ... The victory always goes to necessity. The hero is crushed" [309]. This force always bears down on the tragic hero from outside and it is invariably malevolent. It pours undiluted and unadulterated evil over the characters [310]. The question now is where this power of inevitability resides or with what it must be identified. Raphael is surely correct in saying that some of the greatest works in tragic drama occupy themselves specifically with the metaphysical or theological problem of evil [311]. But at the same time one must realize that tragedy offers no solution.

Is this power of necessity to be identified with the gods? In many places in the dramas this seems to be the case. During their withdrawal the gods fight a rearguard action against man which does not do them great honour : often they are faithless, malicious, even demoniacal. "Since the gods can also be devils, fright is the basic tone of tragedy" [312]. More than once already we have come to the conclusion that the gods are not independent; they too seem to be charmed by an unexplainable force, call it fate or otherwise.

It seems no accident to me that the oldest tragedy, 'Prometheus', points out to the gods that they are limited beings; all other tragedies stand under this sign. Therefore Von Fritz explains the divine command to Orestes to kill Clytaemnestra not as an impenetrable ordinance of the godhead but as the expression of the immanent necessity of the situation. This necessity incites Orestes to his deed. But he would never have performed it if the authority of a divine decree had not helped him to triumph over his repugnance against matricide [313]. Finally, therefore, this force of inevitability remains unexplained and unexplainable.

n. Tragedy and Gnostic dualism

We have assembled sufficient elements now for determining the morphological similarities between tragedy and Gnostic dualism. First of all, their content matter is fictitious and of a literary character. Tragedy preferably draws upon myths, while the Gnosis likes to fabricate stories and in doing so to create a kind of religious mythosophy. An important characteristic of both is the helplessness of man and his utter rejection. Of supreme importance is the withdrawal of the gods to the background where they threaten to disappear from sight; in the Gnosis too the 'secrecy of God' is a crucial element. What man is still able to experience of things divine is of a malicious character; the Gnosis too knows the evil Demiurge. They also share a preoccupation with evil that dominates all things and all men; this evil is the real force of inevitability. However, it does not have its origin in man : in tragedy as well as in the Gnosis the idea of original sin is lacking, a sin for which man himself is responsible.

But it is here exactly that the great difference between tragedy and Gnosis makes itself felt. In tragedy there is no redemption but the Gnosis knows how to effect it : by means of an essential 'knowledge'. This knowledge is lacking in tragedy : Oedipus who knows the ancient riddles is not able to solve them; he is 'blind'. Yet this basic difference contains another resemblance. In the Gnosis only a few elect participate in this redemptive knowledge, in tragedy only persons of the royal blood are burdened with the full weight of suffering. Here too we find an élitist attitude and a very sharp opposition between the highly-placed and the 'common people'. The most essential similarity between tragedy and Gnosis is that both of them recognize 'error'. In tragedy it is the inexplicable 'tragic error' or 'tragic flaw'; in the Gnosis it is a derailment in creation, in the cosmos, as a result of which we live in an evil world.

So, although there is no direct line leading from tragedy to the Gnosis, nevertheless tragic drama is a station on the road to the full development of dualism in the Gnosis. Because it places the problem of evil in such a stark light tragedy also signifies the disappearance of Greek optimism that, in the victory over the Persians, had found its culmination point. When the Greeks had seen an endless number of dramas the flow suddenly dried up. Perhaps they had by then been sufficiently confronted with this question : why is evil supreme in the world? But they had not received an answer.

NOTES TO CHAPTER I

1) It must be noted that not every scholar considers 'Rhesus' an authentic play by Euripides.
2) Contrary to the Orestes of Aeschylus and Sophocles the same figure of Euripides shows an - understandable - reluctance to kill his own mother. But then it is Electra who urges him on to this deed. Eur., El. 982 : "Are you becoming a coward, are you no longer a man?". This reminds one not only of Lady Macbeth but also of Prosper Mérimée's 'Colomba', a Corsican woman who executes the vendetta herself, when her brother recoils from it.
3) In this connection 'Argos' means the kingdom of Menelaus.
4) Eur., Or. 1142.
5) Xen., Mem. I 4.2.
6) Aristoph., Thesm. 451/452.
7) Drachmann 51 sqq.
8) Drachmann ib.
9) Verrall, Euripides 277.
10) Verrall ib.
11) Eur., Troiades 884-889.
12) Eur., Hik. 201-217.
13) Eur., Hik. 212/213 and 230.
14) Eur., Hel. 744/745.
15) Eur., Hik. 399 sqq.
16) In Eur., Hek.
17) In Eur., Phoin.
18) Plut., Them. 13 and Arist. 9.
19) Eur., Phoin. 963-966.
20) Nilsson, Gesch.d.Gr.Rel. I 772.
21) Eur., Her.Main. 1346.
22) Eur., Hel. 17-21; Decharme 65.
23) Eur., Iph.Aul. 795-800.
24) Eur., El. 737-745; Decharme 66.
25) Eur., Troiades 969-982.
26) Decharme 70.
27) Eur., Hel. 16-50. Eur.' idea was not brandnew for it occurred already ca. 600 B.C. in the 'Palinodia', a poem by Stesichorus that is not handed down to us, and later in Her. II 112-120.
28) Eur., Hel. 705.
29) Eur., Hel. 711-745.
30) Eur., Hel. 36-41.
31) Eur., Phoin. 379.
32) Eur., Or. 418.
33) Eur., Or. 955-960.
34) Eur., Troiades 469.
35) Eur., Troiades 989/990.
36) Eur., Iph.Taur. 570-573.
37) Eur., Her.Main. 342-347.
38) Eur., Her.Main. 1265.
39) Soph., fr. 22b4, from 'Thyestes'.
40) Eur., fr. 292, from 'Bellerophon'.
41) Nestle, Euripides 126.

42) Eur., Or. 162-164.
43) Eur., Her.Main. 829/830.
44) Eur., Her.Main. 1303-1308.
45) Eur., Herakleidai 989.
46) Eur., Hel. 608-610.
47) Eur., Hik. 1214/1215.
48) Eur., Hel. 1102.
49) Eur., Hel. 20 sqq.
50) Eur., Hel. 237/238.
51) Eur., Troiades 946-948.
52) Eur., fr. 900.
53) Eur., Ion 894.
54) Eur., Ion 894.
55) Eur., Ion 974.
56) Eur., Ion 436-451.
57) Eur., fr. 286.
58) Eur., Troiades 949/950.
59) Eur., Bak. 225.
60) Eur., Bak. 1037.
61) Eur., Bak. 1092 sqq.
62) Eur., Bak. 1139-1143.
63) See Verrall, Bacchants.
64) Decharme 66. This is not the opinion of D. himself.
65) See Winnington-Ingram, Euripides.
66) "Euripides ... followed the hard path", Winnington-Ingram, Eur. 172.
67) Nilsson, Gesch.d.Gr.Rel. I 778.
68) Eur., Bak. 1348.
69) Decharme 89/90.
70) Eur., Bak. 427-432.
71) Eur., Bak. 200-203.
72) Eur., Her.Main. 505-514. For the role of fate see also Greene, Moira.
73) Eur., Her.Main. 1314-1316.
74) Eur., Hek. 488-491.
75) Cit. Nilsson, Gesch.d.Gr.Rel. I 774 note 15.
76) Nilsson, Gesch.d.Gr.Rel. 774/775.
77) Nestle, Eur. 152-159 argues that Eur. has known a 'dualistische Physik'. Starting from some fragments he shows indeed that, according to the opinion of the poet, everything originates from two principles, the (humid) aether and the (dry) earth. But the term 'dualistic' is not correctly used here since the two 'primary' principles do not exclude each other, and there is also no difference in quality. They are both needed and enter into a peaceful alliance from which all earthly beings come forth. Add to this that the principles are not really primary but are dependent on 'Aphrodite' who brings about the alliance. She is the real primary principle of the cosmos : "Cypris (Aphrodite) is no godhead but something more than a godhead" (Eur., Hipp. 359/360); "everything comes from her" (Hipp. 448).
78) Nilsson, Gesch.d.Gr.Rel. I 779.
79) Nilsson, Gesch.d.Gr.Rel. I 759.

80) Opstelten 205.
81) Soph., Trach. 1276-1278.
82) Soph., Ant. 622-625.
83) Nilsson, Gesch.d.Gr.Rel. I 757 : "... die Vorstellung von den Göttern und ihrem Regiment (ist) abstrakt geworden" ...".
84) Greene 142/143.
85) Soph., Oid.Kol. 1453.
86) Soph., Oid.Kol. 609 and 618.
87) Soph., Aias 646/647.
88) Soph., Oed.Rex 977-979.
89) Soph., Oed.Rex 1080.
90) Soph., Trach. 1266.
91) Aesch., Hepta 702/703.
92) Nilsson, Gr.Rel. I 754.
93) Griffith XI : "The evidence which I assembled shows Prom. consistently behaving quite differently from the six authentic plays of Aesch., and I was driven to believe that another hand was probably at work. This is still my belief."
94) Zawadka in 'Wege zu Aischylos'. She did not know the work of Griffith then.
95) Gagarin 132 : "I see no reason why the presentation of Zeus in different plays should be consistent; Aesch. is a dramatist, not a theologian."
96) Aesch., Prom. 107/108.
97) Aesch., Prom. 233-235.
98) Aesch., Prom. 975/976.
99) Aesch., Prom. 966/967.
100) Aesch., Prom. 762.
101) Aesch., Prom. 578-580.
102) Aesch., Prom. 600/601.
103) Aesch., Prom. 663-668.
104) Aesch., Prom. 759.
105) Aesch., Prom. 515-518.
106) Aesch., Prom. 763-768.
107) Aesch., Prom. 907/908.
108) Aesch., Prom. 940.
109) Aesch., Prom. 956/957.
110) Aesch., Prom. 913/914.
111) Aesch., Prom. 944-952.
112) Aesch., Prom. 987-996.
113) Aesch., Prom. 1094.
114) Aesch., Prom. 180-188.
115) Aesch., Prom. 507/508.
116) Aesch., Prom. 547-550.
117) Aesch., Prom. 526-560.
118) Aesch., Prom. 1036-1039.
119) Aesch., Prom. 311.
120) Aesch., Prom. 309-331.
121) Aesch., Prom. 149/150.
122) See Lloyd-Jones in 'Wege zu Aischylos'. And still more recently Gagarin 135 : "The major achievement of Prom. is this powerful picture of a resister ... The play reveals truths about political

behavior in general."
123) Ehrenberg, Man, State and Deity 41 : "The so-called Prometheic attitude of modern individualists and rebels has no real ancestor in the Greek Prometheus."
124) Grube in 'Wege zu Aischylos' II 306/307.
125) Lloyd-Jones 266.
126) For instance Wilamowitz, Nilsson, Festugière, see Lloyd-Jones 269/270.
127) Grube in 'Wege zu Aisch.' 301-305.
128) Ath. VIII 347e.
129) Plato, Pol. II 19, 380a/b.
130) Plato, Pol. II 21, 383 b/c.
131) Thus Schmid, Farnell, Reinhardt, see Lloyd-Jones 270/273; Ehrenberg, Man, State, Deity 41 says the same : "The gods did not develop".
132) Nestle, Gr.Rel. I 252-254.
133) Lloyd-Jones 295/296.
134) Lloyd-Jones 296.
135) Aesch., Prom. 436-506.
136) Aesch., Prom. 484.
137) Pomeroy 98.
138) Aesch., Hepta 230-232.
139) Aesch., Prom. 200/201.
140) Aesch., Hepta 187-190.
141) Aesch., Hepta 256.
142) Aesch., Eum. 657-661.
143) Diod.Sic. I 80.3-4 mentions this as proper to Egyptian priests. Stobaeus (Hense III.72) says it is Pythagorean - probably this was Aesch.' source -but here the theory does not go so far : in human sexual intercourse the female principle exists on behalf of the male one. "The male begets by sowing life ('psuchê'), the female only provides matter to what originates in this way."
144) Aesch., Eum. 734-743.
145) Aesch., Ag. 351.
146) Aesch., Ag. 1643-1645; Pomeroy 98/99.
147) Gagarin 88/89.
148) Aesch., Ag. 207-214.
149) Aesch., Ag. 11.
150) Aesch., Ag. 910-972.
151) Aesch., Ag. 1439 and 1447.
152) Aesch., Ag. 1435/1436.
153) Pomeroy 98.
154) Gagarin 88/89.
155) Only after having written this sentence I discovered it nearly verbally in Segal 183. And yet I had not read Segal's book then.
156) Segal 183.
157) Soph., Ant. 525.
158) Soph., Ant. 484/485.
159) Trilling 40.

160) "It is characteristic for the human race ... that brothers and sisters have no sexual intercourse, and that parents have no sexual contact with their children", Mair 19. A case on the border between pseudo-incest and real incest is described in the Italian novel 'Gisella' by Carlo Cassola (1974); Gisella and her 'uncle' (stepfather) were, indeed, related to each other. The relationship of these two people is the only one in this book that may be called emotionally satisfying.
161) There exist only very few clearly delineated exemptions from the prohibition on incest; the best known are marriages between brothers and sisters in the royal family of the Ptolemaeans that went on for generations.
162) Gen. 2:24.
163) The fact that the Dutch nazi leader Anton Mussert was married to his aunt, Rie Witlam, a younger sister of his mother and eighteen years older than he himself, made him, during the occupation, the object of endless ridicule, not only by the Dutch population but also by the German authorities.
164) I find the lyrical outpourings between Siegmund and Sieglinde, brother and sister - and they know they are - in Wagner's 'Die Walküre' repellent. From this relationship Siegfried is born.
165) Soph., Oed.Rex 1525.
166) Eur., Hipp. 14.
167) Eur., Hipp. 438/439.
168) Eur., Hipp. 433-481.
169) These plays are Aesch., Choêphoroi, Soph., Electra, and Eur., Electra; in these dramas as in Eur., Iph.Taur. Pylades is only a pale figure.
170) Waldock, Ch. VII, Romantic Tragedy : The 'Antigone'.
171) Soph., Ant. 73.
172) Soph., Ant. 869-871.
173) Soph., Ant. 863-868.
174) Soph., Ant. 909-914
175) Soph., Ant. 891.
176) Pomeroy 103.
177) Aulus Gellius XV 20.6.
178) Ath. XIII 557e, repeated 603e.
179) Pomeroy 107.
180) Eur., Med. 410-420.
181) Eur., Med. 407-409.
182) Eur., Med. 265/266.
183) Eur., Med. 231-237.
184) Eur., Med. 282.
185) Jason presents this to her as perfectly self-evident, 551-568.
186) Eur., Med. 928.
187) Eur., Ion 398-400.
188) Eur., Hik. 786-797.
189) Pomeroy 107.
190) Eur., Or. 552-556.
191) Bullough 72/73.
192) Eur., Phoin. 424/425.

193) Eur., El. 932/933.
194) Eur., Herakleidai 476/477.
195) Eur., Hik. 40/41.
196) Eur., Phoin. 198.
197) Eur., Andr. 944-946; the speaker is Hermione.
198) Eur., Iph.Aul. 569/570.
199) This is a double standard of morals for Athenian men permitted themselves a much larger freedom.
200) Eur., Andr. 220/221.
201) Eur., Hek. 974/975.
202) Eur., Iph.Aul. 1270.
203) Eur., Troiades 860-879.
204) Eur., Or. 606/607.
205) Loraux 75.
206) Eur., Hek. 1178-1181.
207) Eur. Med. 573-575.
208) Eur., Kykl. 186/187.
209) Eur., Iph.Taur. 1005/1006.
210) Eur., Iph.Aul. 1394.
211) Eur., Hipp. 616-667.
212) The 'Old Comedy' is followed by the 'Middle Comedy' of the fourth century B.C. Since it consists only of a number of fragments it is of no importance to our theme.
213) See for this Henderson, The Maculate Muse.
214) Aristoph., Hipp. 1056/1057.
215) Whitman, Ch. VI.
216) Aristoph., Thesm. 383-394.
216) Whitman 221.
217) Aristoph., Thesm. 383-394.
218) Aristoph., Thesm. 466-519.
219) Aristoph., Thesm. 785-847.
220) Auger 88.
221) Aristoph., Ekkl. 106-108.
222) Aristoph., Ekkl. 581-709.
223) Aristoph., Ekkl. 117; Saïd, Assemblée 45/46.
224) Aristoph., Ekkl. 121.
225) Saïd, Assemblée 38/39.
226) Saïd, Assemblée 40/41.
227) Henderson, Lysistrata 186.
228) Rosellini 28.
229) Aristoph., Lys. 1041/1042.
230) Aristoph., Lys. 261.
231) Rosellini 25.
232) Rosellini 25/26.
233) Whitman 215/216.
234) A.Dietrich s.v. 'Aischylos' in PW I (1894), 1065-1084; E.R.Schwinge s.v. 'Aischylos' in Lex.d.Alt.Welt 81-85.
235) Von Blumenthal, s.v. 'Sophokles' in PW XIIA (1927), 1040-1094; E.R.Schwinge s.v. 'Sophokles' in Lex.d.Alt.Welt, 2833-2839.
236) A.Dietrich s.v. 'Euripides' in PW VI (1909), 1242-1281; E.R.Schwinge s.v. 'Euripides' in Lex.d.Alt.Welt, 920-925.

237) I am quoting myself here, from a paper I read in Paris, April 1981, 'Ce que l'enseignement de l'histoire omet. L'histoire et la vision tragique du monde', now in the collection 'Enseigner l'histoire. Des manuels à l'histoire. Textes réunis et présentés par Henri Moniot', Berne, 1984, 112-125.
238) Aristoph., Batr. 1467-1533.
239) Weber 54-56.
240) Weber 64.
241) Weber 39.
242) Weber 59.
243) Weber 85.
244) 2 Sam. 23.
245) Weber 79/80.
246) Weber 82-89.
247) Weber 83.
248) In Vol. I, Ch. III, Section 4, I spoke of the tragic character of the Iliad.
249) Untersteiner, Origini 121; for this part see 80-122.
250) Weber 332.
251) Weber 333.
252) Nebel 164.
253) Weber 330.
254) Weber 334/335.
255) Lev. 16:6-28.
256) Vol. I, Ch. III, Section 4.
257) Ar., Poet. 1448b.
258) Ar., Poet. 1449b.
259) Ar., Poet. 1450a.
260) Ar., Poet. 1453a.
261) Dawe 89.
262) Dawe 123.
263) For instance Darius' tomb in 'Persai', and that of Agamemnon in 'Choêphoroi'.
264) Euripides' 'Alkestis', in which the opposite is the case, is a comedy rather than a tragedy : Admetus, king of Pherae, has lost his wife Alcestis by her death but finally she is brought back to him by Heracles.
265) Nebel 164.
266) Nebel 126.
267) Rosset 13.
268) Rosset 15.
269) Nebel 104.
270) Nebel 53.
271) Rosset, Ch. II.
272) Rosset 37.
273) Rosset 45.
274) Ar., Poet. 1449b.
275) B.Fontenelle, Réflexions sur la poésie, XLV, cit. Raphael 14.
276) F.R.Lucas, Tragedy, London, 1927 (Hogarth Press, the publishing-firm of Leonard and Virginia Woolf), cit. Raphael 14. "... Mitleid ist nicht das letzte Wort in heroischen Angelegenheiten. Wer

das Heroische will und siegt oder untergeht, stellt sich einem anderen Urteil als dem privaten", Otto Flake in 'Hortense, oder die Rückkehr nach Baden-Baden', 1933.
277) Rosset 82 adopts Nietzsche's renowned condemnation of Aristotle's maxim and calls it 'drivel' ('une billevesée').
278) Rosset 7 : "... refus radical de toute idée d'interprétation'.
279) Nebel 242.
280) Nebel 162/163 and 179.
281) Ellis-Fermor 128.
282) Ellis-Fermor 17/18.
283) Ellis-Fermor 146 and 128.
284) Ellis-Fermor 17.
285) Ellis-Fermor 146.
286) I.A.Richards, Principles of Literary Criticism. London, 1924, cit. Raphael 37/38.
287) Nebel 65.
288) In his 'Confessions d'un enfant du siècle', 1836.
289) Nebel 98.
290) Nebel 98/99.
291) Richard Strauss, Ariadne auf Naxos, libretto by Hugo von Hoffmannsthal, 1912.
292) Nebel 99.
293) Nebel 20.
294) Nebel 21.
295) Von Fritz, Trag.Schuld 1.
296) Von Fritz, Trag.Schuld 1.
297) Ar., Poet. 1453a.
298) Saïd, Faute 324-327 and 318-324.
299) Nebel 118.
300) Von Fritz, Trag.Schuld 5/6.
301) Saïd, Faute 327; Von Fritz, Trag.Schuld 7/8.
302) Saïd, Faute 327-447.
303) Von Fritz, Trag.Schuld 1/2 and 15.
304) Ar., Poet. 1453a.
305) Thus also W.Hamilton Fyfe in his translation of Ar., Poet., Loeb Class.Libr. 199.
306) This in opposition to Von Fritz, Trag.Schuld 1/2.
307) Nebel 190.
308) Von Fritz, Trag.Schuld 17.
309) Raphael 25.
310) Raphael 51.
311) Raphael 24.
312) Nebel 24.
313) Von Fritz, Trag.Schuld 9.

CHAPTER II

SOPHISTICA AND SOCRATICA

1. Sophism

a. What is Sophism?

Sophism is one of the very few spiritual movements that have become proverbial, although in an unfavourable sense. The authoritative Dutch dictionary, Van Dale, tells us that a 'sophism' is a 'fine-spun but not a valid argument'; a 'sophist' is 'somebody who advances keen-witted fallacies or mock arguments'. The origin of this far from flattering definition of Sophism is, we may state with some assurance, Aristophanes, who disliked the Sophists intensely. In his comedy 'The Clouds' (423 B.C.) he presents them to us as would-be scholars who occupy themselves with senseless casuistry or even worse; they teach the art of turning wrong into right. Later Plato amplified this by depicting them as dealers who buy wisdom and then barter it away for money; in his 'Sophist' he speaks of 'soul-merchandising which deals in words and knowledge' [1].

Originally, of course, the term is derived from 'sophia', wisdom; a Sophist was a 'sophos', a wise man, a person with a considerable degree of knowledge, an 'expert', to use a modern term. This notion had a long and honourable career : a man like Solon could be called a 'Sophist' without the slightest hint of detraction. In the first centuries A.D. the term was used again, this time as a positive designation for a certain group of scholars whom we would tend to call 'classical scholars'. Nevertheless, Sophism proper is a phenomenon of the fifth century B.C. It would not be correct, however, to say that we have to do here with a philosophical school. If the Sophists were interested in philosophy, they were, at the same time, interested in a great many other subjects. The fields of interest of various Sophists lay often very far apart. Therefore, Sophism must not be called a 'school' but rather 'a trend or movement' [2].

In some respects, however, they are similar to one another. Most Sophists were not Athenians; they came from everywhere and travelled about with their learning. In particular they could be found at the Olympic Games and at other Hellenic festivals. They didn't settle down easily; their attitude, as often as not, tended to the cosmopolitan. However, as if attracted by a magnet they often went to Athens and stayed there for a considerable time; they extended a profound influence on a section of the metropolitan public. They founded schools and taught, especially the 'jeunesse dorée'. For this reason they are among the founders of the European school system.

Their most important subject matter was rhetoric, a word that long remained in use for the final class of the grammar-school, for instance in the French 'lycée'. Rhetoric was a pre-eminently practical art. Whosoever desired to make his way in politics in general or in Athenian democracy in particular had to be well-spoken; especially he must be able to put his opponent out of action by means of words. It will be evident that this led to the accusation that the Sophists were not so much concerned with honesty and exactitude but rather with devious means of persuasion. Every cause has two sides, and the Sophists taught their pupils to defend both of them; this could be done so dexterously that, as Protagoras has it, the weakest argument seemed to be the strongest one [3].

This school-keeping leads us to a third feature the Sophists had in common. They were professionals, in the sense that they had to live by their profession. Because of this necessity they asked money for their tuition, often not a little. "Those who offer it (their wisdom) to all comers for money are known as Sophists", said Socrates spitefully, and he added that he considered this prostitution [4]. This unfavourable and rather general opinion on the payment of teachers has persisted even to the present day : teachers who usually do not belong to the best remunerated intellectuals can never start an action to improve their salaries without being told that this conflicts with their professional ethos.

b. Some famous Sophists

There existed not a few Sophists but of most of them we only know the name and one or two fragments. The most renowned of all of them was Protagoras whom I introduced already in Volume II [5]. He was born in 481 B.C. or perhaps some years earlier in Abdera; there is an old story that, during the time of the Persian invasion, King Xerxes was quartered upon his well-to-do father. He travelled a lot, gave courses everywhere and wrote a number of books. A few times he visited Athens; the remembrance of one of these visits is preserved in Plato's 'Protagoras'. He was a friend of Pericles with whom he discussed extensively. The statute for Thurii in Southern Italy is said to have been his work; in any case he lived for some time in Sicily. Finally he was banished from Athens on account of atheism; later he lost his life in a shipwreck. This happened some time between 420 and 410. He wrote four books, 'On the Gods' - the first book with this title -, 'Truth', 'On Being', and 'Antilogies', a course of dialectics. Of the first two works only the opening sentences remain - an incentive to authors to provide an opening sentence that catches the attention, something like "Scarlett O'Hara had green eyes" [6]. Of the other two books we have likewise only a fragment [7].

Hardly less well-known is Gorgias; he too lent his name to a Platonic dialogue. He was probably born in 485; his birth-place was Leontini in Sicily. He himself was a famous orator; of the model speeches he wrote two have been handed down to us. He was already more than sixty years old when he appeared in Athens for the first time in 427 B.C., as an ambassador of his native town. Immediately his oratorical talents became the talk of the town. He lived to an incredible age, perhaps even to a hundred and nine, for he died between 380 and 376. We still have a few fragments of his speeches; there also existed a textbook of rhetoric from his hand. What is really important for us are the fragments of his book 'On Non-Being' in which he takes Parmenides and the Eleatic School to task, in an ironical way [8].

Hippias even gave his name to two dialogues of Plato, 'Hippias Major' (if this is authentically Platonic), and 'Hippias Minor'. He came from Elis on the Peloponnese and travelled a lot, often as an ambassador of his home town. Many times he visited Athens. Of the years of his life we can only say that he lived in the second half of the fifth century B.C. He was famous for his prodigious memory and for the exceptional extent of his reading; as a consequence he was able to teach the most diverse subjects. He seems, indeed, to have been a man of many talents. He was deeply convinced of his own worth; in all innocence he said to Socrates that he (Hippias) had never yet met any one better than himself in anything. The response of Socrates was : "Isn't that splendid, Hippias!" [9]. What a pity for this great man that so little is left of his writings [10].

Finally Prodicus, who came from the town of Iulia in the island of Keos in the Cyclades and who also lived in the second half of the fifth century B.C. He was an important Sophist of whom, for that matter, we know precious little. In any case he had a reputation in Athens as a giver of courses. Whosoever knows Plato's 'Protagoras' has him already before his or her eyes : lying on a bed in a room of the wealthy Maecenas of the Sophists, Callias, wrapped in an enormous quantity of blankets and furs, probably tormented by rheumatics, while the poor man tried in vain to make himself understood; his deep bass made the room reverberate so much that it was impossible to understand his words. And that was a great pity for he was all-wise and divine, says Socrates [11]. Of his writings too only fragments remain. There was a book 'On Nature', with as a part of it or apart from it 'On the Nature of Man', the 'Horai', a collection of miscellanea, and a work that is said to have been called 'Synonymika', a linguistic treatise on the correct use of words [12]. This last work is said to have influenced Socrates who also was always looking for the right definition [13].

2. The attack on the gods

a. Protagoras' agnosticism

The only sentence that has been handed down to us from Protagoras' book 'On the Gods', is the opening sentence; precisely this sentence earned him a decree of banishment. What he wrote was this : "With regard to the gods I am not able to find out whether they exist or not or what sort of shape they have; this matter is unclear and human life is too short". The offending book was publicly burnt in the agora; the town beadle went around to collect it from those persons who possessed a copy of it [14]. In Plato's 'Theaetetus' the Sophist is reported to have said that he excluded the question of the existence or non-existence of the gods from oral or written discussion [15].

It is evident that this is not atheism pure and simple but rather agnosticism as we know it. It is not credible that Protagoras would have shirked from public veneration of the gods; if this had been the case, he would have been publicly accused [16]. However, he posed the problem of the existence of the gods as an intellectual question; this entailed, of course, that a negative answer was, at least, possible. He must have been the very first to put this question. The mere fact that this happened, says Drachmann, doubtless proved of great importance for the development of thought [17].

b. Prodicus' atheism

Prodicus left the reputation behind him of an atheist [18]. Again the question arises whether this may be stated in such a crude form [19]. He is said to have written : "The ancients accounted as gods the sun and moon and rivers and springs and in general all the things that are of benefit for our life, because of the benefit derived from it, even as the Egyptian deity the Nile". And to this he added that for this reason bread was called 'Demeter', wine 'Dionysos', water 'Poseidon', and fire 'Hephaestus', and so on with everything that was useful in everyday practice [20]. It is not possible to infer a straightforward denial of the existence of the gods from this. The texts in our possession, however, show us that Prodicus thought that the existence of the gods was dependent on human thinking.

Of course this meant striking at the roots of the Olympian creed. What would happen if human thinking took a completely new turn? As perhaps in some quarters it had already done. Graeser calls Prodicus' idea a psychological argument [21], but perhaps we should rather speak of an anthropological argument; if this is true, then it is a piece of anthropology that, in a remarkable way, anticipates nineteenth-century conceptions [22]. The origin of religion is to be found here in agriculture; the first objects of veneration are, in this vision, agricultural products. Prodicus' theory fits admirably into the utilitarian trend of thought of the Sophists. Their turn of mind was not conspicuously speculative - perhaps as a reaction to the metaphysics of natural philosophy, in particular to Parmenides' doctrine of Being. Everything must demonstrably serve some end; religion was no exception to this [23].

c. Critias and the invention of religion

Critias, a cousin of Plato, was a well-known Athenian statesman. He was one of the Thirty who, in 404 B.C., seized power in Athens; very soon this brutal power-politician was the head of this clique that exercised a bloody terror against the Athenian citizens. He fell in 403 B.C. in an attack on Piraeus that was occupied by the democrats. This many-sided gifted man also wrote elegies and plays. Perhaps he was not a Sophist in the proper sense of the word; he did not teach for money for instance. However, his ideas on religion are in line with the thinking of many authentic Sophists.

His reputation as an atheist rests on one of his plays. It is a satyr play, called 'Sisyphus'; only 42 lines of it have been preserved [24]. Once there was a time, this fragments tells us, when there was general anarchy; everybody did what he liked. In order to curb violence people then made laws. Thus an acceptable measure of public order ensued but, nevertheless, evil was still committed in secret. Then a sly dog fell on the idea to frighten people with 'gods' - gods who knew everything and saw everything and heard everything. In order to make this still more impressive he situated these gods in the highest of heavens, in the region where thunder and lightning come from. This too is an anthropological development theory; it will be encountered again in later centuries, particularly at the end of the eighteenth century, in the time of the Enlightenment. Not without good reason the period of Sophism is sometimes called the 'Greek Enlightenment'. What connects both movements is a powerful rationalistic argument : religion has been 'invented'.

This passage too denies any kind of independent existence to the gods. But are we allowed therefore to call Critias an atheist? Drachmann doubts this, first of all because it will not do to lay all the utterances in a play at the door of the author; and next, Critias would have run into trouble with the judges for opinions such as this one. We know that he was not indicted for atheism [25], perhaps also since his position as the virtual dictator of Athens was strong enough to spare him any kind of trouble from whatever source. But apart from this, in any case he would have been able to appeal to the fact that this was said by Sisyphus and not by himself. The real concern of the judges was the maintenance of the public cult and the official recognition of the gods. As long as these were not infringed upon - and Critias did not encroach upon them -, there was no reason for an indictment. However, Sisyphus, as the main character of this drama, denies the existence of the gods in so many words, because he says that the 'inventor' concealed the truth by telling lies [26].

It is hard to avoid the impression that, in Sisyphus, Critias himself is speaking. Sisyphus is not a subordinate figure but the main character; he concludes his exposition in an explosive way : "In this way somebody in the beginning prompted people to believe that there are gods" [27]. Such a theory, with its anthropological, evolutionist and rationalistic character, fits very well into Sophistic thinking. To most scholars, therefore, Critias himself is the spokesman here. I would like to add that this opinion of Critias agrees very well with what we know of him : as the unscrupulous politician he was he must have seen in religion an apt means to keep the citizens in hand. Many a person in power has thought along the same lines. However, this is the very first time that the idea of an 'invention' of religion occurs.

d. Diagoras

Diagoras of Melos too had a reputation as an atheist and as somebody who mocked the mysteries. He is reported to have written an atheistic book which, however, is not known to us [28]. It is said of him that he began with believing in the gods. When, however, he was wronged by somebody who did not shrink from perjury before the judge for which this person was not punished anyway, he roundly declared that the gods do not exist [29]. We saw that Euripides too contended that it is impossible to square the existence of evil with the existence of the gods; this was in a fragment of his play 'Bellerophon'. Diagoras, a contemporary of his, was, therefore, not the first to raise this objection, nor was he the last [30]. One is almost forced to conclude that the whole Sophistic tradition tended to undermine belief in the gods and their veneration. It was yet another stage in the slow process of the destabilization of Greek religion that was steadily going on.

3. General relativism

A certain dogmatism was not alien to the Ionian natural philosophers and to the Eleates who succeeded them. One by one they started from the axiom that everything begins with and can be carried back to a first principle, an 'archê'. Originally these 'archai' had a material character; with Thales it is water, with Anaximander it is an unlimited primary matter, the 'apeiron', with Anaximenes it is air, with Heraclitus it is fire. With 'archai' like air and fire the principles are already getting a more ethereal look. Anaxagoras made the decisive step when he took 'mind' ('nous') as his primary principle, even although Socrates was to complain that he made no further use of it [31]. But the definitive dematerialization of the primary principle was the work of Parmenides, for whom it was 'Being'. The consequence of this absolutizing of Being was, on the one hand, that the concept of 'non-being' became unthinkable, while, on the other hand, philosophy withdrew its attention from all that is moving, coming into being, and growing. This meant that human life and history dropped out of sight.

It was exactly against this that a new generation of scholars protested. To them all was of interest that was directly useful and practical. They turned their backs on Ionian philosophy and its terminal station, the Eleatic doctrine of Being. With them one will not encounter 'first principles' but rather a general relativism. A stage on the road to this was perhaps Empedocles' doctrine that there is not one principle but four - the four elements - and that their mutual relation, their dosage in things, is the decisive factor; this also applies to human beings. Another stage was probably the atomic theory of Leucippus and Democritus. They taught that all things consist of an innumerable mass of infinitesimal particles, the 'atoms'; all configurations we know originate, more or less casually, from this mass. In any case the atomists do not know a general moving principle.

a. Gorgias on non being

I shall begin with Gorgias' little book 'On Non-Being' [32]. It is not the oldest writing of its kind but it contains a direct attack on Parmenides and the Eleatic school. With this booklet the author turned away from philosophy in order to occupy himself henceforward with rhetoric alone. In rhetoric he saw a practical art that served a useful end. Since his lines of argument are at times capricious, one may be justified in presuming that he was deploying them in an ironical way. Presumably what he intended was a 'reductio ad absurdum' of the 'iron ontology' of Parmenides [33].

Gorgias advances three theses : 1 nothing exists; 2 if something exists it would not be knowable; 3 if it were knowable it would not be communicable. Then he begins to juggle in an imposing way with the verb 'to be' using it in the way that Parmenides did, as an absolute statement, like 'I am who I am'. We may call this way of using 'to be' meta-language but he also uses it in the normal manner as copula. For example, in the sentence "the wheather is fine", the predicate 'is fine' refers to the condition of the wheather. Thus Gorgias is using the verb 'to be' in a way that contrasts completely with that of Parmenides. His conclusion is that if it is absurd to assume the existence of 'non being', it is just as absurd to speak of 'being'. "For if

Being does not exist and neither Non-Being nor both of them (at the same time), and, moreover, nothing else (no tertium between Being and Non-Being), then nothing exists (is)" [34]. Of course, Gorgias did not believe for a moment that nothing exists; this is simply a way of emphasizing the futility of indulging in such ontological speculations. According to him, they fall outside the scope of our knowledge and experience (they cannot be 'thought') [35].

This scepticism becomes fortified by the second thesis, viz. that if anything did exist it would be unknowable. Untersteiner calls this the 'tragedy of knowledge' [36]. The dilemma is expressed very aptly by Gorgias when he says : "Being remains unknown unless it acquires a shape; this shape is vague unless it partakes of Being" [37]. I use shape here as the translation of 'dokein' [38]. 'Dokein' refers to the (sham) objects of this world that were dismissed by Parmenides since they have no true ontological status. Nor did this philosopher believe that the 'doxa'-world could partake of Being. According to this quotation, however, Gorgias seems to have been of the opinion that this might be possible. On the strength of his first thesis that an ontology or philosophy of existence is impossible we must assume that, in his opinion, there can also be no philosophy (no real knowledge) of the things of this world. This would mean that no conclusive statements may be made on human affairs and history. This, in any case, was the opinion of Plato.

Gorgias, however, does not accept the 'archai' of Parmenides and Plato, Being and the Forms; instead he comes very near to a general relativism. We must not characterize this attitude of Gorgias as dualistic. He dissolves Parmenides' dualism of Being and Seeming on the supposition that both Being and Seeming are uncertain things. It is not possible to make dogmatic or axiomatic statements about Being but neither is this possible of things (Seeming, doxa). "For if we are not allowed to make systematic distinctions between that what appears (or seems) but is not, and that what is but does not appear (takes shape), then the notions we need to formulate such a dualism (i.e. of Parmenides) have no longer any sense", according to Graeser

[39]. This is, of course, very correct. But at the same time it is highly remarkable that, with Gorgias' anti-doctrine, we have no longer a tertium, a connecting link, between the ontological dogmatism of Parmenides and the Eleates on the one hand, and the total relativism of the Sophists (and of Democritus) on the other. Only Plato will try to indicate a road leading from visible things to the invisible.

Finally, if there existed anything and if it were knowable, it would not be communicable. Gorgias says that the means we have to indicate objects is language; but language is not the same as the objects outside us. Therefore, what we signify to our fellow-beings is not real objects but language (words), and words are not the same as objects [40]. We touch here upon Sophistic nominalism, if I may dub it thus, the antithesis, that is, between objects and the labels (nomina) we attach to them. I intend to return to this later. What is important in this respect is that all observations and all communications are relative. "For even if it is possible to know things, and to express what one knows in words, how then can the hearer have the same things in his mind as the speaker? The same thing cannot be present at the same time in a number of individual persons, for this would mean that one would be two. If, however, the same thing could be present in two different persons at the same time, then there is still no reason why such an object would seem identical to both of them; otherwise we must assume that they themselves were identical persons and present in exactly the same spot ... To all intents and purposes, however, it looks like this : even the objects that are observed by one and the same person at the same moment are not at all identical; his hearing and his vision make him observe different things; and also what he is observing now and on a later occasion is different. Therefore, it is hardly possible that one person should observe the same things as another person" [41]. It is, indeed, tragic that human beings are not capable of making reliable communications (in a logical sense); nevertheless, it is precisely this failure that serves as a starting-point for a general relativism that may explain, perhaps, why Gorgias and other Sophists preferred rhetoric so much : to be able to convince is much more important than to be able to prove.

b. Protagoras' phenomenalism

The banner under which this relativism marches on is the famous and well-known sentence of Protagoras : "Man is the measure of all things". Like many other famous quotations this one too is incomplete. The words cited are followed by : "of the things that are as they are, and also of the things that are not as they are not" [42]. This is the first and only remaining sentence of his book 'Truth'. It is, of course, no wonder that the second half of this so-called 'homo mensura' (man the measure)-sentence is nearly always omitted. For what does it mean that man is the measure of all things 'that are not as they are not'? Because of the succinctness of this basic dictum and the disappearance of all that followed every translator may only hope that he has hit the real meaning of Protagoras. Perhaps it is possible to interpret 'man' in this sentence as 'mankind, humanity', not as an individual person. In Plato, however, Socrates cites the homo mensura-sentence verbally and then continues in this way : "Is it not true that sometimes, when the same wind blows, one of us feels cold, and the other does not? Or one feels slightly and the other exceedingly cold?" [43]. Here it is taken as entirely self-evident that individual man is meant [44].

Another question is whether 'all things' ('pantoon chrêmatoon') include not only observable objects but also values. In any case, in this lapidary sentence Protagoras did not take the trouble to indicate carefully that, according to him, man is not the measure of all values. Plato even makes Protagoras declare that what is right and just in one particular state, is really right and just (i.e. valid) there as long as that state thinks it is [45]. This notion might be called 'polis mensura' for here evidently the polis is the arbiter of justice ('dikaia'). When it suits her, the polis can change her norms. In this vision ethical norms have a subjective character; therefore, Guthrie concludes that Protagoras' relativism also covers the field of ethics [46].

Untersteiner who characterized the position of Protagoras with the modern term 'phenomenalism' [47], translates the phrase 'the things that are not as they are not' as follows : 'the non-phenomenality of what is not real', and, in accordance with this 'the things that are as they are', as 'the phenomenality of what is real' [48]; of all this man, individual man, is the measure ('metron'). Things (phenomena), ethical values included, are as they seem to a particular person - a reality that is not necessarily identical with that of another person. Each individual decides for himself how extensive this reality is, how far it stretches, what it contains, and what significance it has for him. His individuality becomes apparent from the fact that every person decides for himself what is 'not phenomenal', what does not appear real to him, what does not exist (for him), what has no meaning. In this particular world of phenomena everybody is the sovereign ruler ('the measure of all things'). In this way I interpret, with Untersteiner's assistance, Protagoras' famous dictum.

A quotation from Aristotle, who was a candid but not always reliable historian of philosophy, proves that this interpretation cannot be far wrong : "(Protagoras) said that man is the measure of all things, by which he meant simply that each individuals's impressions are positively true (in other words : everybody's reality is *the* reality to him - F.). But if this is so, it follows that the same thing is and is not (that is : for one person it exists but for another it does not - F.), and is bad or good (for different persons bad or good - F.) ...; because often a given thing seems beautiful to one set of people and ugly to another, and that which seems to each individual is the measure" [49].

If this is not total relativism then it is a subjectivism that is pushed very far. Its consequence is, of course, that 'on every matter two opposite opinions are possible' [50]; the art of arguing in this way was doubtless the subject of Protagoras' 'Antilogiai' (= 'counter-arguments') [51]. It must, however, not be lost from sight that an absolute relativism does not exist, if only because it is a contradictio in terminis. Even Protagoras has an 'archê', a principle; his principle is 'man', not even as a category but as an individual. This means that he posited 'man' as a philosophical subject, although the whole of philosophy up till then had neglected him almost completely. Socrates would later follow the same track.

c. Radicalization

The relativism of Protagoras that still knew some restrictions was asking for radicalization by lesser gods. Xeniades, a Corinthian, of whom we know absolutely nothing, taught that all that exists emanates from what does not exists; all that perishes dissolves into the non existing [52]. Every thinker, up till then, had asssumed that all what exists proceeds from what already existed. Parmenides had confirmed this by declaring that non being is absolutely nothing at all and, therefore, cannot produce anything at all [53]. The doctrine of Xeniades boils down to this : everything is untrue (no indubitable utterances are possible) and hence every presentation ('phantasia') and every opinion or conception is untrue. Thus we cannot appeal to any reliable criterion of truth. Untersteiner terms this 'absolute phenomenalism' [54]. This point of view would, indeed, liquidate the whole of philosophy.

Cratylus is said to have been a contemporary of Socrates; Plato who made him into the namegiver of one of his dialogues knew him personally [55]. This Cratylus carries to an extreme Heraclitus' famous saying 'panta rhei' (everything is moving). He contends that if all observable things are in permanent movement, knowledge ('epistêmê') is impossible. What he really means is : reliable knowledge [56]. For it is not possible to make true statements about things that are continually changing. Here short work is made of all science. This proved no problem for Cratylus, for in his opinion it is better to avoid general statements of any kind. Heraclitus had said that it is not possible to descend twice into the same river (since the river streamed on and, therefore, one could not step into it a second time). Cratylus said, however, that it was not even possible to descend once into the same river [57].

d. The bankruptcy of philosophy

It will be clear by now that the Sophists declared a whole period of science and philosophy closed; what is more, they declared it bankrupt. What they aimed at was something utterly different; their point of departure is entirely new. However important this may be - Socrates and Plato will react very strongly to it -, this is, for the moment, not the principal point. What interests me is that these attacks on religion, in combination with this relativism, must have created a sphere of great uncertainty, probably somewhat camouflaged by cynicism. The principal victims were the intellectual youths who crowded into the schools of the Sophists.

I want to repeat here a supposition that I also brought forward in Volumes I and II : Gnostic dualism (especially with regard to the history of religions) will originate when an established religion shows serious flaws or when it falls seriously into decay. The established religion of these centuries was the Olympian one, and this showed very great failings : the gods are neither eternal nor omnipotent, they behave immorally, and they handle human beings in an utterly arbitrary manner [58].

This system was attacked, first by the Ionian natural philosophers, and then by the Sophists. They drove the gods back, if not from public life, then at any rate from the hearts and minds of the educated. Tragedy will show how great the distance had already become. Sophism was another stage in the destabilization of Greek religion. It is now of the utmost importance to see how Plato reacted to this. First, however, we should explain that in two fields the Sophists showed clearly dualistic tendencies, first in the area of linguistics, and secondly in the area dominated by the opposition nomos-physis.

4. Greek nominalism

As great orators and as teachers of rhetoric the Sophists were, of course, deeply interested in language and the phenomena of language. They may even be considered as the founders of the science of linguistics. They were deeply impressed by the power of language : "The word ('logos') is a great power ..., it can chase fear and take away sorrow, it can cause joy and evoke pity" [59]. Their admiration is so great that, with them, language sometimes seems to lead a life of its own; for verbal artists such as they were this would not be surprising from a psychological point of view. Gorgias sighs : "If only it was possible to make, by means of words, the truth about reality pure and limpid, how easily judgments would result then from the spoken word but it is not so" [60]. The conclusion is evident : words conceal reality rather than reveal it; there is, therefore, a difference between words and reality.

In Plato Socrates says that Sophists are people who understand the correct use of words [61]. What interests Socrates here is clearly something deeper than the correct use of words in an oratorical context. The question that interests him is, as he makes perfectly clear to us, whether 'names do possess a certain natural correctness', or whether they are only 'conventional signs' [62]. Or, to phrase it differently, do words and names tally with things? In 'Cratylus', a dialogue on the correctness of names, Hermogenes, an amateur-Sophist and the brother of the rich Callias, the Maecenas of the Sophists, denies that there could be any correctness in names, unless by convention and appointment (therefore not 'by nature'). "If you give up that name and change it for another, the latter name is no less correct than the earlier - ("a rose would smell as sweet by any other name") - ..., for I think no name belongs to any particular thing by nature, but only by the habit and custom of those who employ it and who established the usage" [63].

Just as in the theory of knowledge of the Sophists reality tends to become somewhat less real here. In contrast to Cratylus, who contends that a celestial lawgiver keeps things in their places with the help of names, Hermogenes posits that reality is completely beyond our grasp. What Cratylus and Hermogenes mean may be demonstrated by reference to a dream that is told in 'The Night Bride' (1909), a psychoanalytical novel by the Dutch author Frederik van Eeden. In it somebody has a nightmare in which the furniture in his room starts moving in an uncontrollable way. He is thoroughly terrified but cannot do anything about it till, finally, the names of the pieces of furniture come back to his mind. When he then says 'table, seat!', they immediately return to their usual places and remain there immovably.

Antisthenes, a pupil of Socrates and a near contemporary of Plato, wrote a book 'On Education', or 'On Names', of which precious little remains. Aristotle mentions followers of this Antisthenes ('unlearned', he calls them) who are of the opinion that it is impossible to define what a thing is. One could enumerate elements or part of a thing but not the thing itself : "We cannot say what silver is, but we can say that it is like tin" [64]. Antisthenes' repugnance against general definitions is illustrated by his sneering remark to Plato that he indeed saw a horse but no 'horseness'. What he observed was a concrete thing but not an abstract concept [65].

May this be called 'nominalism', a manifestation of the doctrine that there is a gap between names and the things indicated by those names? Guthrie denies this and says that the opinion of Antisthenes does not resemble that of Hermogenes. For Antisthenes is also reported to have stated that nothing can be described adequately unless by its own name [66]; this would, of course, soundly contradict the opinion of Hermogenes. Nevertheless, the suspicion of nominalism attaches to him also. He declines general definitions, certainly in the sense that 'opposite abstract terms stand concrete things', to quote Graeser; this scholar also thinks that later commentators, like Simplicius and Ammonius, took this for a nominalistic position [67]. If this is correct - although we know very little of Antisthenes -, then his nominalism was of another brand than that of Hermogenes since, according to the first named, specific names belong to things. However, as Gertrud Stein might put it, a horse is a horse is a horse. And nothing more. Perhaps there is no separation between names and objects, but in any case there is one between concepts and objects.

5. The dualism of nomos and physis

'Nomos and physis', according to Heinimann, is a pair of concepts that easily may grow into an antithesis [68]. In the fifth century B.C. this opposition became so strong indeed that it proved no longer possible to keep them together; then, as is the usual result in dualism, two worlds came about, that of 'nomos' and that of 'physis'. 'Physis' is one of those classical terms the rendering of which presents considerable difficulties. 'Nature' is an adequate translation, so long as we equate 'nature' here not with 'flora and fauna' but with 'given reality', that on which human beings cannot exercize any influence. 'Nomos' is usually translated by 'law' and is the regulating principle to which people adhere, the agreement, the convention. For a long time nomos was preferred over physis; without laws, norms and traditions mankind would be badly off; it would be the prey of blind natural forces or of human greed and ambition. States and populations can draw up 'nomoi'; these need not be the same everywhere. However, there is also a 'nomos' for all mankind; this proceeds from the gods. The authority of this nomos is divine.

But belief in the gods is tottering; they are no longer the absolute authority behind the nomos. In the fifth century the opposition is becoming sharper. Nomos is becoming something artificial, invented by men; physis, on the contrary, is now what is natural, spontaneous and authentic. In fact, before very long nomos is seen as something that oppresses physis. In this view people damage their real being by adhering to their self-made prescriptions. How far this 'Umwertung aller Werte' (or 'Entwertung aller Werte') had already gone is proved by a quotation from Archelaus (480-410), a pupil of Anaxagoras : "According to him, good and bad do not spring from our nature but from the nomos" [69]. This certainly is the oldest utterance in which the two concepts are opposed in an irreconcilable way. Our basic ethical notions are seen by Archelaus as a product of convention.

However, the fact that there is an opposition does not necessarily entail that an author chooses the side of physis. In Volume II I digressed on the anthropological theories of the fifth century. Earlier scholars had taken the view that mankind now found itself in a serious state of decay; compared to an hypothetical original situation it had deteriorated considerably. However, in Protagoras and others we encounter a far more optimistic idea : humanity is progressing to ever higher levels. To Protagoras this means that mankind is freeing itself from the shackles of that original human condition which, in his eyes, is more or less identical with degeneration. This progress is impossible without agreements, conventions, regulations, in short, 'nomoi' [70]. This will not surprise us in the man who was asked to draw up the statute book of Thurii. To a lawgiver like him it is evident that everybody has to stick to laws and stipulations. However, this does not mean at all that he ascribes a divine origin or a religious authority to nomos. Good and wrong, just and unjust, sacred or not, in a polis these are only legal terms, the meaning of which is defined according to every polis' own insight; "in this respect no man and no citizen is wiser than another" [71]. In this point the Sophist positively deviates from older opinions.

According to Heinimann, Protagoras is trying to safeguard in this way the nomos from the fierce attacks that were directed against it. However, this attempt was doomed to fail in advance since Protagoras too was of the opinion that nomos is made by men and is, therefore, something temporal and relative [72]. This also applies to others who considered justice and written law as closely related concepts. Even Socrates was convinced that it is man who makes the laws, with the consequence that they are changeable. But as long as such general agreements are valid, one must adhere to them [73]. Socrates showed that he meant this in earnest when he got the chance to leave his prison but, nevertheless, remained in his cell since the law had to be obeyed [74].

In these decades of Greek history the tide ran exactly in the opposite direction. The right of the strongest, in these centuries of permanent warfare easily the prevailing rule, now got a theoretical foundation; for people with brains and some education it was no problem to produce a theory that justified their deeds. They also found a following for it : "All these are views ... which young people imbibe from men of science ..., who maintain that the height of justice is to succeed by force; ... these teachers attract them towards the life that is right according to nature ('kata phusin'), which consists in being master over the rest in reality, instead of being a slave to others according to legal convention" ('kata nomon')" [75].

The man who is the spokesman in this Platonic text is a well-to-do young man, a certain Callicles. We only know him from Plato;

perhaps he invented him. But historical or not, this does not matter, for surely his opinions were shared by many an unscrupulous power figure. Straightforwardly Callicles states that nomos and physis are irreconcilable entities. Socrates' fine ethic that it is better to suffer injustice than to commit it, is a slave's morality in his eyes. "The makers of the laws are the weaker kind of men, and the more numerous. So it is with a view to themselves and to their own interest that they make their laws ... So this is why by convention (nomos) it is termed unjust and foul to aim at an advantage over the majority, and why they call it wrong-doing. But nature (physis), in my opinion, herself proclaims the fact that it is right for the better to have an advantage of the worse, and the abler of the feebler ... Yes, by Zeus, follow the law of nature, though not that ... which is made by us (i.e. the nomos)". Callicles reverses the roles here : what has been called 'nomos' up till then is not the nomos, the rule to which all must adhere, no, nature herself (physis) is the law (and is even called 'nomos' by Callicles).

He then continues : "We mould the best and strongest among us, taking them from their infancy like young lions, and utterly enthral them by our spells and witchcraft, telling them the while that they must have but their equal share and that this is what is fair and just. But, I fancy, when some man arises with a nature of sufficient force, he shakes off all that we have taught him, bursts his bonds, and breaks free; he tramples underfoot our codes and juggleries, our charms and laws which are all against nature; our slave rises in revolt and shows himself our master, and there dawns the full light of natural justice" 76)

Was Plato thinking of Alcibiades here? Whether he was or not, his 'man of sufficient force' is only too recognizable in the contemporary world. The lion's cubs have grown up unimpededly and live on with us as Nietzsche's 'herrliche blonde Bestie', the linear descendant of Callicles' young lion [77]. As I read such or similar words, I suddenly have a picture of burning Warsaw before my eyes : people are driven on like cattle, and before the sea of flames stands, straddle-legged, an SS-officer with a broad grin on his face. For Callicles' words did not fall upon deaf ears. "In the last resort this means that some people have the right to realize themselves at the cost of others, and to press their interests without paying any attention to those of others" [78]. The breach with the older nomos-concept could not be more complete.

A certain Antiphon of whom we know next to nothing wrote a book 'On Truth' of which some fragments remain. There has been some discussion whether these fragments render his own opinion or that of others. This need not occupy us for, anyhow, they represent current opinion. Some of it has already been discussed in the foregoing. He begins very innocently as follows : "Justice consists in this that one does not contravene the legal stipulations of the polis of which one is a citizen". But then he continues : "A man may profit (sic) from justice, if he respects the law when he is in the presence of witnesses; in other circumstances he had rather obey the urge of nature. Laws are artificial; the commands of nature are necessary. Stipulations of law have been agreed upon and have not grown. Natural prescriptions have grown and have not been agreed upon ... Legal prohibitions are just as harmful to nature as the commands of the law ... Everything that comes on top of it (i.e. of the natural disposition) are shackles and bonds to nature; everything that comes from nature is free" [79]. In Volume II, Chapter IV, Section 3k, I cited this in order to show that a gap between the polis and the citizens was coming into being; here the quotation serves to prove that nomos and physis have grown apart so that now they were radical, even dualistic oppositions.

6. Socrates : the man

a. His life and death

In the decades before 400 B.C. the passer-by could, in Athens, often witness a small gathering. In the midst of a number of idle citizens who did not want to miss this spectacle stood a man; he was discussing with one or more others as though he had nothing more important to attend to. And very probably he had not as he used to asseverate regularly. He was an ugly man, corpulent, with a snub nose, thick lips and protruding eyes; according to one friend he had a speaking likeness to a ray, and, according to another, to a satyr [80]. His attire was in accordance with his outward appearance. He possessed only one old coat and usually went about on naked feet. If he, occasionally, looked every inch a king, even his best friends were dumbfounded [81]. His position in Athenian society was rather unclear. He was married, very probably at a late age, and had three sons. His wife Xanthippe whose bad temper became proverbial will have had some reason for not always being pleased with her husband. Not only he was seldom to be found at home but he also had no profession. He had no pupils like the Sophists and took money from no one.

Although he sometimes argued in a downright Sophistic way and did not eschew dialectical tricks, he was, nevertheless, no Sophist in the proper sense of the word. The cosmopolitism of the Sophists was alien to him; Athens hardly had a more stay-at-home citizen than he was : he had only the faintest idea how the landscape right before the walls looked like. His only form of 'tourism' was that he, as a faithful citizen, took part in a number of campaigns in the Peloponnesian War; he was an hoplite, and on more than one occasion this Socrates proved himself an exceptionally courageous soldier.

In view of the improbable accusations of the indictment one can only say that Socrates was eliminated with the help of juridical means. But why? One may assume that many persons found him irritating to an extreme. Not everyone had pleasant memories of a discussion with him since only too frequently Socrates would not hesitate, even in public, to expose the self-conceit and superficiality of his conversational sparring partner. He was perfectly aware of this for he called himself a 'gad-fly' that, ready to sting, buzzes about its victim [82]. Then he was, in spite of himself, classified with the Sophists. Aristophanes who, by the way, did not specifically call Socrates a Sophist, saw in him, nevertheless, a dangerous modernist and attacked him unscrupulously in his 'The Clouds' [83]. Such people Socrates called 'dangerous enemies', and rightly so, for, as he himself was to realize, the accusation of being a Sophist could imply that one was an 'atheist'. The real reason of his condemnation must be sought in the political field.

The process against Socrates took place in the year 399 B.C., in the tense atmosphere of the period after the fall of the Thirty and the restoration of democracy. Socrates, from motives of principle, did not play a role in politics - perhaps in some circles this was an object of criticism -, and had, at great risk of his life, ignored an order of the Thirty. Nevertheless, many people saw in him the man who had greatly influenced Critias, the tyrannical and bloodthirsty leader of the Thirty. "He was the teacher of Critias, one of the Thirty, and that is why Socrates was put to death" [84], - this represents, in all probability, current opinion [85]. Socrates' friendship with Alcibiades did not do him much good either. Not without reason the latter was considered to be the politician who had plunged Athens into catastrophic adventures; moreover, the suspicion of sacrilege and profanation of the mysteries still hung about him. Probably this was the background of two of the counts of the indictment, the 'spoiling of the youth', and 'not venerating the gods'. But these things could no longer be said openly and clearly since, after the end of the dictatorship in 404/403, a general amnesty had been promulgated [86].

b. Which Socrates was the historic one?

Because we know so little of the historic Socrates the question is justified which Socrates we actually mean when we refer to him. For there are several Socrateses, as they are variously presented to us by Aristophanes, Xenophon, Plato, and Aristotle, and even others. In a recent booklet Fresco subjected the available source material to a careful scrutiny [87]. Socrates himself did not leave behind a single written word; therefore we must rely totally on secondary material. "When we ask for the objectives of our sources, these are scarcely ever limited to providing information about the historical Socrates" [88]. It is a fact that Plato was the most prolific author on this subject. According to Fresco, "to most of us Plato intuitively seems a convincing source. The way he paints Socrates is so true to life, it must have been like that" [89]. In his opinion "Plato's picture of Socrates is so convincing because it is based on a real encounter with the man (underlining by Fresco) Socrates" [90].

And, indeed, Plato did know the man Socrates personally, he loved and venerated him, and finally immortalized him in writing. Moreover he presents him to us in connection with his own life and thought. Now it would seem that the most sensible thing to do would be to follow Fresco and take the younger Plato as our starting point. Then we can incorporate 'circumstantial evidence' from other sources [91]. This would be to concur with Guthrie's opinion, and that of many others, that the young Plato, allowing for all the peculiarities and wilfulness of Platonic literary production, has faithfully portrayed not only the man Socrates but also his way of teaching and his thought [92].

The question, however, is which particular dialogues are those of the younger Plato. There exists a great deal of difference of opinion on the problems of grouping and dating these dialogues, at least of certain of them. It is impossible to go into this argument here; I am content to associate myself with the opinion of an authoritative scholar like Guthrie whose arguments are supported by ample documentation. He ascribes nine works to the younger Plato : Apology, Crito, Eutyphron, Laches, Lysis, Hippias Major, Hippias Minor, Charmides, Ion. To the existing arguments in favour of gathering these works into one group I should like to add yet another : without exception they all end in failure. In the Apology Socrates does not succeed in changing the mind of the jury; Crito is not able to talk Socrates out of prison. In the seven other works it is stated at the end that the parties to the discussion did not succeed in defining the subject of the conversation. In later dialogues such failures no longer occur at all or not to that extent.

In the following section it is not my intention to describe what is called 'socratics'; this has already been the subject of thorough and meticulous attention. I merely wish to emphasize some points in the line of development which I have traced already, namely that which led to the coming about of the Gnostic-dualistic complex. However, I would not wish to imply that Socrates' way of thought was dualistic or that he was an early Gnostic. But I am basically interested in morphological similarities.

7. Socrates' 'daimonion'

In his apology before the court of justice Socrates mentions the general opinion that he is different from all other people - a conviction that is also his own; he is different in consequence of a mandate. His sense of mission came from outside, it was something divine, it was a 'daimonion' [93]. He said that this 'divine' had been with him since his early years; it was, he tells us, 'a kind of voice that comes to me'. Although this voice had never ordered him to do anything specifically, it had, occasionally, held him back from something that he intended to do [94]. It had opposed him, he said, even in very small matters [95], and the same voice had also forbidden him to engage in politics [96]. Besides 'voice' Socrates also called this 'daimonion', perhaps out of prudence, 'sign' ('sêmeion') [97]. He knew, indeed, very well that, because of this openly confessed 'daimonion', he was taken for 'a maker of new gods' [98].

Socrates also speaks about 'the god, the godhead', without indication of name. This godhead sometimes forbade him to do certain things - for instance to escape from prison [99] - and, in contrast to the divine voice, sometimes gave him concrete instructions. 'The godhead' who told him to interrogate people is, to all intents and purposes, Apollo [100]. It is for this reason that he does not desire to be acquitted on condition of remaining silent; he has to remain obedient to the godhead [101]. The godhead, indeed, imposed some difficult restrictions, and one of them, certainly, must have been a burden on his family - he was not allowed to accept money for his teaching. Several times he testifies that he is as poor as a church-mouse [102].

In Plato, and also in Xenophon, Socrates speaks so often of his 'daimonion' that we may safely assume that we are in the presence of the authentic Socrates. How must we conceive this 'voice'? This certainly is an interesting question for the psychology of religion. What is important for us, however, is what the voice meant to Socrates himself. One thing seems clear : for Socrates at any rate the voice of the daimonion came from outside his own being and was no part of his own psychology. "I am clever against my will", he says somewhere [103]. He obviously means that in some respects he is subject to an external power. Nevertheless, he saw this also as an enrichment of his own personality : "In everything else I may be a poor useless creature, but there is one gift that I have somehow from heaven - to be able to recognize quickly a lover or a beloved" [104].

Voices that speak to people from above -, these are, in the history of Greek civilization, not too frequent, but, at the same time, no exception. Poets often feel addressed by the Muse; in many cases there is no need to see this only as a literary device. Even a philosopher like Parmenides attributed his way of thinking to divine inspiration. In Socrates, however, the relationship seems closer : the daimonion does not come once or twice, it accompanies him during his whole life, it is his personal daimonion. It does not bestow inspiration on him, it does not inspire his words or actions, but it guides him, rules him, intervenes in his life. This places him in that very special position that makes him different from all other people : he is thirsting after something that does not interest others, that is, after knowledge. This knowledge is not the practical know-how of the Sophists, but the essential knowledge of the regulative concepts that must determine our lives.

Morphologically and partly also conceptually this phenomenon is similar to the conviction of many esoteric groups, especially Gnostic-dualistic ones, who consider that they possess a very special knowledge - a knowledge, that is, that came to them by way of inspiration. It is, however, with regard to his life, not with respect to his philosophy, that Socrates appeals to a voice from outside. Moreover, he is more generous than esoteric groups that keep their 'Geheimwissen' painstakingly to themselves; he, on the contrary, is ready to make everyone a partner to it. Nevertheless, we begin to detect a gap here, between knowledge and knowledge : on the one hand the commonplace knowledge that was fashioned by the Sophists into a highly perfected instrument, on the other hand, the essential knowledge that man cannot acquire without divine help.

8. Socratic knowledge

The Athenians are not interested in this knowledge, the wisdom that Socrates aims at; they are too busy for it [105]. They are like sleeping people, he says, and when they have killed him they may pass the rest of their lives in slumber, unless the godhead, in his care for them, sends someone else to sting them [106]. Socrates examined those who were called wise. But it came apparent to him that the politicians, the artisans and the poets know nothing at all; at best they understand something of their own profession, in particular the artisans, but nothing outside it [107]. It is not so much that Socrates excels them, not at all, he too knows nothing [108], and this in spite of the fact that the oracle of Delphi called him the wisest of all men [109]. But there is one thing he knows : "Human wisdom is of little or no value" [110]. It is for this reason that he goes about and questions those who believe they are wise but are not really wise [111].

For what he means by this kind of knowledge Socrates uses several words, 'sophia', for instance, and 'epistêmê' ('comprehension') but not the word 'gnosis'. The very special esoteric knowledge of Gnosticism played no part for him. On the other hand, his knowledge cannot be learned; it is not an ability that can be taught. Indeed, Socrates, who, in any case, is wise enough not to think that he knows what he does not know [112], has had no teacher himself [113]. Now what is this particular knowledge? To know what is 'aretê', excellence, the right way of living [114]. "An (on this point) unexamined life is not worth living", Socrates declares categorically [115]. Everything begins with excellence; it seems that Socrates expressed this in the lapidary formula : 'aretê epistêmê', knowledge is excellence [116]. "Socrates thought that the end is to get to know what is excellence", according to Aristotle [117]. He reproaches him for his intellectualism; Socrates, however, never meant to imply that a purely intellectual knowledge leads to the good life. This is the practical side of Socrates the Sophist for he, just like other Sophists, was out for tangible results. However, for him the goal was of a totally different order.

The essential knowledge is that of good and evil [118]. But only the gods know what is really good. "I go to die, and you to live; but which of us goes to the better lot, is known to no one but the godhead", with these moving words Socrates concludes his apology [119]. It appears that to him knowledge is of a higher kind, far from self-evident, not easily acquired by men. It is for this reason that he puts his partners so severely to the test; they must know that they are in for a lot of trouble. "Whatever statement we advance, somehow or other it moves about and won't stay where we put it", sighs Euthyphron [120]; "whoever comes into close contact with Socrates is bound to be drawn round and round by him", says Nicias [121].

But even Socrates sometimes needs a teacher - at least so he tells us [122]. Indeed, in one dialogue after another he confesses his incapacity to attain the desired knowledge. With might and main Socrates, and Plato with him, emphasize that commonplace knowledge is useless for the real aim; the acquirement of the necessary wisdom is a matter of the greatest effort and devotion. This is exactly what the Pythagorean movement taught. Not everyone was ready to take such pains. According to the Sophist Hippias, Socrates occupied himself with 'mere scrapings and shavings of discourse, divided into bits'; whereas for him, Hippias, nothing is finer than 'the ability to produce a discourse well and beautifully' - the art of the rhetor, that is [123].

We encounter two portents of the future here. The first is the distinction between commonplace knowledge and another, higher knowledge; between a knowledge that can be taught, and another knowledge that is not teachable. It is not yet a fully developed dualistic opposition, but it is clear that it may soon grow into one. The second is that there is a distinct difference, not yet between the initiated and the uninitiated, but rather between those who are devoted to real wisdom and those who could not care less. Again this is not yet a dualistic opposition between the elect and the massa damnata, but here too our patience will not be tried too far.

9. The right word for the right concept

a. The Socratic doctrine of definitions

Socrates shows affinity with Sophistic linguistics when he again and again presses for the correct definition. "Make clear to what thing it is that you attach such-and-such a name" [124]. This question is raised continually : what is ...? What is courage, what is friendship, what is prudence - always, as we have seen, without drawing a conclusion. The pre-eminent question, of course, is : what is excellence [125]? We have the testimony of Aristotle that two things may be ascribed to Socrates without any reservation : the art of reasoning inductively, and general definitions, both of them as starting-points for science. He adds that Socrates did not confer a separate existence on universals or definitions; by this he very probably means that such Socratic definitions are not identical with Platonic ideas with their very peculiar ontological status [126].

Socrates was not interested in the practical abilities of the Sophists nor in knowledge of the universe according to the natural philosophers (these did not make him any the wiser, he thought). He limits himself to ethical questions, and in this field he was in great need of universals [127]. How can people strive after excellence and choose the right way if they do not know beforehand what justice is or courage or piety? In order to arrive at a good definition, that is to say, at an exact rendering of the general aspect, he uses the inductive method : the principle of this is that he makes his partner in the discussion begin with a concrete detail. What is courage? "Anyone who is willing to stay at his post and face the enemy, and does not run away, you may be sure, is courageous" [128]. From this starting-point Socrates argues towards the final objective.

For this kind of argumentation he dearly needed the dialogue form, from a pedagogical as well from a didactical point of view. For he wanted his partner to develop the whole argument himself. If he were to try to teach him, in the usual sense of the word, about the matter in hand, he would be proceeding deductively. This he had no wish to do. The conclusions are not given ready to hand; Plato tries to avoid the suspicion (but often without much success) that the party to the discussion is steered towards a foregone conclusion. The fact that in not one of the early dialogues a conclusion is reached may prove that the road to the goal is seen as more important than the goal itself. In 'Lysis' Socrates even overturns completely the result that had already been reached [129]. Repeatedly he confesses his own ignorance and incapability. Do not think I have answers to questions, he says to Critias [130].

Again it is Aristotle who assures us that Plato, with his doctrine of Forms, was a disciple of Socrates with his definitions [131]. And indeed, although Socratic definitions and Platonic Forms are not identical, there is a connection between them. If it is true that, inherent in Plato's doctrine of Forms, a dualistic element is discernible - as I intend to demonstrate later, - then Socrates' doctrine of definitions, albeit not dualistic in itself, is, nevertheless, an important step in this direction. We perceive already a flicker of the doctrine of Forms when Socrates, according to Aristotle, is speaking of 'whiteness' [132]. However, this might be a small chip from Plato's block.

b. The 'basic aspect'

In 'Eutyphron' Socrates mentions 'the basic aspect' - here the translation of 'eidos' [133]; in a moment or so 'idea' is used as a synonym for 'eidos'. Platonic terms? Or rather Socratic ones? In any case Socrates says that he wants to use this 'eidos', if one were able to define what it is exactly, as a 'paradigma', as a model, in order to determine what a definition means in concreto, and what not [134]. The fact that people do not know the definitions of the most basic concepts, like good and wrong, makes them into enemies of one another [135]. Even the gods disagree on such things; even they ignore the essentials - for instance, they do not know what holiness is [136]. What is holy is, therefore, not holy because it is dear to the gods [137]. This proves that, for Socrates too, what is universal has a status of its own. What status this is is not as yet apparent, but in any case, holiness as a universal concept is not based on the Olympian religion.

Whether 'Hippias Major' is authentically Platonic or not (it is doubted by many but not by every scholar [138], this work also contains important data. Socrates is speaking here of concepts as if they had a status of their own. The question is 'not what is beautiful, but what the beautiful is' [139]. Somewhat further on he says : "If a beautiful maiden is beautiful (the example Hippias has brought forward), there is something by reason of which these things would be beautiful" [140]. And he goes on to speak of 'the beautiful (in) itself' ('auto to kalon') : things are beautiful when this 'eidos' ('the beautiful') is added to it [141]. At the same time it is valid for all and for ever [142]. Beauty, therefore, is not a quality characteristic of beautiful things; rather they derive their beauty from a general 'shape' ('eidos') with which they, so to speak, are draped. Socrates does not explain what the relationship is between the general and the particular; he left this tricky problem as a legacy to Plato.

Although Socrates broke with the natural philosophers who preceded him, he remained faithful to them in one respect. He too is asking for an 'archê', a general viewpoint, or rather, for 'archai', for the definitions are 'archai' to him. If we speak of friendship, he says, we must "arrive at some first principle which will not keep leading us from one friend to another" (what he means is arguing without being in possession of a definition), "but will reach the one original friendship ('to proton philon'), for whose sake all the other things can be said to be friends" [143]. The words that immediately follow will prove of the utmost importance for the future : if we do not possess the original definition, if we have no idea what 'friendship' really is, then the concrete things may be deceiving us 'like so many phantoms ('eidola') of it" [144]. Here the first shadow of dualism is falling over the explanations - the distinction between being and seeming - that later, in Plato, will deepen into a full shadow.

NOTES TO CHAPTER II

1) Plato, Soph. 224C-D.
2) Copleston I 1, 307.
3) DL IX.51; DK II Prot. A21 and C2.
4) Xen., Mem. I 6.13.
5) Vol. II, Ch. IV, Section 3e.
6) First sentence of Margaret Mitchell's 'Gone with the Wind' (1936).
7) Olof Gigon s.v. 'Protagoras' in Lex.d.Alt.Welt 2458; Von Fritz s.v. 'Protagoras' in PW XXIII.1 (Stuttgart, 1957), 907-921.
8) Olof Gigon s.v. 'Gorgias' in Lex.d.Alt.Welt 110/111; E.Wellmann s.v. 'Gorgias' in PW VII (Stuttgart 1912), 1598-1604.
9) Plato, Hipp.Min. 364A.
10) Olof Gigon s.v. 'Hippias' in Lex.d.Alt.Welt 1302; Björnbo s.v. 'Hippias' in PW VIII (Stuttgart, 1913), 1706-1711.
11) Plato, Prot. 315C-E.
12) Plato, Euth. 277E.
13) Plato, Meno 75E, Lach. 197D, Charmides 163D. For Prodicus see Olof Gigon in Lex.d.Alt.Welt 2439.
14) DL IX 51-52.
15) Plato, Theaet. 162D.
16) Drachmann 41.
17) Drachmann 42.
18) He is called 'atheos' by Sext.Emp., Ad.Phys. I 51, among others.
19) Drachmann 43/44.
20) Sext.Emp., Adv.Phys. I 18.
21) Graeser 57-60.
22) Guthrie III 239-242.
23) Drachmann 44.
24) DK II Kritias 88B25.
25) Drachmann 46.
26) DK II Krit. 88B25:26.
27) DK II Krit. 88B25:41-42.
28) See Aristoph., The Birds 1072/1073, where a prize is set on his head, and The Clouds 839, where Socrates is called 'Melian' = atheist.
29) Sext.Emp., Adv.Phys. I 53.
30) See Drachmann 31-34.
31) Plato, Phaedo 97B-98C.
32) DK II Gorgias 82B1-4.
33) Copleston I 1, 14.
34) DK II Gorg. 82B3:76 = Sext.Emp., Adv.Log. I 76.
35) Untersteiner, Sophists 147.
36) Untersteiner, Sophists 145.
37) DK II Gorg. 82B26.
38) Guthrie III 199 translates 'appearance', DK has 'gelingen zu scheinen' = 'to succeed in looking like'; this must mean 'to take on a shape'.
39) Graeser 41.
40) DK II Gorg. 82B3:84 = Sext.Emp., Adv.Log. I 84.

41) MXG 980b = Pseudo-Ar., De Melisso, Xenophane, Gorgia = Bekker II G Ar. 1B.
42) DK II Prot. 80B1.
43) Plato, Theaet. 152A-B.
44) Copleston I 1, 108.
45) Plato, Theaet. 167C.
46) Guthrie III 187.
47) Untersteiner, Soph. 48.
48) Untersteiner, Soph. 42.
49) Ar., Met. 1062b.
50) DK II 80B6a.
51) Copleston I 1, 111.
52) Sext.Emp., Adv. Log. I 53/54.
53) Guthrie III 200.
54) Guthrie III 163.
55) Ar., Met. 987a.
56) Ar., Met. 987a.
57) Ar., Met. 1010a; see Graeser 45 who enumerates the arguments.
58) Vol. I, Ch. IV, Section 3.
59) Gorgias, Helenês Enkomion, DK II Gorg. 82B11:8.
60) Gorgias, Palamêdou Apologia, DK II Gorg. 82B11a:35.
61) Plato, Crat. 391B-C.
62) Guthrie III 205.
63) Plato, Crat. 384D.
64) Ar., Met. 1043b.
65) Simpl. in cat. 8625.
66) Ar., Met. 1024b.
67) Graeser 55.
68) Heinimann 110.
69) DK II Archelaos 47A1 = DL II.16; see Heinimann 110-114; Guthrie III 58/59.
70) This is how Plato presents it, Prot. 327A.
71) Presented as Prot.' opinion by Plato, Theaet. 172A.
72) Heinimann 119.
73) Xen., Mem. IV.4:12-13.
74) In Plato's Crito.
75) Plato, Laws 890A.
76) Plato, Gorg. 483B-484A.
77) In 'Die Genealogie der Moral', see Graeser 75.
78) Graeser 75.
79) DK II Antiphon 87B44a:1-4.
80) Plato, Meno 80A, Symp. 215B.
81) Plato, Symp. 174A.
82) Plato, Ap. 30E.
83) Socr. refers to this in Plato, Ap. 19C; his resistance to the Thirty in Plato, Ap. 32C-D.
84) Aeschin. I 173.
85) Copleston I 1, 135.
86) Copleston I 1, 135.
87) See Fresco, Socrates.
88) Fresco 23.
89) Fresco 47.

90) Fresco 48.
91) Fresco 64.
92) Guthrie IV 67/68.
93) The texts of Plato and Xenophon do not speak of a 'daimoon' since they have the apologetic intention to safeguard Socrates from the accusation that he wanted to introduce new gods.
94) Plato, Ap. 31D.
95) Plato, Ap. 40.
96) Plato, Ap. 31E, Rep. 496C.
97) Plato, Ap. 41D.
98) Plato, Eutyphr. 2B.
99) Plato, Crito 54E.
100) Plato, Ap. 30A.
101) Plato, Ap. 29C-D.
102) Plato, Ap. 23B, 31B-C, Hipp.Maj. 300D, Eutyphr. 3C.
103) Plato, Eutyphr. 11E.
104) Plato, Lys. 204C.
105) Plato, Ap. 29D-E.
106) Plato, Ap. 31A.
107) Plato, Ap. 21E-22E.
108) Plato, Hipp.Min. 372B.
109) Plato, Ap. 21A.
110) Plato, Ap. 23A.
111) Plato, Ap. 33C.
112) Plato, Ap. 20D.
113) Plato, Lach. 186C.
114) Plato, Lach. 190B.
115) Plato, Ap. 38A.
116) I do not think that this combination occurs in as many words in the nine dialogues I am using here but we meet them in more or less the same form in Xen., Mem. III 9.51 : "He (Socr.) said that justice and every other virtue is wisdom (sophia)", and also in Aristotle : "He regarded the Virtues as departments of science" MM 1182a (MM often considered as post-ar.). EN 1144b29-30 : "S. thought that the virtues are principles (logoi), for he said that they are all of them forms of knowledge". Idem in EE 1216b6/7.
117) Ar., EE 1216b3-4.
118) Plato, Charm. 174D.
119) Plato, Ap. 42.
120) Plato, Eutyphr. 11B and D.
121) Plato, Lach. 187E.
122) Plato, Lach. 201A.
123) Plato, Hipp.Maj. 304A.
124) Plato, Charm. 174D.
125) Plato, Lach. 190B.
126) Ar., Met. 1078b27.
127) Ar., Met. 987b1-4.
128) Plato, Lach. 190E.
129) Plato, Lys. 218C.
130) Plato, Charm. 165B.
131) Ar., Met. 987b4-8.

132) Plato, Lys. 217D.
133) Plato, Eutyphr. 6D.
134) Plato, Eutyphr. 6D.
135) Plato, Eutyphr. 7D.
136) Plato, Eutyphr. 7E-8A.
137) Plato, Eutyphr. 10D-E.
138) Guthrie IV 176.
139) Plato, Hipp.Maj. 287D-E.
140) Plato, Hipp.Maj. 288A.
141) Plato, Hipp.Maj. 289D.
142) Plato, Hipp.Maj. 292E.
143) Plato, Lys. 291C.
144) Plato, Lys. 219D.

CHAPTER III

PLATONICA AND ARISTOTELICA

1. Plato : the man and his work

a. His life

Born in 428/427 B.C. Plato belonged to one of the most prominent families in Athens [1]. We do not know much about the way he spent his life, in spite of the fact that he is one of the greatest philosophers ever brought forth by mankind. He seldom speaks about himself in his work. Although we may be sure that he knew Socrates well, it is by no means certain that he ever was his student. As we have seen already, Socrates did not take pupils in the proper sense of the word; Plato, indeed, does not call him master' but 'my older friend'. Undoubtedly he loved this older friend, he venerated and admired him. "I would hardly scruple", he tells us, "to call him the most just of the men then living" [2]. He was never to deviate from this judgment. When Plato was twenty-nine, Socrates was executed. For the younger man this was a stunning blow that made him averse, once and for all, to that career in Athenian practical politics to which, in line with his descent and his family connections, he had formerly aspired [3]. Moreover, after the death of Socrates in 399 he also felt himself threatened, and he disappeared for some time to Megara. After this, he travelled for some years, probably to North-Africa and Egypt, but certainly to Southern Italy and Sicily. When he arrived there for the first time he was forty years of age.

In Syracuse he came to know Dion, the son-in-law and at the same time the brother-in-law of the ruler of that town, Dionysius I. This was the beginning of a long and sad story that need not be retold here. Plato's interest in politics had not disappeared completely but had assumed a pedagogical rather than an active character. He now tried to exert influence on the court, first on Dionysius I, then on Dion, and later, by means of this man, on Dionysius II. He did, indeed, teach this ruler, and he submitted his political plans to him. Either Dionysius II or Dion, who became tyrant of Syracuse in 357 (but was murdered already in 353 B.C.), was destined to become the ideal 'philosopher-king' of whom Plato was dreaming. Only after two more voyages to Sicily he was to abandon his plans in a mood of disappointment. Yet it was in Sicily and Southern Italy that he came into contact with members of the Pythagorean fraternities, among them the famous mathematician Archytas in Tarent. Their way of thinking was to effect his own philosophy.

After his return from his first voyage, probably in 388/387, Plato founded the 'Academy' in Athens after which all other academies are called. It got its name from the 'grove of Akadêmos' where the building stood; this grove in its turn was called after a legendary hero, Akadêmos. Taylor regards the establishment of the Academy as 'in some ways the most memorable event in the history of Western European science', since the Academy was 'the direct progenitor of the medieval and modern university' [4]. Plato's institution corresponded to the schools of the Sophists in this respect that it too wanted to turn out practically schooled people, in particular politicians and administrators. But it was also a totally new foundation because science was taught here as an end in itself. Apart from philosophy mathematics was the most important subject, but astronomy was also studied. Pupils came from everywhere; the most famous was Aristotle who arrived in 367 B.C. Plato taught here himself and found the time to write a great many of his works. When he died in 348/347 B.C. he was about eighty years old. He never married.

b. The 'Corpus Platonicum'

Plato is the first philosopher or scholar in Antiquity whose works we possess in toto. However, this does not mean that all the writings in his name are authentically his. The 'corpus platonicum' consists of

Socrates' Apology, thirty-four dialogues and thirteen letters. After decades of the most minute criticism it is assumed at present that the Apology and twenty-three dialogues are authentic; six dialogues are not by Plato (although they fit into his train of thought), and five are of doubtful origin, albeit they are not infrequently attributed to Plato; the authenticity of some of the letters is also a point of discussion [5].

Plato taught regularly in the Academy. We know his philosophy from his dialogues. However, Aristotle speaks somewhere of Plato's 'so-called unwritten doctrine' ('agrapha dogmata'), although in a way that suggests some written document [6]. Plato was hostile to the idea that his doctrine should be disseminated by others, by means for instance of written reports of his lessons. For, he says, "it does not at all admit of verbal expression like other studies" [7]. Somewhere else he adds that he has written nothing at all on certain subjects; all that is written finally is disseminated. "Beware lest these doctrines be ever divulged to uneducated people ... The greatest safeguard is to avoid writing and to learn them by heart" [8].

This sounds peculiar in the mouth of a man who wrote such a lot. For it evokes the impression that he does not take the dialogues seriously and that, apart from these dialogues, yet another doctrine existed - Plato's so-called 'secret doctrine' - accessible only to the initiated [9]. The consequence of this would be that his teaching would go along a double track and would not be really coherent. Luckily Plato himself has provided us with an explanation. Of course, he says, or rather, he makes Socrates say, that the practice of dialectics in itself is the most noble occupation imaginable. But why then did he write these dialogues? His answer is that it is a kind of literary diversion for the philosopher. "The garden of letters he (the philosopher) will plant for amusement, and will write, when he writes, to treasure up reminders for himself ... and for others ..., and he will be pleased when he sees them putting forth tender leaves. When others engage in other amusements, refreshing themselves with banquets and kindred entertainments, he will pass the time in such pleasures as I have suggested" [10].

This quotation clearly proves that Plato enjoyed writing the dialogues; however, they may scarcely be called 'popular' since they make heavy demands on the reader. At the same time, it is evident that he did not regard them as final. As everyone who has published a great deal and has taught for a long time knows, in a small circle of devoted and talented pupils one can add, expend, explain and comment, far more than is possible in writing. The gifted teacher will try, under his inspiring leadership, to conduct his best pupils much further in comprehension and insight.

Like every other author, however, Plato knew that he threw his bread on the waters : many would shrug their shoulders, other would fancy that they really understood him [11]. But only they would attain to the goal who continuously applied themselves to the subject. The essential thing they had to perform themselves, for "it is brought to birth in the soul on a sudden, as light that is kindled by a leaping spark" [12]. This applies, however, to readers and hearers similarly, although the pupils were privileged because they, under the guidance of the master, reach so much farther. I believe, therefore, that Plato saw his dialogues as a kind of preparation, not so much for admission to the Academy but for the ascent to the light. Even the reader might be brought to contemplation, and, finally, to the contemplation of what Plato called 'the sublime mysteries' [13].

c. Why the dialogue form?

Another question is why Plato preferred the dialogue form above that of the learned treatise. The evident answer is, of course, that this enabled him to put into practice the dialectical method; by alternating arguments and counter-arguments he was more able to come nearer to the truth. But this does not explain it completely. I believe one is justified in calling Plato a 'romancier manqué', or, to put it another way, he was a man who might easily have become a tragedian or perhaps, better still, a writer of comedies [14]. It was said of him that he actually wrote tragedies and that he even competed for a prize for the best tragedy. But after hearing Socrates (apparently for the first time) delivering himself in front of the Dionysus-theatre, he threw his manuscript into the fire [15].

His tragedies no longer exist, but some of his so-called dialogues are really rather plays, with a lively interchange between the actors; sometimes they are even provided with stage-directions. They resemble Aristophanes more than Aeschylus or Sophocles (Lamb rightly spoke of 'the Aristophanes-side of Plato's nature' [16]). Their tone is light, they are full of comical incidents, and they sketch the parties to the discussion mercilessly, especially their weaker sides. The dialogues contain a number of delicious vignettes : Meletus (later the prosecutor of Socrates), a man 'with long hair and only a little beard, but with a hooked nose' [17], or Stesilaus who, provided with a weapon of his own invention, a scythe fixed to a spear, handled it so fiercely that its point stuck into the rigging of an enemy ship. Stesilaus, who did not want to lose his device, was forced to run along in his ship's gangway holding on to his spear while the ships were passing each other; finally, however, he had to let it slip through his hands, amidst the loud laughter of both crews [18]. And who is able to forget the memorable scene, worthy of comedy, in which all those present want to seat themselves next to beautiful young Charmides and in doing so knocked each other off the bench [19]?

Perhaps this may explain too why Plato himself never appears in his dialogues, not even as as sparring-partner to Socrates, but leaves everything to him [20]. In some respects, certainly, he did this out of veneration and admiration for his great master. Yet even if he had been of the opinion that his own typically Platonic ideas were the necessary consequence of Socrates' conceptions, he nevertheless put tenets into the mouth of his predecessor that Socrates himself never held. In fact, the further we advance in the dialogues, the more Socrates turns into 'Socrates', the spokesman of Plato. This difference between Socrates and 'Socrates' he explains in the second letter in a very charming way. There he says that there do not exist nor will ever exist treatises by Plato; "those which bear his name belong to a Socrates become young and fair" [21]. It is possible that he never mentioned himself because he was somewhat ashamed of the frivolous, the artistic side of his nature. Socrates had been a well-known as well as a controversial figure, and, therefore, these things could better bear his name. In any case, in the course of time Plato frees himself more and more from the figure of Socrates; in 'The Sophist' and in 'Laws' - we meet Socrates no longer, and in, for instance, 'Timaeus' not Socrates but Critias is the spokesman.

2. From Socrates to Plato

Guthrie groups five dialogues together : Protagoras, Euthydemus, Gorgias, Meno, Menexenus; he believes that these belong together because they are longer (with the exception of Menexenus) and more elaborated than those of the preceding series. Moreover, their common objective seems to be to settle the account with the Sophists once and for all [22]. The decisive point, however, is that in these works the authentic Platonic themes begin to emerge by means of which Plato will differentiate himself from the historic Socrates.

It is, of course, not my intention to give a complete picture of Plato's philosophy; the central emphasis will fall on the dualistic element, an emphasis that, from the standpoint of my thesis, will prove extremely important, even essential and decisive. I do not pretend to have mastered the secondary literature on Plato; anyone who has stood on the shore of this almost infinite sea will understand this. A great help was the first half of Simone Pétrement's book on dualism [23]. Yet even if certain valuable articles or books have escaped my attention, at least I can claim that, in preparing this section, I have read or reread and annotated all the dialogues.

In the following sections there is a clear connection between the line of thought I pursue and the arguments presented in my first and second volumes. Plato's work is a reaction to all those who preceded him as well as a recapitulation of their work. He opposes himself to the natural philosophers and their materialism, but he takes over essential tenets from Heraclitus. He knew the Pythagorean movement and was influenced by it. He knew what happened in the mystery religions and felt affinity with them. He distances himself from the iron ontology of the Eleates but leans nevertheless on Parmenides. He rejects Sophism and its utilitarism but has learned much from the

Sophists. He will forbid the poets and the tragedians to enter his ideal state but he himself shows a remarkable artistic trait and cites the poets endlessly. Finally, he rejects Athenian democracy but his political interest remains undiminished.

3. The open and the closed society

In Plato the opposition between two forms of society, the open and the closed one, is irreconcilable and, therefore, dualistic. He has been the very first thinker to sketch a Utopian model of a closed society. In this respect Popper was not wrong first to direct his incendiary arrows at the Greek philosopher (the following volleys descended on Hegel and Marx). As Popper was the man who made the notions 'open and closed society' the fashion, we shall consult him for a number of definitions.

A closed society is characterized by magical practices, by strong ties to the tribe or by collectivistic ideas. It strongly resembles an organism because semi-biological bonds (like kinship) are so powerful in it. Its institutions are sacrosanct, taboos are important, everyone's status is defined and clear. The claims of communal life largely determine the mode of existence of individuals. In contrast, in an open society the individuals are constantly confronted with the necessity of personal decisions. The members of such a society are united by objective and juridical regulations; therefore their mode of living together has to take account of general or abstract considerations. Every individual relies mainly on himself; he may change his status and ascend or descend the social ladder. To this description Popper adds that the transition from a closed to an open society is one of the greatest revolutions through which humanity may pass (although a few lines further he says that the process has only recently begun). At its commencement stand the Greeks [24].

Plato allows the venerable Sophist Protagoras to take the floor in order to recommend the open society as the self-evident result of the process of civilization. Protagoras begins his disquisition with the optimistic anthropological theory I mentioned earlier, according to which mankind, starting from a wild and anarchic primeval condition, climbs upward to ever better ordered forms of society. Finally he arrives at the polis Athens (he says this in as many words) and then indicates a basic principle of the open society. "People in cities, and especially in Athens, consider it the concern of a few to advise on cases of artistic excellence or of good craftmanship, and if anyone outside the few gives advice they disallow it ... But when they meet for a consultation on civic art, where they should be guided throughout by justice and good sense, they naturally allow advice from everybody, since it is held that everyone should partake of this excellence, or else that states cannot be." And as if to banish all doubts he adds that it is believed actually that everyone partakes of justice. When "they happen to know that a certain person is unjust, if he confesses the truth about his conduct before the public, that truthfulness which in the former arts they would regard as good sense they here call madness ... since it is held that all without exception must partake of it (i.e. of justice) in some way or other, or else not be of the human kind". In this field confessions of inexpertness or incapability are simply not allowed. Therefore, the Athenians have every good reason also to seek the advice of the smith and the cobbler [25].

Plato seems to make an important step in this direction when, with regard to the opposition nomos-physis, he rejects the option for the physis, that is to say, for the right of the strongest. This he does in another dialogue, the 'Gorgias' [26]. And yet this step may be more apparent than real; in any case, he does not seem ready to defend the (Athenian) open society. It has been remarked sometimes that Plato, in his presentation of Callicles' voluble defense of the right of the strongest, shows a certain (surpressed?) sympathy for it. When he, indirectly, answers Protagoras, it seems to me that it is Plato who takes the floor rather than Socrates - the Plato who was full of bitterness against the Athenian democracy that had killed his friend. What else is democracy than adulation of the public, than rhetoric, than demagogy [27]? Be careful that "our choice for power in the city may not cost us all that we hold most dear (by this, of course, is meant the immaterial goods of the soul)" [28]. In the soul of

Callicles, however (Socrates tries in vain to influence the ambitious young man), love of the 'dêmos' has already riveted itself so strongly that he is no longer able to change his course [29].

Who wants power in Athens "will find himself possessed of the greatest evil, that of having his soul depraved and maimed as a result of his imitation of his master (i.e. the people) and the power he has got" [30]. Plato even ventures to attack the reputation of Pericles by stating that he left the Athenians worse than he found them - whereas it is the task of the good statesman to make people better [31]. In fact there has never been a good statesman in Athens [32], with one exception : Aristides [33]. And then Plato states his aversion to the free play of the politicians. In Tartarus those who are most heavily punished are the kings, the rulers, the tyrants, and those who controlled the affairs of the polis (the democratic politicians, that is). "It is among the powerful that we find the specially wicked men", and it is exceedingly hard for a politician to be a good man at the same time [34].

It is true that all this does not yet mean that Plato expressed predilection for a closed society in this way; however, he is already coming close to it. During this stage of his life he had not yet de-developed his ideal state. Another point, however, is worth stressing. When Socrates, at the end of the 'Gorgias', declares categorically that he does not desire a political career (in the traditional sense) but prefers to search for truth [35], it is Plato who speaks rather than Socrates. For 'Gorgias' is the manifesto in which Plato accounts for the foundation of the Academy. His devastating attack on Gorgias makes it clear that his institution will not be an ordinary Sophist school; at the same time he gives his reasons why he renounces a traditional political career. If it is true that his school will also train politicians, then this will be done in an utterly unconventional manner. He makes his Socrates define his own (Plato's) position as rector of the Academy in the following terms : "I think I am one of the few, not to say the one, in Athens who attempts the true art of statesmanship ('politikê technê'), and the only man of the present time who manages affairs of the state" [36]. What he is striving after is the good, that is the absolutely good, and the road to this is the road of philosophy.

4. Philosophy and knowledge

This may be all well and good, says Callicles, who then goes on to say that "it is really a fine thing to partake of philosophy just for the sake of education, and it is no disgrace for a lad to follow it, but when a man already advancing in years continues its pursuit, the affair becomes ridiculous ... An elderly man still going on with philosophy ... that is the man whom I think in need of whipping ... It is bound to become unmanly through shunning the centres and marts of the city; he must cower down and spend the rest of his life in a corner with three or four lads, and never utter anything free or high or spirited (a self-caricature of Plato?)" [37]. Callicles, however, does not understand at all what philosophy is about. He is told that "we have a duty of inquiring what we do not know, and this will make us better and brave and less helpless" [38]. Knowledge does not so much provide a man with good luck ('eutuchia', what is meant is success) as with good discernment in all that he possesses and does [39].

A primary distinction between kinds of knowledge begins to emerge at this point. These kinds differ in the respect that they are directed to different objects, and it is even implied that the various sorts of knowledge are related to different faculties, since Socrates says that he knows 'with his soul' [40]. There is even a field of action that lies below the level of knowledge : politicians do not act on the strength of what they know but of 'eudoxia', that is to say, of what they think they know. In other words, they are guided by suppositions, and this places them on the same level as soothsayers [41].

Here we see one of the greatest oppositions in Plato's theory of knowledge come to light : the opposition between 'epistêmê' and 'doxa', between knowledge and opinion. The philosopher always speaks denigratingly of 'doxa'. However, between knowledge and opinion there is still an intermediary form, namely the 'right opinion', 'orthê doxa';

both, knowledge and right opinion, can show a man the way to follow [42]. Right opinion is useful and a good guide for acting in the right way [43], but philosophically it is not on the same level with knowledge. For right opinions exhibit the tendency 'to run away from the soul'; they must be properly established by philosophical argument. When this is the case, they turn into knowledge and become durable. "This is why knowledge is more prized than right opinion" [44]. This goes to show that knowledge rests on a much firmer basis than right opinion.

For Plato faith without works is dead. "Every form of wisdom when sundered from justice and the rest of virtue is seen to be plain roguery rather than wisdom" [45]. The good must be the goal of our actions [46]. For happiness is brought about by education and justice [47]. In this group of dialogues the concept 'knowledge' is already assuming a somewhat philosophical shape, as an element in a theory of knowledge. Sometimes something like a Platonic idea suddenly emerges, like 'roundness' for instance [48], although the well-known terms 'eidos' and 'idea' are not used yet. There are a few indications of the later doctrine of Forms : something beautiful (the concretely beautiful) differs from beauty itself ('auto to kalo' = the absolutely beautiful), although everything beautiful has something of (absolute) beauty in it [49].

5. Can excellence be learned?

Man is not good by nature, says Plato [50]. If people are good, then this is because they have learned to be (by 'mathêsis') [51]. Is excellence (virtue, aretê) then a form of knowledge, can it be learned [52]? One must pay attention to the fact that Plato does not speak here of 'excellences', of virtues, in the plural, but of 'excellence' in the singular, referring to a general concept. "However many and virtuous they may be, they all have one common character (here the term used is really 'eidos') whereby they are virtues" [53]. This too is an important step in the direction of the doctrine of the Ideas. Plato, however, asks whether excellence can be learned [54]; after a protracted discussion of the problem he makes Socrates conclude that this is impossible [55].

Because, however, Socrates continues to contend that virtue is knowledge even although we can neither learn it nor possess it by nature, it must obviously come from some other source. Well then, it is imparted to us 'by a divine dispensation without understanding in those who receive it' [56]. Here we see the origin of Plato's 'mysteriosophy', and this immediately has a dualistic character. For, he adds, "he (the man who has received this divine dispensation) may be fairly said to be among the living what Homer says that Tiresias was among the dead : 'he (Tiresias) alone has comprehension; the rest are flitting shades' " [57]. These are already favourite Platonic terms, real understanding, divine dispensation, and in contrast to this, the world of shadows!

6. The doctrine of the soul

From this period onward Plato shows himself influenced by Pythagorean ideas and tenets. In Socrates we do not notice such influences; they are proper to Plato who, during his first voyage to Sicily and Southern Italy, came to know Pythagoreans. In 'Gorgias' he quotes 'a wise man' who presumably is the Pythagorean Philolaus, and then goes on to speak of some Sicilian or Italian Greek who, clearly enough, is also a Pythagorean [58]. A very important element, typical for the Pythagorean movement, is that the soul of man is immortal [59]. This again is a dualistic dogma, for the body does not share in this immortality. Indissolubly connected with this is another dogma of the Pythagoreans, that of rebirth : the soul is reborn into another body, many times even [60]. Plato adopts this theory eagerly, among other things because he can use it as the basis of his theory of knowledge.

In a world other than this and also in this world during our previous lives, our souls have already beheld a great many things. As a consequence of this we know already everything - in principle that is -, not only about excellence but also about much else. It is stored in our memory, and it can be restored to consciousness. For this it is not even necessary that we remember everything at the same time; no, by remembering one thing we are able to discover all the others. This means that we learn by association, or, to use a modern (German) term, 'exemplarisch'. For, says Plato, the whole of reality ('phusis') is mutually related. In fact learning is, therefore, the same as remembering [61]. This is what we call the 'theory of recollection'.

In support of this Socrates calls a slave (who is uneducated by definition) and makes him prove a mathematical problem by means of a game of question and response (what the boy is asked to do in fact is to prove the theorem of Pythagoras [62]). Then the mental process that is being demonstrated is explained : the slave carries these 'opinions' ('doxai'), of which he knew nothing, in himself; it became evident that they were 'right opinions'. They were in him 'as in a dream'; by means of this interplay right opinion developed into exact knowledge ('epistêmê'). This winning back of knowledge is recollection; the process might recover, with equal success, every form of knowledge [63].

From this point of view the body will not seem very important. Death and life exchange places; we believe that we live but actually we are dead. "The body is our tomb", according to Plato in 'Gorgias' [64]. The idea that our body is our tomb - soma-sêma - is presumably Pythagorean, or else it comes from Orphic mysticism. Anyhow, it is undilutedly dualistic. Here, in 'Gorgias', Plato for the first time reveals himself as 'mythopoiês', as a creator of myths, for he makes Socrates relate the myth of body and soul. A myth? "You will regard it as a fable, I fancy, but I as an actual account; for what I am about to tell you I mean to offer as the truth", says Socrates to Callicles [65]. It is the fable that the souls appear naked in the nether world, that is deprived of their bodies, for the judges down there must not be misled by make-believe. The soul is wrapped in the body as in a veil. Death parts body and soul for ever. Now when somebody is dead his soul shows her real nature, all the qualities she has, both innate and acquired, and on the ground of these qualities she will be judged [66].

7. The first blossoming of Plato' great ideas

We may assume that a third group of dialogues was written between the foundation and the Academy (not before 387 B.C.) and Plato's second visit to Sicily (367 B.C.), in the twenty years of his middle life when he was between forty and sixty years old. This group contains Phaedo, Phaedrus, The Banquet, Cratylus and The Republic. The dating of the first book of The Republic and of 'Cratylus' has been disputed, but neither of these books happen to be of great importance to us. Socrates is still speaking but now very evidently as Plato's spokesman. The Republic is undoubtedly Plato's magnum opus in this period, and it is worth pointing out that it is only formally a dialogue. From a point in Book II onwards Socrates' partner in the discussion has hardly anything else to contribute than 'of course, Socrates!' and 'my opinion too'; at the uttermost he is allowed to interject a 'this I don't fully understand'.

8. The doctrine of the soul further developed

The following argument is a direct continuation of section 6. One of the most striking points of the doctrine of body and soul is that they do not really belong together. In order to have an existence on earth a soul does not especially need this particular human body; she may also descend into another human body and even into that of an animal. There is, therefore, an essential distinction between body and soul. To the soul a greater durability is assigned; bodies pass away after having been 'used' once. On account of the recollection theory Plato assumes that souls have a pre-existence [67]. For instance, how do we know that two concrete things are similar to each other? This is only possible because we have an abstract idea of similarity [68]. Since this and other abstract concepts cannot be acquired by means of the senses, we must be in possession of them already before birth [69]. The inescapable conclusion, therefore, is that the soul has a history of pre-existence [70]. The whole dialogue 'Phaedo', the conversation between Socrates and his friends in his cell on the last day of the Master's life, has as its objective to convince the friends that the soul will continue to exist even after the death of the body. Plato's argumentation on this point is irrelevant to us. What he has to say about the soul, however, is highly important for our theme.

Plato states unambiguously that we consist of two separate parts : there is the body, and there is the soul, and they are not identical ('allo ti') [71]. The body directs itself towards the visible order of things, and the soul to things invisible; this is self-evident since the body is visible and the soul invisible [72]. Therefore, their functions are different. But they are different in quality too, as it must be in a dualistic relationship. For the soul is the lord and the body the servant, the one is divine, the other is mortal [73]; the association between them, moreover, has never been voluntary [74]. The soul is related to all that is divine and immortal, to that which is intellectual and uniform, to that which is unchanging and indissoluble; the body is coterminous with the human, the mortal, the multiform, the unintellectual, the dissoluble, and the ever changing [75]. And this poor soul of ours must live in this body that is squarely called a 'misery' ('kakon') [76], caught as she is 'as an oyster in its shell' [77]. The intercourse of the soul with the body is a great hindrance to her for she is forced to pick up her sensations by means of the senses; these, however, draw her downward [78], for they are full of deceit [79].

Only when the soul is left to herself may she come to the pure contemplation of things eternal [80]. Only then, unhampered by the body, is she able to understand the essentials. The body and the senses are no more than impediments [81]; they are utterly incapable of bringing the soul to truth and wisdom [82]. And then Plato bursts forth in a tirade against the body in which nothing good is to be found. It keeps us constantly busy by reason of its need of sustenance, while when diseases come upon it they hinder our pursuit of the truth. The body fills us with passions and desires and fears, and these are the causes of wars and factions. And because of all this we have no leisure for philosophy [83]. The conclusion is now obvious : real wisdom is impossible as long as we draw the body with us [84]. The solution is death, for death separates body and soul radically and for ever [85]. Plato says expressly that in the hereafter no bodies exist : Hades is so great and wise that he refuses to receive people as long as they still have bodies [86].

But what is to be done when we, still remaining in our bodies, nevertheless want to acquire wisdom? Must we commit suicide in order to free ourselves? Far from it! "We men live here in a kind of prison but we must not set ourselves free or run away" [87]. It is remarkable that Plato, when he speaks of the soma-sêma-idea here, speaks of a 'doctrine taught in secret'; evidently he is appealing to esoteric, in particular to Pythagorean and/or Orphic tenets. The beginning of wisdom here is not 'the fear of the Lord' but that we must not be afraid of Death. Death is no evil; it is not something horrible [88]. All those verses that give a sad and unfavourable idea of the nether world must be erased, even if they are to be found in Homer [89]. The opposition between life and death is sharpened and accentuated and then the values are reversed : it is not human life that is desirable but death [90].

Whosoever understands this and lives up to it is a philosopher, for all philosophy is a study of death [91]. Whoever, while still in this life, understands that he should keep body and soul apart is a true philosopher [92]. As far as he is able, he must avoid contact with the body [93]. Isn't this vintage dualism? A man who is not a philosopher, not a lover of wisdom, cannot possibly come into contact with the gods [94]. Philosophy effects liberation by concentration on what is essential [95]. Therefore, a philosopher is an exceptional person, his soul has wings, he is able to ascend to heavenly things. Because he has no great interest in normal human matters people think he is mad. But this is not at all strange. For he is the real lover, and Eros is a form of madness, according to Plato. It is as if the philosopher has been initiated into a mystery cult. Only he who is 'initiated' may go over to the other life; therefore, the philosopher is a 'bakchos', he is the real initiate [96]. In 'The Banquet' Alcibiades calls Socrates 'a philosopher of frenzy and transport ('bakcheia' = the mysteries') [97]. At the same time a form of Gnostic thought is looming up here : the knowledge meant is a very peculiar, very special kind of knowledge; only a few are in possession of it, and most people are debarred from it.

9. The parts of the soul

a. The parable of the two horses

All created things are complex wholes constructed from parts and are destined, in course of time, to fall back again into the parts from which they were constituted. But the soul is of divine origin; she cannot perish [98]. But reading very carefully one sees that Plato qualifies the words 'the soul is entirely indissoluble' ('adialutos'), with the addition : 'or nearly so'. This is his means of escape, not from the supposition that, after all, the soul might prove to be mortal, but from the possibility that the soul might possess some sort of complexity. We must not exclude in advance that Plato's doctrine of the soul contains some basic contradictions. Let us see whether this is true.

In the Republic Plato says that the soul has two parts, a good one and a bad one; the good part must rule the bad one and keep it in check [99]. This bipartition runs parallel to that in Plato's ideal state, where the sensible minority must rule the inferior majority (women, children, slaves and rabble) [100]. This somewhat illogical element in Plato's doctrine of the soul probably stems from the fact that, in dualistic theories, a complete, an absolute separation is nearly unthinkable; in any case, it is impossible in practice. Is it really possible to think of man as of two parts that exist separately from each other, body and soul? Somewhere there must be a connection between them. And if there is a connection, then it must be that one part influences the other. Plato's aversion to the body was so great that we cannot expect that it could be improved under the wholesome influence of the soul. Rather the reverse is the case : the inferior body, with its corruption, penetrates into the soul. On the other hand, it is impossible that the soul, which is so noble and superior and intellectual, should be completely overpowered by the body. Thus one arrives automatically at an intermediate solution : only the nether half of the soul becomes corrupted.

This is made abundantly clear in the parable of the two horses (Plato warns us that it is a 'muthos') [101]. Here - and one has to take due note of this - the soul already consists of three parts : the charioteer (discernment), the good horse (the higher part of the soul), and the bad horse (the lower part of the soul). The good horse is a magnificent animal, with a noble nature, lightly coloured, and with dark eyes; the other is crooked, ugly and disobedient, his colour is dark (pay attention to the sharply whetted oppositions!). When the charioteer beholds the great vision (of the good and beautiful), then it is easy for him to lead the white horse upward, but the dark horse prances and offers resistance with the result that the charioteer must cause him pain by pulling on the bit and the reins, until he finally obeys and follows the other horse.

b. The threepartite soul

Somewhere else Plato speaks more directly of the three parts of the soul, and then it is no longer a parable. Do we really do everything with our whole soul, he asks himself [102]. The answer is negative, since there are three parts in the soul. The first is the rational part by means of which we reason and learn. The second part of the soul is in particular the domain of angry feeling. The third part is more inclusive but one is justified in referring to it as the 'appetitive' division of the soul. It is the domain of desire - desire, for instance, for food, drink, love, money [103]. This partition into three strikes us as rather forced : why should the middle part, 'the Thumos or principle of high spirit, that with which we feel anger', not be identical with the appetitive part (this, indeed occurs to the partner of Socrates) [104]? But here again the matter is settled by the resemblance to the ideal state. Plato's state is based on the situation where everyone has a job of his own and performs this without meddling with the occupation of others. In the soul too 'justice' (that is balance, harmony) can only operate when each of the three parts sticks strictly to its own task [105].

Plato's state has three population groups : the rulers, the guardians, and the citizens; as a consequence of his predilection for the parallelism of micro- and macrocosmos, the soul too has three parts. State and soul are both governed by intellect and defended by courage and 'high spirit'. Of their third part Plato has no high opinion. In the state it is the mass ('hoi polloi' [106]), in the soul it is 'to pleiston' [107] - a word with similar connotations. It is exactly this 'mass' of the soul that forms the link with the body; it is, therefore, also the part that is most easily contaminated by the body. Vigilance should be exercised in order to prevent this lower part from dominating the higher faculties [108].

c. Platonic love

The parable of the two horses is directly linked up with an argument of Plato on Eros which is, as I have already pointed out, a form of 'mania' [109]. This Eros, however, is by no means the Eros that in Athenian society ranked as Eros par excellence, namely pederasty. No, it is the passion of the soul (not that of the body) for the good and beautiful, and the urge to ascend towards them at all costs [110]. It is evident, therefore, - and this fits remarkably well into an esoteric and dualistic ideology - that Plato's judgment on common sexuality is not favourable. In the first of 'The Republic' old Cephalus quotes a word by the likewise aged Sophocles who is glad to have escaped from 'the service of Aphrodite'. He has 'run away from a raging and savage beast of a master'. "When the fierce tensions of the passions and desires relax, then ... we are rid of many and mad masters", says Cephalus, and Socrates (Plato) admires him for it [111]. No pleasure is more mad than the sexual one; one must not allow it to come even near the real love that strives after the beautiful and the just. Real lovers must remain far from the lower forms of love : the relationship between a lover and a beloved must be like that of a father and his son [112]. This is the origin of what came to be called 'Platonic love'.

Plato condemns pederastic love. He blames this Eros on the promptings of the disobedient, black horse - once again forcing his imagery somewhat; the beautiful horse and the charioteer are dead against it, they 'oppose it with modesty and reason' [113]. This attitude is well illustrated in 'The Banquet'. Here Alcibiades relates that Socrates rejected his erotic advances for the very simple reason that he seemed to have no idea what Alcibiades was aiming at [114]. Alcibiades concludes that the night he passed with Socrates did not differ at all from one with his father or his elder brother. One should notice that Plato never speaks of the love between man and woman; his model of Eros is exclusively that of male homosexuality.

10. The rebirth of the soul

In the dialogues of this group too Plato confirms his belief in the return of souls. In principle it would be possible for every soul to return to 'the place from where she came' (the divine realm of the Ideas) but this can only happen after ten thousand years. This period will only be shortened for the real philosopher and for him who has loved in a philosophical (= Platonic) manner; these souls get their wings back already after three periods of a thousand years each. All others are judged after their life on earth; some will have to do penance in Tartarus, a place of chastisement under the earth. A passage in 'Phaedrus' makes it clear that hardened criminals who end up in Tartarus will never leave this sombre region again; they will not be reborn [115].

Others go to some place or other in afterlife; there they lead a life that resembles that which they had when they still wore a human shape. In an intriguing passage in the myth of Er, Plato asserts that souls will only come to heaven after they have expiated their iniquities during a stay under the earth; this period of expiation will last a thousand years (ten times the maximum of human life). When, after these thousand years, the soul comes to heaven, she must choose a new existence on earth. When she makes the wrong choice, she herself is to blame, for 'the godhead is blameless' [116]. Any kind of shape may be chosen, even an animal one; "a soul which was once human may pass into the life of a beast ... For the soul which has never seen the truth can never pass into human form". But if one were to ask Plato how such a soul could ever free itself from an animal shape - for how can an animal see the truth? - , he would answer that it is not the animal shape that sees the truth but the soul inside this shape [117].

However, says Plato, it is ordained that the soul never begins her first existence on earth in an animal but always in a human shape. The kind of man she becomes depends on what the soul saw in heaven. There are nine ranks. Who has seen most of the divine mysteries becomes the soul of a philosopher, a lover of beauty, or somebody who has a loving or a musical disposition. The second rank is that of the rulers, the princes and the warlords; the third that of the politicians, the businessmen and the bankers; the fourth that of the gymnasts and of those who are charged with the cure of the body; the fifth that of the prophets and of those who are initiated into the mystery cults; the sixth that of the poets and of the plastic artists; the seventh that of the artisans and peasants; the eight that of the Sophists and the demagogues; the ninth that of the tyrants [118].

It will be clear that this list contains a number of unambiguous value judgments. Here again the highest rank is that of the philosopher, for "a man who employs such memories (e.g. of the divine mysteries) rightly is always initiated into the perfect mysteries and he alone always becomes perfect" [119]. These words demonstrate that, inside this order, yet another order exists, caused by the radical separation of the philosophers from all others. Here too Plato employs the language of the mystery cults to indicate the significance of philosophy. Since philosophy is so evidently of a higher order than every other occupation, it is clear that we are very near to a dualistic distinction.

11. The doctrine of Forms

a. The essence of things

Is man the measure of all things? Or does there exist for each individual a separate, a personal reality, so that things are as they appear to me and for another as they appear to him? Or have things a reality of their own, apart, that is, from the person who observes them? With these questions that are put into the mouth of Socrates, Plato opens his great attack on the relativism of Protagoras and the other Sophists [120]. One extreme gives rise to another : as Protagoras showed a tendency to dissolve reality into the observer, so Plato leans towards a drastic separation of observer and reality, a first glimpse of a dualistic theory of knowledge.

The first response goes as follows : yes, indeed, there exists for every object a name that belongs to it in an essential way, and what this means is that all things have their own being [121]. Such names belong to things 'by nature'; the 'giving of names' is no trifling matter, they are not given capriciously by men [122]. Or to put it in other terms : it is not men who determine the essence of things. It is not so much the names of persons that must interest us, for these are often deceptive. No, instead of speculating on these we must try 'to find the correct names in the nature of the eternal and the absolute'. Such names have been given most carefully, some of them even 'by a power more divine than that of men' [123]. "For clearly the gods call things by the names that are naturally right" [124]. In this way, however, the essence of (the most essential) things is brought beyond the reach of men.

Plato mocks those philosophers according to whom everything is in a constant flux [125]. If all things are changing, than they cannot be known, then there is no knowledge [126]. It is extremely important to note that, for 'knowledge', Plato employs the word 'gnosis' in this text. This is the spearhead of Plato's attack on the doctrine of Heraclitus ('panta rhei' = everything is streaming, e.g. everything is constantly changing) that is mentioned expressly here [127]. No, everything has an 'ousia' that is not subject to change [128]. "Shall we assert that there is any absolute beauty, or good, or any absolute existence?", Socrates asks in the name of Plato [129]. Plato, therefore, posits general principles, concepts, that, in his usage, bear the name of 'ideas' (or 'forms') and which have an ontological status. We call something beautiful, because, in some way or other ("call it what you may please", says Plato [130]), it partakes of absolute beauty, of the essence of what is beautiful, or the 'idea' of beauty [131]. The ideas, therefore, cannot conflict with one another [132]. According to Plato, they form a harmonious whole.

The Platonic doctrine of the Forms is a highly important stage in the ancient philosophical controversy of the One and the Many. Parmenides emphasizes the One - with him this is Being - in such a manner that the Many becomes almost non-existent; in any case it is no object of philosophy. Heraclitus, on the other hand, is the great protagonist of permanent change. In Volume I, I characterized both points of view as dualistic. Plato follows neither Parmenides nor Heraclitus completely. For him the Forms are principles of unity under which the numerous concrete manifestations of things are subsumed. How can we know that something is beautiful, if we have no 'idea' of beauty?

But we may go still further. We would not know either what tables and chairs and all other concrete and material things are, we would not be able to call a piece of furniture a 'table' or a 'chair', if we did not possess the 'idea' of a table, of a chair, or of whatever else [133]. But men are not the creators of these ideas, since, as we have already seen, they are not capable of giving names to the being of things; in no way can they control what is essential in things. The 'Forms', therefore, are no concepts or models postulated by the human mind; they are not developed for every occasion anew; nor, indeed, are they innate. However, our capacity to know the ideas is inborn, for "there is in every soul an organ or instrument of knowledge ..., a faculty whose preservation outweighs ten thousand eyes, for by it only reality is beheld" [134].

Plato's conclusion is now obvious : the Forms have a distinct existence of their own [135], or, to use the terminology of a much later date, they have an ontological status of their own. This means that their existence is not dependent on human thought. Every Form stands on itself and is one [136]. However, one migt make the objection - Plato himself also saw the problem - that the Forms taken together are still a multiplicity rather than a unity. Hence he perceives some sort of hierarchy in the world of Forms. To begin with, he is not especially interested in the Forms of material objects. Of these he speaks rarely; his favourite theme is always the good, the beautiful, the just, and other lofty entities - the usual abstractions the Greeks loved so much.

b. The Good and the godhead

Among the Forms there is one that rises above all others, takes the lead, and thus becomes a general principle of unity; this is the Idea of the good. "The greatest thing to learn is the Idea of the good by reference to which just things and all the rest become useful and beneficial" [137]. "This reality that gives their truth to the objects of knowledge, and the power of knowing to the knower, you must say is the Idea of the good, and you must conceive it as being the cause of knowledge" [138]. It is even the case that what is knowable (e.g. the Forms) derives its recognizability from the good; it exists because of the good [139]. The good, therefore, supersedes all other Forms, but - and this is a typically Platonic turn of thought - Plato states expressly that the good in itself is no essence ('ousia'); it is, therefore, something different from the Forms [140].

But what is 'the good'? Is it God? It is clear that we are stepping across the frontiers of philosophy now; but it is not so much theology as contemplation we need for further exploration. Plato is not particularly interested in the Olympian gods; he is indignant about the way they are spoken of in literature but he himself hardly ever mentions them. It appears that his belief in them was never very strong. But this does not make him an atheist. On the contrary. Again and again he speaks of 'the god, the divine' and even of 'god' (without an article); these words are used here not as specific but as generic and abstract terms. The philosopher pleads for a purified concept of god that has to be much more metaphysical than the current Greek notions (this, however, does not mean that Plato's concept was monotheistic). Of this metaphysical concept of god, the good is a principal manifestation.

c. Between being and non-being

"We dwell in a hollow of the earth and we think we dwell on its upper surface ... By reason of feebleness and sluggishness we are unable to attain to the upper surface of the air. For if anyone should come to the top of the air or should get wings and fly up, he could lift his head above it ... and would see things in that upper world. And, if his nature were strong enough to bear the sight, he would recognize that that is the real heaven and the real earth" [141]. This forerunner of the famous myth of the cave shows that Plato had no high opinion of our commonplace way of knowing; according to him, it is obviously not given to everybody to come to know the higher things. Hence he develops a particular theory of knowledge the goal of which is to learn to contemplate the Forms, especially that of the good.

But even the most solid training in ways of thinking will not be sufficient to attain to the higher things; Plato's theory is by no means built on an intellectual basis. It is for this reason that the wise woman Diotima says to Socrates that he is 'initiated' - into the mysteries of Eros, that is; he will come to learn their 'rites and revelations' [142], terms which Plato borrows from the mystery cults. For it is Eros that makes us ascend from the concrete things to the Forms. When somebody loves a beautiful boy, it will strike him that there are other beautiful boys; thus he will arrive at a general concept 'beauty'. The next stage will be that he values beautiful souls more than beautiful bodies; in this way he will mount upwards to ever higher forms of beauty, till suddenly a wondrous vision is shown to him - 'the final object of all those previous toils' -, the essence of the beautiful, 'divine beauty itself, in its unique form' [143].

It should be now almost self-evident that, in Plato's vision, those who are able to contemplate real beauty, the essence of beauty, will be few in number. A man who is capable of such contemplation is awake, while the others live as though in a dream. The awakened man has knowledge, the others only have an opinion ('doxa') and are mentally, therefore, not really sane [144]. This means that Plato is making an extremely sharp, even dualistic, distinction between two kinds of knowledge ('knowing' and 'fancying') as well as between two sorts of people ('guardians' and 'dreamers', those who are sent from above, and those who are not). What wholly exists is at the same time entirely knowable; what does not exist, the non-existent, obviously cannot be known - our relation to it is one of total ignorance ('agnoia').

Yet between these two terms - valid knowledge ('epistêmê', the sole knowledge worthy of that name) and 'agnoia' (that actually does not exist since it refers to something that does not exist) - there is a middle term, 'doxa' = opinion [145]. Because it is clearly impossible to have an opinion about something that does not exist, 'doxa' must have an object that lies between being and non-being, something that partakes of both. This object is the fallible, the world of concrete but changeable things about which we may easily err. True knowledge refers to the infallible, to the eternal and unchangeable substances. This is what the philosophers are destined to contemplate; the others are rather 'philodoxai', unable to see the beautiful and other Forms, and never arising above the concrete things [146].

One might call this a relative dualism. The really absolute distinction is between being and non-being, à la Parmenides, but in Plato it is impossible to climb up from concrete things to the contemplation of the Forms. On the other hand, not many do this. They roam aimlessly around in their lives, they never arise above everyday existence or open their eyes to the things above; they will never ascend to the contemplation of the Forms and they are saturated in an inessential way with inessential things. In vain they try to nourish that part of themselves that really exists with unreal things [147]. Our term 'relative dualism' should not, therefore, lead us to infer that Plato took a hopeful view of the possibilities of the 'Erziehung des Menschengeschlechts'; the organization of his ideal state, indeed, has as one of its aims to keep the ignorant mass in check.

12. Plato's terms for knowledge

It may be useful now to examine some of the specific words Plato used for 'knowledge'. Of course, I am not in the position to start a semantic inquiry but even a perfunctory inspection of the terminology, with the help of the Plato lexica, yields interesting results. Plato's usage is very varied : 'mathêsis, mathêma, epistêmê, gnomê, phronêsis', these and still more are his words for knowledge. But also, and this is what interests me most, 'gnosis'. 'Gnosis' is a normal Greek substantive, originally without ideological connotations. It signifies 'inquiry' (also in a juridical sense), then the result of this inquiry, 'knowing', 'knowledge', that is, and because of this also 'decision' and 'explanation'. It may further signify 'means of knowledge' or 'acquaintance with'. From these meanings the term starts to move towards the specific meaning it acquired in the history of religion : acquaintance with higher things, a particular esoteric knowledge. This finally has led to modern terms like 'Gnostic' and 'Gnosticism'.

I have not discovered a special monograph on Plato's terms for 'knowledge'; however, this does not mean that it may not exist somewhere in the immense literature on Plato or that there are no relevant passages in one or other of the more general works [148]. The general opinion (doxa!) is expressed by White when he says that Plato scarcely, if ever, draws careful distinctions between these various terms for 'knowledge' [149]. Hence Perls found it unnecessary to enter the word 'knowledge' in his lexicon of Platonic concepts [150].

In contrast to those who think that Plato used his terms 'knowing' and 'knowledge' in an undifferentiated way, we find scholars who believe that he makes some distinctions. Neither they nor I would wish to assert Plato used the word 'gnosis' as the 'terminus technicus' it was to become some centuries later. There is no more than a first step in that direction. If this is correct, then 'epistêmê' would mean 'knowledge' and 'gnosis' 'comprehension'. Even the sceptical White is ready to admit that much; in doing this he takes a step in the direction I have indicated [151]. The English linguist John Lyons devoted a careful semantic study to Plato's usage; in this the words for knowing play the main role. He too concludes that Plato uses the verbs for 'knowing' in a somewhat unspecified manner; nevertheless, he believes that the verbs 'gignooskein' and 'epistathai' are not in all cases interchangeable. He even quotes one passage in which they evidently are opposites : there 'gignooskein' means 'knowing' ('connaître') and 'epistathai' 'to be able to' or 'to learn' ('apprendre') [152]. According to him 'epistêmê' is a general word for 'knowledge' that covers two fields : 'technê' = ability, and 'gnosis' = insight [153].

Checking some passages in which the word 'gnosis' occurs we meet with the following curious distinctions : "If a man has a science ('epistêmê') that knows ('gignooskei') itself, he will be similar to that which he has. For instance, he who has swiftness will be swift, he who has beauty will be beautiful, and he who has knowledge ('gnosis') will know ('gignooskei'). And when he has knowledge ('gnosis') that is of itself, he will then, surely, be in the position of knowing ('gignooskoon') himself" [154]. What this proves anyhow is that 'gnosis' is a special case of 'epistêmê', a very conscious way of knowing, of knowing what knowledge really is; such knowledge brings one who knows onto a higher plane.

Once again I will refer to the passage from 'Cratylus' [155] in which Plato is polemizing against Heraclitus : no knowledge would be possible if things are constantly changing. In that case knowledge would change, but knowledge that changes would be no knowledge. The result would be that nobody would know anything at all, for the very reason that there would be nothing to know. In this text Plato uses the term 'knowledge' nine times, and every time it is 'gnosis'. Since Plato does not believe that unchangeable things are unknowable but, rather, that we may acquire some knowledge of them, 'gnosis' means here that special kind of knowledge that enables us to rise above the changeable world. And indeed, he states straightforwardly : "Being is known by 'gnosis' " [156]. Those who do not possess this gnosis are blind souls; they are unable to open their eyes towards the absolutely true [157].

This is an opinion that would do honour to a Gnostic. Two other times he repeats that gnosis is knowledge of that which is [158]. To this he adds that our knowledge (doxa) of sublunar things is no gnosis [159]. To conclude, a careful inquiry into Plato's words for 'knowledge', in particular his employment of 'gnosis', would be thoroughly justified.

13. Plato's dualistic scheme of knowledge

It is impossible to acquire the necessary knowledge by studying assiduously; its source cannot be reached during our life. But when once the soul is freed from the body, she rises upwards as a winged horse, into the highest heaven; while she follows there the revolutions of the cosmos, she 'beholds the things outside of the heaven' [160]. What the soul contemplates there are the Forms, justice, temperance, and knowledge of absolute being [161]. Many, however, are unable to climb so high; their wings are clipped, and they fall back to earth [162] without carrying with them knowledge of the Forms.

Again and again Plato emphasizes this dualistic bipartition of mankind into those who have seen and know and those who have seen nothing and remain blind. At the same time, this rests on a dualistic bipartition between the intelligible world, the realm of the Forms, that, to Plato, is reality proper, and the world of the changing phenomena that we erroneously equate with reality although in fact it consists only of shadows. This appears extremely clearly in the renowned myth of the cave [163].

In this parable men are dwelling in a subterranean cave, with legs and neck fettered so that they can only look forward. In front of them is a wall, and along this wall, as in a kind of wajang-presentation, images of men and implements are carried. What the prisoners see is nothing but shadows but they believe that they see real things; they don't know any better. Now, if somebody would succeed in escaping from his fetters and from this cave, it would be very difficult for him to become accustomed to the light. First he would prefer to look at the shadows and then at the reflections of men and things, and only later at the things themselves; then he would find courage to raise his eyes to the stars and the moon at night, and, after this, he would feel confident enough to contemplate the sun in the full blaze of the day. Yet if he should go back into that cave and tell the fettered prisoners what he has seen, they would not believe him, and still less they would follow him. This world-famed parable presents to us, on the one hand, a blind humanity that is content to take appearances for being itself, and, on the other, the lonely philosopher who has viewed the Good but finds no hearers. The cave - our own world - is painted in sombre colours; the real world is to be found outside and above it, the world of the Forms. There is not much of a connection between these two worlds.

Plato presented his dualistic theory of knowledge in yet another way. In 'The Republic' he gives us a hierarchy of knowable objects. The lowest class is that of the 'images' or 'shadows', things of which we have only a very vague notion or that exist only in our imagination; an unjust sentence, for instance, is but a 'shadow' of justice. Next comes knowledge of real things, of living beings and the like; this kind of knowledge is called by Plato 'pistis', that is something like 'reasonable conviction'. Our shadowy images are, of course, in no way what Plato would call 'knowledge' but 'pistis' does not deserve this ascription either; it is still 'doxa' = opinion, and it does not really matter whether or not this opinion is correct.

Most people leave it at this, since in order to advance further one has to break through a very strong palisade. Who succeeds in crossing it leaves the visible world behind him and arrives in the region of the really knowable things, the 'noêta'; they are knowable only with the mind. The first class of these includes the objects of mathematics. This science still has some connection with the visible world because it uses concrete forms like triangles. However, the concreteness of these forms is hardly of importance since the mathematician employs them in order to draw abstract inferences. Mathematics is, therefore, an indispensable exercise for learning to contemplate the objects of thought. This is rightly called 'knowledge'.

But Plato in no way imagines that every mathematician, by practising his science, automatically ascends to still higher levels. For he who wants to go on finds himself confronted with yet another obstacle; when he succeeds in breaking through this he may call himself a philosopher. Beyond this palisade lies the essential and highest field of knowledge, the abstract and absolute world of the Forms [164]. No matter how Plato explains his theory, it invariably becomes a dualistic scheme.

14. Plato's threedimensional state

Plato's description of his ideal state in 'The Republic' contains some elements that are important for our theme. For Plato this state is the best possible one, because it is ruled by justice [165], and the concept of justice is synonymous with the fact that everybody in the Republic limits himself strictly to his own task [166]. Quite another question is, of course, whether Plato thought such a state possible [167]; his answer is that he does not intend to show that his ideals might become reality [168]. "Don't insist that I must exhibit as realized in action precisely what we expounded in words. But if we discover how a state might be constituted most nearly answering to our description, you must say that we have discovered that possibility of realization which you demanded" [169]. The model of Plato's state, as he says himself, is to be found in heaven but not on earth [170]. It is good to keep this constantly in mind.

Another point should be made. In our own time Plato's ideal state inspires many people in the western, democratic world with deep aversion, it even terrifies them. We have been through so much ourselves; we have seen the appalling results when certain aspects of Plato's ideal are carried into practice by men who have probably never read The Republic, that we cannot avoid a certain repugnance to his idealized state. It is not a blueprint that appeals to us. Indeed, it is frequently stated - and rightly so - that Plato outlined his Republic out of aversion to Athenian democracy. However, we must not lose sight of the fact that, basically, this democracy contained the elements that Plato carried through to their extreme consequences. With regard to the fact that for the higher classes of his society, the rulers and the guardians, he abolishes family life and advocates community of women and children, Hans Bogner maintains that the philosopher "draws inferences from what the innovations of Clisthenes already contained as possibilities - and he did this consequently, radically and without paying attention to human nature; if the Greek polis was such a firm political unity, why did it need also the natural family?" [171]. In Volume II I tried to show that the idealized and all-embracing polis functioned at the expense of the individual and his family [172].

a. Plato's threepartite society

The first important point is the partition into three of Platonic society. Especially in Volume I and here and there in Volume II I have indicated that this notion of 'partition into three' is, so to speak, a divining-rod that may help us to detect esoteric tendencies. For three is the pre-eminently mystical number. The usual pattern of a social partition of human society into three is that in which two priviliged classes, the 'initiated', stand over against the 'massa damnata' of the unknowing; so it was, for instance, in the Pythagorean movement [173].

Plato begins his description with the middle group of the 'guardians', the 'phulakes'. They form the professional army of the state, an army that does not consist of mercenaries but of citizens. They have to be professionals because of the principle 'one man one job' : just as a shoemaker cannot simultaneously be a good farmer, he cannot be made into a decent soldier [174]. They form a priviliged class that for food and maintenance is totally dependent on the citizens. Every child that is to become a guardian is educated very carefully. Plato has not the slightest need of a troop of raw fire-eaters; on the contrary, his guardians have to be cultivated people. They receive a thorough physical training. But Plato would not be Plato if the real aim of this training were not so much the body but rather the unimpeded functioning of the mind. Physical imperfection was not allowed to obstruct it. To poetry a great educational role is assigned. However, the great Greek poets will be presented only in expurgated editions since they write so many things that are not wholesome for the souls of the little ones. Musical schooling is necessary too, for music is supposed to be benificial for mental harmony. A selected group of the guardians receives a prolonged training comprising study of mathematics. From this limited number finally a select company is chosen from those between thirty and thirty-five years old, who are to study philosophy. From this very restricted body the rulers are selected.

The guardians live separately from the other citizens in a fortified camp; there they live an extremely sober life and have their meals in common. Of course the reader will be strongly reminded of the Spartiate barracks - and rightly so - but there is one important difference. The guardians are not permitted to have private possessions. They do not even receive pay, for the state provides for all their needs.

b. Women in Platonic society

Plato does not often mention women. But in his earlier dialogues we find a number of 'obiter dicta' with the same denigrating judgments on them that were typical of the Greeks. As a group - although he is perfectly ready to admit exceptions - he finds men more sensible than women [175]; women are more inclined to emotional outbursts [176]. In fact, it is difficult to think of any area in which men do not excel women, unless in the arts of cooking and weaving [177]. The consequence of this is that women must stay at home, manage their households and obey their husbands. They are not really equal to appearing in public and taking the floor; they hang back from this with all their might [178]. These are the usual arguments but in his personal quiver Plato has still some extra-sharp arrows. With respect to 'aretê', to excellence, women are positively inferior to men; they "would not so much as listen to the mention of the right rule without shrieks of indignation" [179].

However, the position of women in Plato's republic differs from the sketch he gave in earlier works. The differences between the sexes that Plato used to stress so much are reduced here to the fact that the man begets the children and the woman bears them. Nevertheless, we must not lose from sight that he only speaks of the wives of the guardians; there is no mention at all here of the other female citizens. The female guardians receive the same training and education and perform the same functions as the male, 'save in so far as the one is weaker, the other stronger' [180]. In Plato's state the guardians are not married and have no families. They only consort to beget progeny; the children are a common possession, the parents are not permitted to know who their offspring are nor may these know who their parents are [181]. The education of the children is taken care of by state employees. One will recognize here the ideas of Aristophanes' 'Lysistrata'. However, Plato is not saying here that men and women have equal rights but that women are the common possession of all the men [182]. He has no intention of effecting the complete equalization of men and women but he wants to make an end of the dualistic situation that prevailed in his Athens. It is a remarkable thing that no Greek of this period has ever found a harmonious mean between the historic situation and promiscuity without marriage.

Plato, for that matter, has some propositions to make that are not to be found in 'Lysistrata'. In 'The Republic' he is pleading for eugenesis since the best men must sleep as often as possible with the best women; the weakest must remain apart as much as is feasible [183]. The ages for procreation are officially limited; for women those between twenty and forty years, for men between thirty and fifty-five. After this everyone may have intercourse with whom he or she likes so long as there are no children; offspring born in these later periods of life will be killed [184]. Personal feelings and relationships too are undesirable; they only serve to corrode the unity of the state. Mothers in particular are not allowed to entertain private contacts with their children [185]. This is all for the best, since offspring who are unfit will not be raised : "that is the condition of preserving the purity of the guardians' breed", these are Plato's own words [186]. The guardians must call as many things as possible 'mine' [187], which means that there is collective ownership of everything. The only private possession they have is their body. Everything else they have in common for they must share one conviction and one aim [188].

It will be evident that the idea of the closed society has been brought to perfection here. All the criteria which Popper enumerated may be applied to the guardians : the coercive demands of a common life, no private roles for individuals, the domination of collectivistic notions, a strictly determined status for everybody, and a course of life that is fixed by the authorities. With this description Plato distances himself as far as possible from all forms of open societies; the opposition is fiercely dualistic, and that is precisely what he intends.

c. The rulers

The rulers of the state are chosen from the best-tried and best-educated guardians [189]. The office of ruler is by no means heriditary within the guardian class; it is perfectly conceivable that a guardian's son who lacks the qualities of an administrator becomes an artisan or a peasant [190]. The reverse is also possible; a promising child of the labouring classes might be elevated to the guardians and might eventually be raised to a ruler [191]. Of the three groups in this society the rulers are the smallest, which is understandable enough since the ruler must be at least fifty years of age [192]. Plato does not even exclude the possibility that only one person may be found capable of governing the state, but, he says, one is enough, 'if he has a state that obeys him' [193]. Only the rulers possess that special form of knowledge that may be called wisdom [194].

d. The great mass of the people

What remains now is a nondescript medley of people, the great mass of artisans and peasants, of shopkeepers, businessmen and bankers, and of housewives (it calls for special attention that in Plato's state slavery has not been abolished). The philosopher does not estimate these people highly, they are not initiated, they are no lovers of wisdom, and they are by definition incapable of contemplating the One or the Forms [195]. He admits that they may be converted and brought to better insights [196]. Eminent children of this group can be, as we have seen, promoted to the guardians. Nevertheless, Plato is not particularly optimistic about the members of this lowest group of the citizens. This is proved by the fact that they have to restrict themselves to only one occupation; the shoemaker makes shoes, the peasant tills the land, and that is all there is to it. Plato has, of course, no problem with the cobbler who has a kitchen-garden of his own; what he means is that cobbler and pesant must stay out of politics completely.

This principle of 'one man one job' conflicts with the principle proclaimed by Pericles that even the shoemaker is capable of passing judgments on the affairs of the state. It seems to me that every time that Plato arrives at a somewhat more favourable idea of the mass of the people, the image of the Athenian dêmos rises up before his eyes; then he immediately becomes filled with disgust. Did he not compare the enfranchised citizens of Athens to a great wild beast [197]? Did he not speak of the madness of the populace [198]? Actual politics are good for nothing, not only in Athens, no, everywhere! Not one existing state is ripe for 'philosophy' [199].

How can this situation (as it actually exists) be improved? We are now confronted with some unpalatable facts. It is, for instance, ominous enough that the new state can only be established by the purification of the old [200]. One is reminded unavoidably, and very probably justly, of the drastic purges that are a feature of totalitarian ideologies. Plato tells us that the new state must begin with a 'clean slate' [201]. Now why does he say this? The most merciful explanation is that, since nothing can be done with the adults, a start must be made with the youngsters. This is supported by another passage where we are told that all children below the age of ten are to be placed under the guardianship of state in order to unlearn the 'bad' habits and customs of their parents. All the rest of the population, that is everyone above the age of ten, is to be sent to the country [202]. Those who are ailing or invalids may die in peace; those who have an incurably bad nature will be executed; that is what is best for them and the state [203]. The new state does not shrink back from the use of force [204].

In this description of the condition and the fate of the masses two points strike us forcefully : 1 the radical puritanism that is proper to all dualistic esoteric movements - what is not sound must be done away with : "Let us tear out these weeds!" [205]; 2 the separation and opposition between the mass of the population, and the guardians + the rulers. While this is not perhaps a watertight demarcation, since children of the working class may become guardians, it is beyond any doubt a case of relative dualism.

e. Philosophers and non-philosophers

The distinction between philosophers and non-philosophers grows out of the partition into three and is also dualistic. It was Plato's ideal that his new state would be ruled by the 'philosopher-king' till his painful experiences with the tyrants of Syracuse brought him to the insight that the actual 'kings' - the then ruling potentates - showed very little affinity with 'philosophy'. Plato had a very lofty, not to say an exalted idea of philosophers. His philosopher is an artist who works after 'the heavenly model' [206]. He (the philosopher) identifies with the divine order of the world and in that way becomes divine and 'cosmic' himself, in so far as this is possible for mortals [207]. Plato never tires of summing up the excellent qualities of the philosophers : they have a good memory, they are quick-witted, generous, kindly disposed and friendly; they are 'akin to truth, justice, bravery and sobriety' [208].

Of course there are only very few people of this kind for most human beings are bad - this is what Plato says literally : 'hoi polloi kakoi' [209]. There is not the slightest prospect of improvement; the only remedy is that somebody who 'bears the stigma of uselessness' - a philosopher that is - takes the helm of the state [210]. In the background we find always that thoroughly corrupted 'massa damnata' [211]. The (true) philosopher "stands aside in winter under the shelter of a wall in a storm and blast of dust and sleet and sees the others full of lawlessness, content if in any way he may keep himself free from iniquity and unholy deeds throughout his life" [212]. Was the Academy Plato's 'wall'?

15. Plato's later works

In the last period of his life Plato wrote another eight works, Parmenides, Theaetetus, The Sophist, Politicus, Philebus, Laws, Timaeus, and Critias. The last three are works of his old age. Evidently his energy remained undiminished. 'Critias' was left unfinished but 'Laws' is an enormous work, much more voluminous than 'The Republic'. They are rather different in character from the earlier works, in particular because Socrates, as the main party to the discussion, had to concede a lot of ground. The last dialogue in which Socrates leads the discussion, the 'Philebus', lacks the vivacity of the earlier ones. In 'The Sophist' and in the 'Politicus' Socrates' role as interrogator is taken over by the (Eleatic) 'stranger'; in the 'Timaeus' and the 'Critias' the persons who gave their names to the dialogues are the spokesmen; in 'Laws' Socrates does not even appear (these three works are dialogues only in a formal sense). What is important is that Plato, in this last phase of his life, looks back on his earlier work, in the 'Parmenides' on his metaphysics, and in 'Laws' on his ideal state.

16. Criticism of the doctrine of the Forms

In form the 'Parmenides' may be thought of as a kind of 'novel', written in indirect speech. The spokesman of the dialogue is a certain Cephalus, a citizen of Clazomenae. The rather complicated background is as follows. This Cephalus had been given an account of a conversation between the still very young Socrates and the venerable philosopher Parmenides by Plato's half-brother Antiphon. This conversation was also attended by Zeno. It was a second hand report since Antiphon had not been present himself, but had learned it from a friend of Zeno [213]. Thus Cephalus is giving us a third hand report.

This meeting between Socrates and Parmenides is supposed to have taken place about 450 B.C. but whether it is authentically historical is an open question - a question that, however, is not important for us. Much more interesting is that the roles are reversed here : it is not Socrates who drives his partner up the wall with his acute and ironical questions; no, 'Socrates' is thoroughly put through his catechism by Parmenides. It is a 'Socrates' who has not yet really found himself. "You are still young, Socrates", says Parmenides, "and philosophy has not yet taken hold upon you, as I think it will later" [214].

Parmenides appears to doubt the doctrine of the Forms. He asks whether there exists a distinction between the abstract ideas and the concrete things which partake of them [215]. This is an arrow aimed at the heart of the doctrine of Forms, and Socrates retorts hastily "yes, I do think so". In order to emphasize this distinction between Forms and objects, Parmenides uses twice the word 'choris' that signifies 'apart, separated, totally different'; in doing this he points to a possible dualism of Forms and things. Then Parmenides rips open an old sore : are there Forms of such matters as hair, mud and dirt? O no, not at all, says the shocked Socrates, that would be absurd! Though, he adds hesitantingly, if I am consequent, I must admit the possibility of such Forms, I am much troubled about it [216]. For why should there be an Idea of the beautiful and not of hair?

Parmenides now raises the question of 'partaking'. Socrates may say that concrete things and concepts 'partake' of their Form but how must this be imagined? If many things partake of the same Form - for instance, that many people are beautiful by their participation in the Form 'beauty' -, then this Form is divided. Thus it is not possible for it is one. And if it entirely enters into one given thing, then there remains nothing for other objects. "By Zeus!", says the dumbfounded Socrates, "I think this is a very hard question to determine" [217]. This point is of the highest importance for our theme too. For, by Zeus! if Plato does not succeed in finding a solution, the dualism between the metaphysical Forms and the concrete things will be complete. Socrates makes a guess : "The most likely view is that these Ideas exist in nature as patterns (or models, 'paradigmata'), and the other things resemble them and are imitations of them" [218]. Does Socrates realize that he lowers the status of the Forms by a few steps? Is he aware of the fact that they are no longer metaphysical if they are part of nature?

But Parmenides assembles still heavier guns in position. It forms a very great difficulty that the Ideas should stand wholly on themselves. He even uses the word 'aporia' here, a problem with no way out [219]. The Forms are absolute, so he continues, they exist totally outside us, they have their relations with one another and not with concrete things. "These concrete things, which have the same name with the Ideas, are likewise only relative to themselves, not to the Ideas, and belong to themselves, not to the like-named Ideas" [220]. Parmenides could not state more clearly that to him Plato's doctrine of the Forms is dualistic. Or must we rather say that Plato himself tells us here that his cherished doctrine is dualistic? Moreover, continues Parmenides, absolute ideas require absolute knowledge, and such a knowledge we do not possess; this means that the Ideas are unknowable [221].

A normal person, says Parmenides, would of course infer that the Forms do not exist. Only somebody of exceptional talents is able to comprehend that everything has its own nature and its own being; it is really a marvellous person who can explain this to others. Socrates is clearly relieved - "what you say is very much to my mind" -, for he sees Plato's philosopher looming up, Plato himself indeed, the marvellous person who is able to explain everything [222]. Now Parmenides makes a big concession : if the Forms do not exist, no philosophy would be possible [223]. Plato recognizes implicitly that not all problems with regard to the doctrine of Forms have been solved; however, this doctrine remains the foundation of his philosophy. He is not able to do without this doctrine since it contains the solution to the age-old problem of the One and the Many.

17. The One and the Many

a. Can the Many exist without the One?

The second part of this dialogue is about the problem of the One and the Many. Parmenides is leading the discussion, and he presses the still inexperienced Socrates as hard as the latter was later to do with his own partners. The starting-point of the old philosopher is that one should carefully explore the consequences that would ensue if the Many exists. The consequences he means are the relations of the Many to itself. What Parmenides means are probably the following questions. Is the Many a disorderly mass of unconnected things? Or is there coherence in it? If there is coherence in it, of what kind is it? Is there also a relation to the One? What are the relations of the One to itself and to the Many? This means, if there is a relation of the One to the Many, does that imply that the Many is subsumed under the One, and in what way? If the Many did not exist, what would happen then to the Many, in relation to itself and to the One 224).

What this means is as follows. Suppose somebody asserted that the One does not exist, what would then be the consequences for the Many? Can the Many (that is the world of concrete things) exist without the One? Is this conceivable? But suppose now, in contrast, that one were to place the highest priority on the One, without paying much attention to the Many. While one might not deny the existence of the Many, one would not consider it an object of philosophy. This is, by the way, Parmenides' own philosophical position. We must not forget, however, that it is not the historical Parmenides who is speaking here but Plato. Now if we give this high priority to the One, what would be the consequences for the Many? Can the One exist, is the One conceivable without the Many? In other words, is a dualism of the One and the Many possible?

With regard to the answers Parmenides begins by excusing himself on account of his old age [225], although he starts to argue in the most perfect dialectical manner, so much so that he sometimes seems to have been apprenticed to the Sophists. His disquisition is long, exacting and tiring. He is all the time aiming at two conclusions :
1 If the One exists (is) - that is to say, if it is exclusive, and the Many, therefore, does not exist -, then the One is everything (all that exists is lost in the One). At the same time the One is nothing with regard to itself and to all other things [226]. This does not mean that the One, in that case, is identical to 'nothing', but then no meaningful pronouncements about the One, its qualities and its relationships

to the Many, are possible.

2 If the One does not exist (is not), then it is impossible to ascertain of other things (the Many) either whether they are one or manifold or whatever qualities the Many may have [227]. Without assuming the existence of the One it is impossible to pronounce valid philosophical judgments on the Many. What this implies is that Plato considers the philosophical positions both of Parmenides and Heraclitus as untenable. In the very last words of the dialogue Parmenides and Socrates agree in this final conclusion : "If the One is not, nothing is" [228]. The existence of the One is, therefore, postulated as a pre-existence for the existence of the Many. But what we still do not know is how they are related to each other, and this is the real 'aporia'.

b. A personal problem for Plato

This second part of the 'Parmenides' reads as a highly abstract dissertation, as an exercise in pure thought. Under the surface, however, one can detect an acute personal problem for Plato. In 'The Republic' the problem of the multiplicity of the Forms (each of them considered as one in itself) seemed to have found a solution because the Good had been made into the all-embracing unity. Yet the solution is only apparent. Again and again Plato tells us categorically that the Forms are absolute, abstract and independent realities. Subsequently he extols the Good to such a degree that it is almost as though he has lost touch with reality, and the basic question remains unsolved. In what manner do things partake of the Forms, do they, indeed, partake of them? In 'The Republic' Plato was bold enough to say that God is the creator of the ideal bed, that is to say, of the Idea of bed [229]. But now he is no longer so sure; such a notion suddenly strikes him as banal.

At this point Parmenides intervenes, not so much Parmenides, the Eleatic philosopher, but Parmenides, the highly venerated predecessor, the philosopher par excellence, whom Plato would readily accept as his teacher. The Dutch novelist Louis Couperus once said that all his personages are 'splits' of his own being; in the same way Parmenides is here the mature Plato who is able to review his own position with a critical eye. 'Socrates', having suddenly become 'young and fair again', and unexpectedly placed in the situation of the pupil, is that Plato who is prepared to learn from himself and to reconsider everything. When 'Parmenides' says that 'Socrates' surely will become a real philosopher some day [230], what Plato means is that he (Plato) doubtless will be able to solve the problems that are still presented to him by the doctrine of Forms. There is no question here, as is sometimes supposed, that Plato takes his leave in this way of the Forms as separate entities, or that he would henceforward see them as concepts dependent on the human mind. On the contrary, he keeps affirming that the Forms have an ontic reality (that they possess 'being'). But confronted with the problems of his dualistic position and fully aware of the consequences of this, he is now looking for an intermediate link, a connection between being and non-being. The result of this would be that the world of concrete things could be defined more satisfyingly. In that way a conciliation between Parmenides ('only Being') and Heraclitus ('only change') might be effectuated. However, Plato did not live to realize this.

18. Plato's criticism of his ideal state

a. The second-best state

In his longwinded book 'Laws', a product of his old age, Plato renounced some characteristic projects of 'The Republic', without, therefore, waiving his most crucial concepts. His love of democracy has not grown; government belongs to a few, preferably to one man, the 'monarch' [231]. But bitter experience in Syracuse had taught him that this would not necessarily turn out to the good of the state. Hence he is now of the opinion that the monarch must have a first-class lawgiver beside him [232]. It is one of the strongest characteristics of this book that everyone and everything is subjected to the rule of the law. As ever the rule of the wise man (the philosopher) remains the ideal, for law is not better than knowledge, and reason must be supreme [233]. But alas, no human being is capable of ruling as sole master without becoming guilty of injustice and presumption [234]

However, this does not mean at all that Plato is now evolving in the direction of the legality of the democratic state. The 'lawgiver' is given the most complete power over the life of the citizens [234], with all the sanctions belonging to this; the law covers even the most intimate spheres of life, such as marriage and the education of children [235]. The first task of the law is to educate the citizens [236]; the law is the great pedagogue. It will accomplish this by teaching and convincing rather then by punishing [237]. Nevertheless, there is a wide spectrum of punishments, from fines and prison via banishment to capital punishment. Stalley says that more crimes were liable to the death sentence than was usual in Athenian law [238]. Plato will not pardon offences against the state - his state! - : capital punishment will be put in effect also because of corruption, contempt of court, and similar offences [239].

This proves very clearly that Plato has now abandoned his ideal state : it is not practicable because of 'the general infirmity of human nature' [240]. What is now present to his mind is the second-best state [241], and the ideal citizen, the pre-eminently virtuous man, will be he who lives carefully up to all the laws and regulations [242]. These laws are very detailed, because human nature is utterly incapable of comprehending what is best for social life. And even if someone were to understand this, he would not be able to practise it [243]. If Plato is literally implying that there are no exceptions, one thing is clear : the ideal of the 'philosopher-king' has been dropped [244].

b. The 'guardians of the law'

The great partition of society into three, as presented in 'The Republic', is not recapitulated in this later edition. Plato's aversion to the commercial, restless and greedy Athens of his days is expressed in his demand that his state must lie far from the sea : preferably no harbours and no commerce [245]. The ideal size of the population would be 5040 households, that is 40. to 80.000 inhabitants [246] in all, more than in the usual Greek polis but far less than in Athens. The possession of gold and silver is prohibited together with commerce [247], industry and crafts [248].

The principle of 'one man one job' is maintained, on the understanding that everyone now has to be a farmer; every citizen is allotted a piece of land [249]. In this way poverty is banished. It would be a great thing, says Plato, if everyone possessed as much as everybody else, but this will not be practicable [250]. However, excessive wealth must be made impossible; there are four classes of property, in the ratio of 1 : 2 : 3 : 4 [251]. Who acquires more must cede it to the state [252]. Is this a Utopian thought? In my country, the Netherlands, progressive income-tax makes it impossible for 99 % of the citizens to earn netto more than four times the netto minimum wage. The division into property classes makes no difference in political rights. All citizens have the vote for the Council, which consists of 360 members, ninety from each property class [253]. It is evident that Plato endows the citizens with more influence than formerly was the case. Perhaps we might say that every citizen has now become a 'guardian'.

Nevertheless, part of the guardian group remains. There is in the state a number of high officials and administrators who will be chosen by all citizens liable to military service [254]. The most important of these are the 'nomophulakes', the 'guardians of the law'. They watch over the correct execution of the laws [255]; eventually they may act as lawgivers but exclusively with regard to amendments and additions [256]. 'The law' itself is given from on high and is inviolable. Guardians of the law must be at least fifty years old and must resign when they have reached the age of seventy [257].

Because the laws not only cover the public life of the state but also the entire private existence of the citizens the power of these guardians over the citizens is accordingly great. They have acquired a sinister reputation since their council is called the 'Nocturnal Council' which reminds one of the Ku Klux Klan; in reality the council assembles at sunrise [258]. The 'minister of national education' has to be one of these 'nomophulakes' [259].

c. How free are Plato's citizens?

The life of the citizens is strictly regulated for it is the task of the lawgiver to bring everything, to the smallest detail, under the law : nothing must be left uncontrolled [260]. An important difference with 'The Republic' is that Plato abandons his ideal of common possession of women and children, albeit with a sigh of disappointment. Normal family life has been restored [261]. Still, meals must be taken in great common 'mensae', but afterwards everybody may go home [262]. Another pastime is communal too, paramilitary training with the lighter weapons that takes place every day [263]. In spite of the restoration of family life, the children still belong to the state rather than to the parents [264]. All children go to school, the girls too, and compulsory ('coercive', says Plato openly) education is provided by the state. Men and women are equal, the women are liable to military service no less than the men [265].

The state penetrates very deeply into the private existence of the citizens [266]; Plato says literally that it is necessary to regulate everybody's time, from one sunrise to the other, and so on [267]. It is true that, according to the philosopher, the lawgiver must not bother himself with details, but this is immediately followed by the prescription that nobody must sleep too long : that is dishonourable for free people [268]. But one may well ask how 'free' these people are. It is even the case that all children must play the same games at the same time, and both the games and the time are stipulated by law [269]. The state does not even stop at the bedroom door. Marriage is compulsory for everyone, not for his or her own advantage but for that of the state that needs children for its continuance. He or she who does not marry is fined and will be discriminated against openly [270]. With regard to sexuality Plato again shows himself a true puritan; he is afraid that indulging in sexual desires will keep people from their duties towards the community. Once again he calls the sexual urge a pathological phenomenon, a form of unrestrained madness [271]. Sexuality is solely permitted in marriage and exclusively to beget children. When no children are born, the marriage partners must divorce [272].

Because children are begot for the well-being of the state, they must be as good and beautiful as possible [273]. Procreation is, therefore, a matter that must be attended to very carefully and sensibly. It is kept under close control by female inspectors who survey married couples during the ten years that are destined for the 'production of children'; they see to it that the married couples do not neglect their task. These inspectors are even allowed to enter the homes and point out their duty to the couples. When they remain negligent both man and wife will be exposed to public humiliation [274]. From the age of three onward children are placed under public supervision [275]; when they are six they have to go to school.

d. Dualistic distinctions

Since every citizen is responsible for the maintenance of the state, no one has time over for commerce, industry and crafts [276]. Since these activities are indispensable in society, it is necessary to enlist resident foreigners and slaves. The older partition into three has nearly disappeared and is replaced by a bipartition; this again is dualistic, especially since it has a qualitative character. For Plato says that such occupations, in particular commerce, are unworthy of a free citizen - so much so that a person who is caught in retail trade must be punished [277]. Let those people indulge in such vile and low activities whose moral decline does not present a disadvantage to the state - strangers, 'metics', that is -, he says pitilessly [278]. (This dualistic distinction between honourable and dishonourable occupations, such as commerce, was to have a great career before it). The consequenc for Plato's own Utopia would be, naturally enough, a great number of foreigners inside its frontiers and also an enormous mass of slaves. He fully maintains the classical dualistic division of society into free and unfree. He tells us that slaves must not be treated badly but for the rest slavery in his eyes is a perfectly normal institution [279].

What does this new edition of Plato's ideal state teach us? That it is less dualistic than the former one? By no means! True enough, as I said, the distinction between the two privileged classes and the mass of the workers has been allayed to a great extent. But it has been replaced by a new and far more formidable one, utterly dualistic, by that between 'the Law' and the citizens. The Law is sacred and sacrosanct; it is divine, it even seems to have taken the place of the gods. But of the citizens Plato has no high opinion; compared to 'the Law' they are only an inferior lot. The question is justified here whether such a state can really exist? Perhaps not, Plato admits, but we must try to come as closely as possible to the ideal [280]. And then, in the thick of his argument, this revealing remark slips from his pen that human affairs are unworthy of earnest effort; the only object really worthy of all serious and blessed effort is the godhead [281]. But why then does he thus regulate human life in the smallest detail?

Although in his long work Plato hardly ever speaks of the great themes of his philosophy, nevertheless, albeit indirectly, the dualistic distinction between being and non-being comes to the fore again. Human life belongs to what is non-essential. It is exactly because of this that it must be regulated so strictly. Life is a plaything, says Plato [282], but it must be played as beautifully as possible. No wonder that somebody criticizes Plato's principal spokesman, the Athenian stranger, on the grounds that he has a mean opinion of the human race. The stranger does not even deny this forcefully. True enough, he takes the point of view that the human race is not a mean thing in itself, but then he goes on to say that we are merely puppets in the hands of the godhead, although we do share, occasionally, in truth [283]. The opposition is sharpened considerably here.

Perhaps Plato's 'Laws' does not make any great difference between the 'lawgiver' who is constantly quoted, and the godhead. From all sides the sublimity of the law is radiating at us. Human nature is frail, that is what we know already, and no human being is capable of understanding fully what is good for public life [284]. But the 'lawgiver' knows this and communicates it to the citizen by means of the law. The enormously extensive and detailed legislation that occupies several books of the work consists for a small part of stipulations from a 'civil code' and for the larger part of articles from a 'penal code'. Evidently Plato thought his citizens capable of everything, from patricide to desecration of temples. In consequence he exposes them to a shower of penal provisions. Opposite the sacred and inviolable laws stands worthless humanity, capable of nothing good.

In this society too there is no lack of dualistic oppositions. The basic opposition, however, just as in 'The Republic', is that between the closed society (his Utopia) and the open society - we need scarcely argue that a society whose members are so strictly regimented, to the most intimate details of their private existence, must be dubbed as 'closed'. Plato himself would certainly not deny it but would, at the same time, attempt to persuade us that if the aim of the state is virtue - and what other aim could it possibly have? -, such regulations and institutions are indispensable. The closed character of this society appears very clearly from Plato's aversion to contacts with foreign countries. We have already seen that the state must be situated far from the sea (and for the Greeks the sea was the communication par excellence). Under no condition may persons under forty obtain permission to visit other countries; above this age it is possible but only in official functions, never for private reasons. Envoys who have visited foreign countries are asked to explain to the youth that the political institutions of all other countries are inferior to their own [285]. In the most literal sense the gates of the ideal state remain closed.

19. One world or two?

a. A 'vitium originis' in the cosmos

When we read what Plato writes about the cosmos, there is, at first sight, only one judgment possible : "The All is ordered like a cosmos" [286] - hence the idea of a second cosmos is a contradiction in terms. At least, this is the impression we derive from the 'Laws', although in fact most of what Plato has to say on the cosmos comes from the 'Timaeus'. Here he tells us that the cosmos is not only beautiful but also the best possible one; its architect - whom we shall henceforward call, with Plato, the 'Demiurge' ('dêmiourgos') - constructed it after a pattern that may be comprehended by reason ('nous') and thought : thus it is at once intelligible and identical with itself [287]. The architect of the universe is himself good and wants it to resemble him. This is the principle ('archê') - the principle of the Good - from which the cosmos and all coming to be originated [288].

However, already some elements have crept in that must make us cautious. The cosmos is not the original creation; it is a copy of something else. This is necessary, says Plato [289]. Why is this necessary? Because the cosmos has a body, it is a physical construction, it has an origin and it is visible and tangible [290]. In this work of his old age Plato still remains faithful to his doctrine of the Forms : the cosmos has been built on the pattern of a Form. For the rest the philosopher is extremely vague about this Form; he gives us very little relevant information. He merely informs us that the model cannot be a 'part', for in that case it would not be perfect. The model is a living being that encloses in itself all conceivable living beings; it must needs be one, and therefore there is only one cosmos [291]. For the Demiurge wanted our cosmos to resemble the perfect living being that at the same time is absolutely unique. The cosmos, moreover, is a true globe, for the globe is the most perfect shape and is identical with itself; it turns regularly around its own axis. It is a closed system that comprises all forms of existence; outside it there is nothing [292].

But at this juncture the opposition between Form and concrete shape makes itself felt. In the beginning of the 'Timaeus' the spokesman formulates the subject of this metaphysical cosmology in the following words : "What is that which is Existent always and has no Becoming? And that which is Becoming always and never is Existent?" [293]. In this work Plato is trying, for the last time, to connect Being and Becoming, the One and the Many, with each other. But the moment he embarks on the subject, he puts himself in arrears. The Demiurge - who in this passage is called 'god' - did not create the cosmos but ordered it.

"He (the Demiurge) took over all that was visible, seeing that it was not in a state of rest but in a state of chaotic and disorderly motion." The Demiurge is, therefore, working with existent matter; we are never informed who it was that created this original matter. "For the god desired that, so far as possible, all things should be good and not evil" [294]. What is good in the cosmos is the result of the ordering by the Demiurge; it is no effect of that primeval matter itself. One must also pay attention to the almost casually added phrase 'as far as possible'; with such refractory material even the Demiurge is not able to build a perfect universe. This means that there is a 'vitium originis' in the cosmos.

b. The world-soul and the human soul

The true architectonic element of the cosmos is reason (or the mind, 'nous'); the Demiurge planted reason into the soul and the soul into the body (of the cosmos). "The cosmos has verily come into being as a living creature endowed with soul and reason" [295]. After what we have seen in the foregoing sections of the relations between soul and body in the philosophy of Plato, it will not surprise us to find them back here again. The first thing he tells us is that the (world-)soul is older than the (world-)body and that the soul, therefore, has to be the mistress [296]. Here suddenly a new opposition appears, that between the Same and the Other (obviously corresponding with being and becoming). The Demiurge made a compound of them, but it proved so difficult to mix them that he had to 'force them into union', says Plato [297]. From this equal mixture the world-soul is made. We shall encounter the opposition Same-Other again. But first let us consider the following.

When the Demiurge wanted to make the human soul, the mixture had already lost much of its original purity [298]. In other words, the human soul is not an undiluted part of the world-soul; she is of a lesser quality. There are as many human souls as there are stars; every soul is assigned to a star of her own where she stays until she is united with a body [299]. Here we meet once again Plato's favourite tenet of the pre-existence of the soul. It is 'of necessity', he says, that they come into terrestrial bodies. In passing Plato sketches here his hierarchy of values. Everyone first becomes a male but those who do not live justly return as females, while those who fail to improve themselves in any way finally end up as animals [300]. It is worth noticing that the Demiurge does not create human beings himself. He leaves this to younger gods; otherwise mortals would become equal with the gods [301].

In the cosmos we can distinguish between a higher and a lower creation; it is a more or less balanced equilibrium of chaotic and unspecified primordial matter and reason. In man, as the microcosmos, both elements are present, and they cause opposite movements in human beings. The rational element may be completely subdued. Take, for example, a newborn child. Although a soul is infused in his body, the child is as blind and senseless as the primordial matter of the cosmos. But this is only a stage. By means of education, the light of the soul may be, as it were, kindled [302].

Next, Plato describes how human beings come into existence. "They (the lesser gods), imitating him (the Demiurge), on receiving the immortal principle ('archê') of the soul, framed around it a mortal body, and gave it all the body to be its vehicle" [303]. In this construction too the body is secondary and subordinate to the soul. And now something curious! Into this body they now inject a second shape of the soul, a mortal one; this is the seat of the passions and desires. In order to prevent this soul from polluting the original, the divine soul - 'unless through absolute necessity' -, the divine soul is lodged in the head and the mortal soul in the great cavity of the body, with the neck as 'isthmus' and frontier between them.

Earlier in this chapter I have already pointed out that the mortal soul also consists of two parts. The first part is the seat of courage and 'panache'; it is open to the guidance of reason. The second part is the seat of the lower appetites. Since it is resistant to reason, it must be forced to obey it. These two parts are separated by the midriff, 'as if to fence off separate chambers for men and women', says Plato, and this comparison too speaks volumes. In the lower part we find the urge to eat and drink and indulge in all bodily appetites; hence this part must be kept as far away from 'the citadel of reason' as is possible [304]. The older Plato, no less than the younger, still looks with great aversion at what is physically human; even now he regards man as a construction that can only be kept together with great difficulty.

c. The dualism of Demiurge and cosmos

When we keep in mind that in Plato the macrocosmos (the universe) and the microcosmos (man) are always analogous, we may expect to find patterns in the universe that bear a close resemblance to those we find in man. In this connection I must draw the attention of the reader to a highly significant passage from the 'Laws. Plato's spokesman, the 'Athenian stranger', states categorically that the world-soul is primary and the cause and ruler of all things. But then he asks all of a sudden : is there only one world-soul or more? And in fact there is more than one world-soul; there are actually two : the beneficent soul, and the soul that is the total antithesis of the beneficent [305]. It is as though Plato suddenly realizes that there is also evil in the world and that he must not ascribe this to his all-good godhead. As long as everything goes on in the right way, that is to say, as long as the universe follows its circular course, it is reason (nous) that controls everything. When, however, the other soul, in combination with senselessness ('anoia'), gets the upperhand, then, in every respect, the opposite happens. Then there is no longer a regular movement, since the bad soul (Plato uses the word 'kakên') acts foolishly and in a disorderly manner [306]. The cosmos is one indeed but contains, nevertheless, two opposed principles.

Plato expresses this in still another way. He does this by opposing Reason and Necessity ('anankê'). By 'Necessity' we must understand primordial matter or the blind forces of Nature. "This cosmos in its origin was originated as a compound of Necessity and Reason. And inasmuch as Reason was controlling Necessity by persuading her to conduct to the best most of the things coming into existence, thus and thereby it came about, through Necessity yielding to intelligent persuasion, that this Universe of ours was being in this wise constructed in the beginning" [307]. Reason persuades Necessity but with difficulty and not in every respect : even in this ordered universe there are things over which Reason has no control. Plato says expressly that everyone who is speculating on the origin of the cosmos cannot pass over 'the form of the Errant Cause' [308]. By 'errant' ('planomenês') he means : irregular, not circular, and as such not committed to an ideal or harmonious course.

In this way we arrive at a highly intriguing passage from the 'Politicus' that shows clearly that, according to Plato, in the universe two contrary movements are possible. I am referring to the story of the earth turning back on its course [309]. Plato calls this a 'myth' but we must not forget that by 'myth' he does not mean something that is not true [310]. The cosmos revolves in a course from right to left, in an east-west course according to the movement of the sun, directed by the Demiurge. When, however, it has reached 'the measure of its allotted time' (the period in which the Demiurge travels along with it in the original direction), the Demiurge leaves it to itself and then it begins to revolve in the reverse direction. Reason steps back and 'fate and innate desire' take the helm [311].

What is the cause of this? The universe has received from its creator many blessed qualities but it has also a physical nature, and therefore it is not safeguarded from change [312]. Plato postulates in an evidently dualistic manner two opposing movements in the universe. But, he adds, one must not say that the godhead moves the universe in different directions in turns, for the godhead is unchangeable and cannot work evil. Nor must one think that two gods who are opposed to one another make the cosmos revolve, for god is good and Plato cannot conceive of a malevolent godhead, a god of evil. In the first instance, therefore, the cosmos is moved by a divine cause (that is not identical with the cosmos itself); in the second instance, the cosmos is left to itself and then it revolves of its own accord [313].

There is an evident dualism of Demiurge and cosmos here : the Demiurge has other intentions than the self-willed cosmos but is not always able to assert his will. One must also pay attention to the fact that the favourable movement is not natural to the cosmos but is imposed on it. Plato says literally : "The opposite direction is contrary to divine law" [314]. Left to itself the universe is rapidly heading towards its destruction. "From its Composer the universe has only received good things; but from its previous condition (i.e. that of chaos) it retains in itself and creates in the animals all the elements of harshness and injustice ... But in becoming separate from him (its Pilot) ... the ancient condition of disorder prevailed more and more and towards the end of the time reached its height, and the universe, mingling but little good with much of the opposite sort, was in danger of destruction for itself and those within it" [315]. But then the Demiurge intervenes and saves the world.

In the 'Timaeus' this mythical rendering gets its scholarly counterpart. In the sphere-shaped universe as it is presented in this late work of Plato there exist two contrary movements. There are two tracks, two hoops, so to speak; the one stands in a vertical position, the other horizontally, with the same hub for both circles. The outward track, the horizontal one, is the track of the Same; the vertical one is that of the Other. The track of the Same turns to the right, that of the Other to the left [316]. The track of the Same contains reason and knowledge, that of the Other opinions ('doxai'), and convictions ('pisteis') that are solid and true; this is Plato's old opposition between 'knowledge ' and 'opinion' again [317]. However, the opposite movements do not have such dramatic consequences here as in the myth; in this more cosmological work Plato needs the track of the Other in particular to explain the irregular movements of the seven 'wandering stars' (the 'planets', sun, moon, Venus, Jupiter, Mars, Mercurius, Saturnus, the last five of these being those planets visible to the naked eye).

20. Was Plato a dualist?

a. Plato's concept of God

It may seem astonishing that, after all that has already been said, the question 'was Plato a dualist?' can still be raised. But this question is asked from time to time; sometimes it is answered in the affirmative but not infrequently in the negative. Even some eminent experts in the field of ancient philosophy may deny that Plato was a dualist. Let us consider, for example, Guthrie and De Vogel. In the indexes of Guthrie's great history of Greek philosophy, Volumes IV and V, the word 'dualism' does not even occur. To the problem at issue he devotes scarcely one page [318]. Guthrie admits that Plato apparently acknowledged two principles, the One and the 'ápeiron', that is the 'indeterminate Dyad'. "True, before time and the world began, they were there." And somewhat further on : "For his act of creation the supreme God, the Demiurge, had to accept the apeiron". But this creative mind, says Guthrie, is itself the first and only cause of all that exists, because it has connected the two principles with one another. And he concludes in these words : "The monism of Plato's latest metaphysics lies in his theism".

Two remarks are apposite here. May one really apply the word 'theism' to Plato's concept of God? In my view this word includes the concept of a 'personal god', a god who is an individual being and who is knowable as such, the Jahve of Israel, the Triune God of orthodox Christianity, the 'God of Abraham, Isaac and Jacob, not of the philosophers', as Pascal wrote in his 'Mémorial'. In common with this God the Demiurge is also a creator but here the similarities end. He is no Father, no Providence, no object of love and veneration, he did not even create mankind himself. He is 'Reason', 'nous', and this is his function with regard to the cosmos.

Plato's concept of god remains abstract; I have already indicated how many names he holds in reserve for his godhead. Its relation to the gods of the Olympian pantheon is far from clear. Plato's concept of god has, perhaps something in common with that of the eighteenth century, with Deism, that is : god, for Plato, as for the 'philosophes' of the Enlightenment, is less a living being than a principle, an abstraction. However, Plato was far more religious than the Enlightenment philosophers. Is this Demiurge, like Jahve, 'a jealous god who suffers no other gods besides himself'? In the 'Timaeus' Plato says that he is speaking of the nature of the visible gods (plural) who have an origin, and his Demiurge addresses them solemnly as 'gods' [319]. The gods meant are the Olympian ones who have their part in the work of creation and who, according to 'The Statesman', each control a department of the world [320]. Hence it would be clearly inaccurate to refer to Plato's theology as 'theistic'; at the same time his system is by no means 'monistic' in a strict sense. Guthrie, it would seem to me, is misleading on both of these issues.

b. Guthrie on Plato's 'archai'

Guthrie, as we have already seen, considers that the 'apeiron' is a particular instance of the 'archai', those primeval principles that exist independently before all other things. Thus it is, as Plato himself says only too clearly, a datum, something given, and Guthrie raises the following question : "Was the One too a datum, used by God as he used the material on which he stamped his imprint?". He answers it as follows : "The One was in himself". Does he mean that the Demiurge participates in the One in a special manner? Or even that he is identical with the One? It appears from the previous quotation that Guthrie meant that he was indeed indentical with the One. But Plato (who remains rather vague about his Demiurge, for that matter) never asserts that he (or the Nous) is the One [321]. Moreover, it seems to escape Guthrie that even if the Nous (or the Demiurge) were the One, there would be, nevertheless, two principles, the Nous and the apeiron. But the Demiurge cannot be the One because he works on a model that is entirely consistent and shows no variations [322]. It seems to me that the introduction of the Demiurge (who is a somewhat mythical figure) is another attempt by Plato to escape the radical dualism of Parmenides. He is engaged in a ceaseless attempt to connect the two principles (whatever names they may bear, the One and the Many, peras and apeiron, being and non-being, the Same and the Other) with one another, here with the Demiurge as the link between them. We may admit so much that this is not radical dualism. But, as the next paragraph will demonstrate, there also exists relative dualism.

c. De Vogel on Plato's dualism

Cornelia de Vogel begins her argument on the question whether or not Plato was a dualist [323] with a statement that is suspiciously similar to a 'petitio principii'. Those who contend that Plato was a dualist base their point of view on second hand knowledge; but those who 'have lived all their lives with Plato' - that is, those who have studied his own texts long and attentively - don't accept this view [324]. The clear implication is that anyone who argues that Plato was a dualist proves that he never has read his works. In so far as this may be called an argument, the author undermines it by observing several times that there actually is some reason for considering Plato a dualist [325]. Here she is right; the evidence for dualism is incontrovertible. Why, then, do scholars close their eyes to it? I cannot help thinking that they associate dualism with something ugly; saying that somebody is a dualist would mean an accusation, an indictment. This charge carries no weight with me; in my eyes Plato does not become a less great and fascinating philosopher if one detects dualism in his work.

What does De Vogel actually mean by 'dualism'? Evidently this : "two realities, the one next or opposite the other, realities of basically the same order, and thus independent the one of the other - which would be dualism" (my underlinings are the original italics by De V.). But, she says, I cannot detect this, there is only a difference in level. "The two kinds of reality which are clearly distinguished the one from the other are not conceived (sc. by Plato) as equal poles. An ontological scheme of subordination can hardly be called a dualistic scheme" [326]. The problem is not that Plato, according to De Vogel, is unaware of two realities confronting one another - she admits frankly that this is indeed the case [327] - but that a scheme of subordination would not be dualistic.

Radical dualism does not often occur in world-history. The reason why is obvious enough. In this case there are two utterly opposed principles, concepts, realities, systems or groups of people that are not connected in any way. For instance, how must one imagine a 'two-worlds-theory'? This means two worlds that are without any links or connections between them. This is beyond the range of what is knowable. What means of knowledge have I, living in one world, to know anything at all of a second world that is totally different from mine and radically opposed to it? If there ever was a person who was aware of this problem, it was Plato. For he saw very clearly that Parmenides really did create insuperable difficulties with his 'iron ontology'. In his doctrine Being stands irreconcilably opposite non-being. Non-being comprises all that is not eternal, not wholly identical with itself - that means changeable and moving things, everything that comes into being and disappears again, in short what Mansfeld calls 'the human world'. Parmenides ignored this world, to him it is no object of philosophy.

But however radical he might be, he was radical only as a philosopher, as a thinker. For as a human being he took part in this human world since he belonged to it. In every radical dualism a backdoor is needed, otherwise it is impossible to live. What is so obstinately ignored exists nevertheless; one is constantly confronted with it. Plato, however, was conscious of this. His significance in the history of dualism is that he mitigated Parmenides' radical dualism. But it would be a mistake to conclude that he was not a dualist : we are confronted in Plato with a vintage dualism since his two realities cannot be reduced to each other and since they differ in quality, the one being superior to the other. True enough, they enter into some sort of partnership but this remains an 'uneasy alliance'.

d. De Vogel on Plato's 'archai'

The second part of De Vogel's disquisition is concerned once again with the question whether Plato really handled two 'archai', two primeval principles. She does not deny this; indeed, she refers to it, somewhat in contradiction to the tenor of her essay, as 'a kind of dualism' [328]. Again the difficult question crops up of the One and the Apeiron, the problem known to philosophy as that of 'peras and apeiron'. What is the 'apeiron', what does it signify in Plato? 'Apeiron' means 'indeterminate, unlimited', while 'peras' signifies 'frontier, limit'. Apeiron is extensiveness, unlimited space, but not empty space for it contains all kinds of primary or primitive shapes that move about in a disorderly way; the apeiron itself moves in the same manner. It doubtless contains the four elements but in vague, chaotic shapes. Rather than 'primary matter' one should call the apeiron 'chaos'. Only then something orderly may result from it - for instance, a 'cosmos' (a word that originally meant 'order') - if somebody (the Demiurge) applies 'peras' to it.

Now Plato had a special term of his own for the apeiron : 'the indeterminate Dyad' [329]. Why he dubs it like this appears very clearly from a passage of the 'Philebus'. He says there that the apeiron, in some way or other, is the Many; this means, everything that may contain a 'more or less'. Therefore, there are no fixed quantities of it. As an example he presents 'warmer and colder', which as soon as they are determined become 'warm and cold' (this means, with a specific degree of warmth and cold) [330]. The indeterminate always contains oppositions and is, therefore, called 'duality' or 'Dyad'. Aristotle says that Plato knew two primary principles, the material principle, indicated as the 'great and small', the Dyad that is, and the formal principle (or essence), indicated as 'the One' [331]. Aristotle formulates this more or less in his own terms ('material principle'), but nevertheless he says clearly that his master knew two 'archai'. Can one doubt this?

Another disciple, Hermodorus, says that everything that is indeterminate, has a greater and smaller in itself, or a broader and a smaller, or a heavier and a lighter, and so on. Opposite these stand those things that are similar and permanent and in harmony with themselves since they are sealed by the 'peras' [332]. This agrees with what Plato himself has said : "God revealed in the universe two oppositions, the finite and the infinite" [333]. In concrete things peras and apeiron come together; such things are a combination of both. Concrete objects, however, do not possess the highest ontological status (for this is reserved for the Forms); concrete things, as well as living beings, have but a passing existence; they disappear again and therefore know no true stability.

All this means that peras and apeiron are two principles of reality and - by definition - opposed principles. Opposite the second principle, the apeiron or Dyad, Plato often places the One, the Monad. 'Peras' is closely related to this and is in fact the same principle. So we have two 'archai' opposite to each other, the One (the Monad) and the Duality (the indeterminate Dyad). The question now is whether the Dyad may be derived from the Monad, or, to put it in the most simple way, whether for Plato 1+1=2 - I mean, of course, from an ontological point of view (for arithmetically it was the same for Plato as for everybody else).

In some stage of his life Plato became influenced by the Pythagoreans and by their mystique of numbers. He himself began to equate his Forms with Pythagorean (ideal) numbers. Now, with the Pythagoreans multiplicity does not follow directly after unity but, in their famous list of oppositions, they stand opposite one another; in this list Unity is good and Multiplicity is bad [334]. The textual proofs that De Vogel quotes in order to demonstrate that the Dyad can be derived from the Monad are of a late date, from Sextus Empiricus in the second century A.D., and from Alexander Polyhistor in the first century B.C. [335]. It is also very important not to lose sight of the fact that these texts are not about Plato but about Pythagoreans. It is equally important that we have yet another and more circumstantial text of Sextus Empiricus in which he points out the dualistic character of the Pythagorean Monad and Dyad [336]. Unity and Multiplicity are clearly distinguished principles there; nowhere it is said that the one can be derived from the other, and this is wholly in accordance with the Pythagorean way of thought. It was this train of thought that influenced Plato so deeply.

But, says De Vogel, although appearances are sometimes against Plato, "a more profound reflection makes it clear to us that an actual dualism is not in line with Plato's thought" [337]. This 'actual dualism' is again that radical dualism that, indeed, does not occur in Plato. For however much the principles may be opposed, the Demiurge succeeds nevertheless in combining them. "Plato's thought naturally tended in the direction of superposing the One over his whole system of Reality and placing the indispensable Indefinite Principle immediately under it" [338]. True enough, but then this is a more mitigated dualism in which one principle is subordinated to the other; however, they are and remain opposed to one another and cannot be derived from or reduced to each other. Sometimes I ask myself how relative Plato's relative dualism is since his Demiurge always remains a shadowy figure and his attempts are not, finally, succesful.

21. Plato's dualistic oppositions

Let us now run over Plato's dualistic oppositions once again. There are many of them. Beginning with the microcosmos we find the opposition of body and soul, and next that of man and society in which the individual person is nearly non-existent. In society there is, according to 'The Republic', the opposition between guardians and citizens, and, according to the 'Laws', that between citizens and labourers, and still more that between the citizens and the Law. This is crowned with the opposition between philosophers and non-philosophers. This last opposition leads us to the cosmic oppositions.

The primary principles in the cosmos, with their many names - amongst others the One and the Many, peras and apeiron, Same and Other, Monad and Dyad - are dualistic. The cosmos as a whole moves in two different directions, and it contains within it also two opposite movements. From the viewpoint of the theory of knowledge there is constant talk of the intelligible and the non-intelligible, of knowledge and opinion, of being and seeming. Finally there is the preeminent opposition, that between the Forms and concrete things.

However, with regard to this last opposition we must be on our guard, for Plato did not mean this as an opposition at all. On the contrary, the concrete objects are knowable and their qualities can be defined precisely because of their relationship with the Forms. The question, however, is whether Plato succeeded in proving this relationship. We have already seen how many terms he uses for it but he failed in making clear what this 'partaking' means exactly, that is, in what way something beautiful 'partakes' of the Form of the beautiful. In the 'Parmenides' he appears to be conscious of this but if he intended to solve his difficulties in a later work, he never executed his plan.

This prompted Aristotle to a criticism that, in my opinion, is irrefutable. He says that the doctrine of the Forms has its origin with Socrates, in the favourite 'definitions' of that philosopher; his intention was to subsume the particular under the general. But, he continues, Socrates did not separate the general from the particular, and in this he was right. Those, however, who adhere to the doctrine of Forms (Plato, he means) take the Forms not only as universal substances but also as separate entities; this causes the greatest possible difficulties. According to Aristotle, therefore, there is an unbridgeable distance between the Forms and concrete things. For these things are in constant movement, and they all disappear again; the universalia, on the other hand, remain and are, therefore, essentially different from things. Aristotle called this the aporia into which Plato had landed himself [339]. In other words, for Aristotle Plato was a dualist.

22. Plato's dualistic mentality

Plato is the first dualistic thinker of whom we know more than next to nothing. Yet even if it is true that the biographical facts are scanty, his writings have been handed down to us complete and intact. These writings are voluminous and they support the contention, as I see it, that Plato without any doubt, was a person with a distinct proclivity towards dualism. One might say that he belongs to a psychological type that is far more common than is often assumed. I wish to say expressly that I am not passing any kind of value judgment. In my opinion certain events in a person's life may predispose him or her to think dualistically or even to act dualistically.

In order to get a grip on reality we group phenomena in terms of similarities (analogies) but also in terms of oppositions (polarities). In our existence such polarities occur in great numbers (day-night, summer-winter, warm-cold, man-wife, old-young, and so on). We have a way of finding some of these oppositions more important than others. Now the more an opposition is sharpened, the closer it comes to a dualistic opposition. Probably some people have a natural bent for thinking in dualistic categories; they detect polarities rather than analogies. In the course of events and because of them this latent bent may become activated.

Perhaps this was also the case with Plato. We have now had every possibility to convince ourselves that he must have had a radical disposition, with a predilection for very outspoken oppositions. His political doctrine proves amply that he was authoritarian-minded to the point of pitilessness. More than once we have noted that he was very puritanical in his ideas and proposals. He was also not married. If need he runs counter to himself for instance when, despite his great knowledge of and affinity with the poets, he nevertheless bans them from his state. In his personal life too we find abrupt decisions, for instance when he throws his tragedies into the fire and when he resolves to stay out of politics. I therefore suspect that there is a link between his life and personality on the one hand, and his writings and philosophy on the other.

23. Aristotle : the man and his work

Aristotle was no native Athenian. He was born in 384 B.C. in the city of Stagira (or Stagiros), a colony of the island of Andros, far to the north, on the peninsula of Chalcidice, bordering on Macedonia. His father was a not unimportant person, the personal physician of the Macedonian king Amyntas III; both he and the philosopher's mother came from a family of doctors. He got his passion for empirical science from two sides therefore. In early life he became an orphan, with an uncle as his guardian. Seventeen years old he left for Athens where he presented himself for study at Plato's Academy. Aristotle remained closely connected with this institution for twenty years. Many years he spent in the company of the Master and heard him expound his doctrines; the influence of Plato on his own train of thought is clearly perceptible.

However, he never became a true Platonist himself. He did not have a marked predilection for the abstract world of the eternal and unchanging Forms; even mathematics did not arouse much enthusiasm in him. His disposition was for observing rather than for contemplation.

His great interest went to concrete things. Aristotle, of course, did not remain a pupil of Plato for twenty years; he also taught in the Academy and did research. When Plato died in 347 B.C., he left Athens. The reasons for his departure were a certain opposition to Plato's intellectual heritage and a distaste for the fiercely anti-Macedonian policy of Athens as voiced by Demosthenes.

Aristotle went to live in a small independent kingdom in the north-west of Asia Minor, Atarneus. A few pupils of Plato had already established themselves there; on his arrival a kind of little Academy came into being, with its seat in the city of Assus. He stayed there for three years and married a near relative of the tyrant of Atarneus. After a short stay at Mytilene in the island of Lesbos Aristotle arrived in 343 B.C. at Pella, the capital of Macedonia. King Philippus II had invited him to undertake the education of his son Alexander. Inasmuch as Alexander, from the age of sixteen onward, regularly had to act as regent of the kingdom, the philosopher's teaching cannot have lasted more than three years. However, Aristotle remained in the north even when his pupil had invaded Asia Minor in 334 B.C.

Somewhat later he returned to Athens and began to teach there in the Lyceum, an already existing academic institution, called after a sanctuary of Apollo Lykeios in the vicinity of which it was established. This Lyceum, that was founded by Theophrastus, is also called the 'peripatetic school', either because teacher and pupils discussed while walking about ('peripatein') or because they sat together in the coolness of the portico. This school was a scientific faculty rather than a philosophical one. The institution possessed a large collection of biological and other material; the students could do research there. When Alexander died suddenly in 323 B.C., a difficult time began for Aristotle who had always been overtly pro-Macedonian. Athens immediately rebelled against the Macedonian domination. The philosopher no longer felt at home there and certainly incurred a risk by staying in the town; therefore he took refuge at Chalcis, in Euboea. A year later, in 322 B.C., he died there, 62 years old.

The numerous writings we possess from the hand of Aristotle are not books in the usual sense of the word. What we have - 445.270 lines, if we may believe Diogenes Laertius [340] - are the lecture notes which the philosopher had lying before him when he was teaching, or notes made by pupils. Partly the writings consist of essays by pupils. All those writings were published by other hands, often in a somewhat edited or redrafted form; of some of them we have more than one version. Aristotle also wrote for a larger public but of these works only a few fragments remain.

The books that are handed down to us show that their author was interested in a great many things. They are concerned with problems of philosophy and ethics, with logic, methodology and the theory of science, and also with the most different branches of natural science, from geology via biology to metereology; and as though this were not yet enough, he also wrote on literature and politics.

24. Aristotle and the oppositions in social life

With regard to Aristotle too the question keeps returning whether he was a dualistic thinker - I shall come back to this. Even those who answer this question in the affirmative tend to forget that this philosopher, in no small measure, gave expression to forceful, even dualistic oppositions in Greek social life. Since he enjoyed a great authority for centuries, especially in the Middle Ages, his opinions were to have the most far-reaching effects.

a. Woman as an incomplete being

Let us start with his attitude regarding women. Aristotle was not an outspoken misogynist; after all he was a married man. Nor was he, like Plato, a puritan in sexual matters. The way he talks of these things is very matter-of-fact, 'clinical' one might even say. There is not the slightest indication that he found sexual intercourse something inferior or humiliating. He says that a woman too may experience pleasure in the sexual act; this he proves anatomically [341]. However, this does not mean that in his eyes man and woman are equals. By no means! For, as he explains to us, a woman is really an infertile man; she is a woman because she lacks the capacity of forming spermatozoa [342]. Hence he concludes that the female is the opposite of the male; it is exactly because of this that the one is male, the other female [343]. This means that man and woman are not complementary but opposites.

Considering woman as an incomplete being Aristotle compares her to a boy who is not yet in the possession of his full sexual potential [344], or to eunuchs who no longer posssess it. This last comparison he bases on a curious but revealing argument. A seminal emission, he says, is similar to thrusting out heat; afterwards one cools down strongly. Now the brains are by nature the coolest part of the body; the effect of the cooling is, therefore, strongest in the head, first in the brains and subsequently in the skin and the hair. The hair becomes, so to speak, 'undercooled', with the result that it falls out. Men with a powerful potency grow bald early in their lives therefore. (Is this an autobiographical allusion? Tradition has it that Aristotle was bald.) But women who do not emit semen do not cool off and do not become bald, just like eunuchs. For eunuchs have in fact become women; they have head hair and pubic hair but no other hair on their bodies; just like women they are unable to grow beards and moustaches. Aristotle plainly calls this a 'mutilation' [345].

This is a highly important text. It is doubtless one of the most principal sources for the viewpoint that a woman is really a sort of castrated person or a eunuch, that she is female because of a deficiency. Aristotle pays a lot of attention to the phenomenon of menstruation and enters into physiological details here [346]. He does so since, contrary to some other authors of his days, he is of the opinion that a woman in no way contributes to the conception anything that is comparable to the male semen. "It obviously follows that the female does not contribute any semen to generation" [347]. However, this does not mean that Aristotle fails to assign some role to woman; he is forced to, in fact, since it is woman, after all, who bears the child.

b. The superiority of the male

Aristotle states that there are two main factors in generation, the male factor being the principle of movement and origination ('genesis'), and the female one, the material principle [348]. The difference is that a man possesses the capacity of generating outside himself in another, whereas a woman can only generate within herself. In other words, she is the one in whom what is generated (the child) and what was present in the begetter (the man) gets shape [349]. In this view too woman is the fertile soil, like the earth for the grain. "This is why in cosmology too they speak of the nature of the earth as something female and call it 'mother', while they give to the heaven and to the sun and to anything else of that kind the title of generator and 'father' " [350]. And now the philosopher says something highly revealing : man and woman do not only differ with respect to their build or to their physiological functions but also and in particular in their 'logos' [351]. This means that, according to Aristotle, both sexes are fundamentally different in their higher abilities, that is in thought and reason. And in these respects woman is inferior.

It will be abundantly clear by now that to Aristotle woman is not the equal partner of man, nor has she, as member of the polis, the same value as a man. "The male is by nature superior and the female inferior, the male ruler and the female subject. And the same must apply in the case of mankind generally" [352]. It is true that in democratically governed states the citizens alternate in ruling and being ruled but this does not apply to the relation between man and woman. Nevertheless, her position is not completely similar to that of a child or a slave, for a slave has no brainpower at all, and a child is not yet ripe for independent thought. The man has 'constitutional authority' over his wife; this means that she is neither his possession nor his passive subject [353]. But on the other hand, the relationship is not 'democratic'. The courage of the man is shown by his commands, that of woman by her obedience. "Silence gives grace to woman", quotes Aristotle from Sophocles with great approval [354].

What Aristotle means by 'constitutional' is shown elsewhere when he says that the relation of a man to his wife is inherently aristocratic. He is the ruler since he is worthy of it, he exercizes his rule in those matters that belong to the male sphere; exclusively female matters he leaves to his wife. "The relationship between man and woman (in marriage) is, therefore, identical to that existing between rulers and subjects in an aristocracy." Each party receives what is proper to it; this means that the better part (the man, that is) gets a larger share of the good for everything is rated according to excellence ('aretē') [355].

Somewhere else Aristotle says that no political justice (no equal rights) can exist between husband and wife. Such justice is only possible between free and equal persons; in case the persons are not equal or free there is only justice for them in a metaphorical sense. The consequence of this is that the position of women, children and slaves is not regulated by law. Law is only valid for those persons to whom injustice may be done, that is to say, only to the free and equal [356]. Nevertheless, the wife is entitled to somewhat more justice than children and slaves. Therefore, and 'pour besoin de cause', Aristotle invents the term 'household justice' [357].

c. Aristotle on barbarians and slaves

In Volume II I stated that Aristotle had a highly unfavourable idea of barbarians [358]. It was the task and the destiny of the Greeks to rule over them. In this respect he disapproved of the policy of the Macedonian princes. He saw it as their principal task to unify the Greeks in a political entity of their own rather than absorb them in a superstate that included barbarians.

Slaves were not rarely of barbarian descent; they were prisoners of war more often than not. It will be evident that Aristotle found them too an inferior lot. The kernel of the matter is that, in his opinion, slavery is a natural institution. As there have to be men and women, because otherwise no children will be born, so there must be, as a natural necessity, people who command and people who execute the commands; this means that there will always be masters and slaves. The master has intelligence and foresight, and therefore he is, naturally again, in authority; the other has only his physical force and therefore is, again by nature, a slave [359]. Once again the solidly rooted conviction of the Greeks is revealed here that physical labour is unworthy of a free man. They looked down on such labour and left it to their slaves if they possessed them. There is not only a dualistic opposition between freedom and slavery but also between freedom and labour. In passing Aristotle prides himself on being Greek, for, he says, with the barbarians women and slaves have the same (low) rank but with the Greeks woman is more highly rated [360]. In using the term 'by nature' so often he opposes those authors (Sophists) who think that nature does not create differences between men; in their view the dominance of the one over the other is based on violence [361]. No, says Aristotle, some people are slaves by nature, therefore some people are slaves always and everywhere, and other people nowhere and never [362].

A slave is a 'live article of property' and as such he is a 'tool', an instrument ('organon'), albeit with precedence over other tools [363]. A slave, however, is more closely related to his master than lifeless tools; he is a member of his master, as though he were a living member of his body, albeit separate from it [364]. He is a part of the master's body, indeed, but not of his mind; for what he has to offer is physical, not intellectual force. A slave possesses reason in so far that he is capable of acknowledging it but no more. So he does not differ very considerably from animals; the similarity is more striking than the difference. Both sorts offer their phsyical power for the performing of indispensable task. To the degree that the body is different from the soul, and man from an animal, the free man differs from the slave [365]. Aristotle even goes so far as to inform us that he can differentiate between the free man and the slave on the basis of their physical characteristics; the erect bearing of the free man, for instance, is a sign of his aptitude for political life, while the slave's build is perfectly suited for hard labour [366].

25. A dualistic element in Aristotle's psychology

a. The composite soul

There is no doubt that, in his doctrine of the soul, Aristotle is trying to eliminate the dualistic distinction of body and soul that characterizes Plato's psychology. In particular in his 'On the Soul' ('De Anima') he gives an exposition of his principles. These principles are his favourite ones, those of form and matter, both of them indispensable to bring about whatever kind of object. Therefore, they are not opposite but complementary principles. We may think of the body in its primary state as matter, and we may think of this matter as a potential human being. It is the soul that gives matter (here that of the body) a unique human shape. It is the act that activates potency and brings about a human person - this singular human person. This union of matter and form, of act and potency, is, therefore, absolutely necessary for otherwise there would be no man. In other words, for Aristotle man is a unity of body and soul. Plato's sombre vision that the body is the tomb of the soul is not his.

However, a few moments ago we heard that the soul differs from the body just as much as a human person differs from an animal and a free man from a slave. One may therefore ask oneself whether this unity is really complete. Aristotle says that the difference between lifeless objects and living beings consists in the fact that living beings have a soul. From this it follows that not only men but also plants and animals are endowed with a soul. Plants possess a vegetative soul; this enables them to adapt themselves to the environment and to multiply themselves [367]. Animals have this lowest form of soul too plus yet another one, namely the sensitive soul that enables them to observe, to strive after something, and to displace themselves. Animals possess also a certain imaginative faculty and some measure of memory [368].

Man, of course, possesses all these faculties in addition to some others of a higher order. He has intellect, a typically human mind ('nous'). By its means he can strive, consciously, after practical and useful ends. He is even capable of neglecting these and devoting himself to speculation and philosophy on behalf of truth. This means that man also possesses an intellective soul; actually 'also' is not correct for every being has only one soul, albeit endowed with a greater or lesser number of faculties [369].

Now all earthly things and beings are transitory. Animals and plants die; at that same moment their souls become extinct since they are indissolubly linked with their shapes. In man who has a composite soul this is totally different. His intellective soul is part of his whole soul, and it is that part - the 'nous' - with which man knows and thinks. This is the highest faculty imaginable; potentially this faculty is the same as its objects (for thought thinks what is thinkable) but, nevertheless, not identical with it. Human brainpower cannot possibly be the same as thought itself; the characteristic of the mind is the process of thinking in itself rather than the thoughts that present themselves, which are the products of thinking. Mind has to rule unobstructedly in order to be able to think. It is, therefore, unreasonable, says Aristotle, to suppose that mind might be mixed with the body; in that case it would be something qualitative (that is to say, a property of the body), and this it is essentially not [370]. In order to explain the question even more clearly, he points out that just as things may be distinguished from their constitutive matter (a wooden seat, for instance, from wood as matter), so the intellectual faculties too are distinguishable from their matter (the body) [371].

b. Aristotle drifting towards dualism

Now this whole section of 'On the Soul' is notorious for its difficulty; it has brought many clever brains into a state of confusion. The reason for this might be that the whole thing was not completely clear to Aristotle himself too. He must have been aware of the fact that he, unwillingly, was drifting in the direction of dualism. Of course he did not know this word - it is a neologism - but he employs in this connection the word 'dyas' that W.S.Hett, in the Loeb Classical Library-edition, translates as 'duality'. The connection in which the philosopher uses this word is that of a concept and its practical applicability. He gives this example : 'right' (something right, a right line for instance) is not the same as 'rightness'. This results in the conclusion that thinking is not identical with the objects of thought [372]. But do we not come very near to the Platonic train of thought here? True enough, Aristotle does not use the word 'Form'; instead he has 'that what is', that is, the essence of things, and this is something different from the thing itself. This is a 'dyas', as he states in so many words [373]. And does he not lay himself open to the criticism he himself brought against Plato, i.e. that there is a 'chorismos', an (unbridgeable) gap between the Forms and the objects that exist because of these Forms?

In this section of 'On the Soul' Aristotle uses the Greek word for 'separation' three times. First he says that the intellectual capacity of the soul is 'separable' [374]. Somewhat further on we learn what he means : it is separable from the body (whereas the sensitive soul is indissolubly bound up with the body). This same word 'choristos' = separable, occurs twice in the passage I quoted a few lines back on the essence of things and the things themselves as an example of the distinction between thinking and what is thought [375]. As to the 'separability' (of the intellectual soul), the philosopher says that this exists either in a spatial sense or according to reason [376]. In other words, is it really possible that the nous exists separately, apart from the body, that is, or is only a logical priority meant?

Somewhat further Aristotle gives an important part of the answer himself. We must, however, not forget that he is not speaking there of the whole soul but of its thinking part, the nous. "Mind in this sense is separable (again 'choristos'), impassive and unmixed (i.e. with the rest of the soul and with the body) ... Potential knowledge is prior in time to actual knowledge in the individual, but in general it is not prior in time (i.e. potency and act occur simultaneously) ... When isolated ('choristeis', i.e. from the body and the lower parts of the soul) nous is its true self, and this alone is immortal and everlasting" [377]. In the interests of salvaging what he can from Plato's doctrine of the immortality of the soul, Aristotle is obviously doing some violence to his own system. Potency and act coincide, they occur simultaneously to bring about a thing or a being. But in this passage he allows potential knowledge to be prior in time to the actual (factual) knowledge. In this way we are very near the position that the nous precedes (mortal) man in time, and this means also in space. This also implies that it has a separate pre-existence.

In another text of 'On the Generation of Animals' ('De Generatione Animalium'), Aristotle elaborates this point. He is speaking here of the three sorts or departments of the soul; it appears that all three of them have a different origin. The rather intricate argument boils down to this. The vegetative soul of a new human being is provided by the woman; this soul is in the material (Aristotle employs this word) that is being supplied by her. The sensitive soul comes from the male; it is part of his semen. But the intellective soul comes from outside. From where? This Aristotle does not tell us in as many words; in any case not from the human side, for it is 'divine'. In itself this origin from outside need not mean dualism but it comes close to it. For then these words follow : "Physical activity has nothing whatsoever to do with the activity of Reason ('nous')" [378].

c. The pre-existent nous

Since Aristotle evidently is not allowed to show dualistic tendencies, some scholars perform the impossible in order to exonerate him from this 'accusation'. Moraux, a well-known Aristotle-specialist, says that the text in which the philosopher posits that the (intellective) soul comes 'from outside' does not express his real meaning [379]. Enrico Berti writes many pages on man, soul and intellect (nous) in Aristotle to prove that there is no trace of dualism in his system. But in the text itself Berti never refers to the passage containing the words 'from outside'; true enough, in a note he mentions the Greek word for it (= 'thuratēn') but does not quote the passage itself [380]. In her afterword to his essay De Vogel expressly draws Berti's attention to this 'thuratēn' [381].

"If indeed," writes Berti, "the intellect, that is also to Aristotle the most essential part of man, is a substance apart from the mixture of body and soul, that is called man, then this man would be composed of two separate substances, the intellect (nous) on the one hand, the compound of soul and body on the other" [382]. Now this is utterly impossible, he says, for in Aristotelian philosophy man is 'one substance, a single one' [383]. It is not possible that the substance which gives to the compound its substantiality (say its definite shape) still remains a separate substance, different from the mixture of soul and body. Inasmuch as it (this substance) gives substantiality to the compound, it (the nous) no longer is a substance itself (a substance that is separate from the human shape). "During the period in which the intellect (nous) is combined with the compound, this (the compound) is the true substance ... A human being exists exclusively during this period but not before and after it" [384]. According to Berti, therefore, Aristotle does not acknowledge the pre-existence of the soul.

What Berti overlooks is that plants and animals which, according to Aristotle, have a soul too, do not need a 'nous' to be a substance (= to have a concrete shape). The case of man is, therefore, peculiar : to make him into the substance 'man' (= to give him or her this concrete shape) yet another substance is needed that comes 'from outside'. In my opinion Aristotle is certainly causing problems with respect to his concept of substance but this is not my centre of intertest. The point is that nobody would dream of asserting that the nous, when it is not lodged in a human shape, is a human being. Nevertheless, nous exists, it is pre-existent and it is post-existent and it is transcendent and divine. Berti himself admits that much. "The intellect leaves the compound (this concrete human being) and takes its substantiality away, whereas itself continues to exist as an immaterial substance" [385].

In this particular concept of nous there is certainly an element of dualism. In another passage Aristotle says : "The physical part, the body, comes from the female (literally : out of the female), and the soul (psuchē) from the male (out of the male), since the soul is the essence (substance, 'ousia') of a particular body" [386]. Here we have not only a sharp opposition between man and woman but still more so between body and soul (without soul no human being). However, there remains a problem. It is woman who provides the vegetative soul. The sensitive soul comes from the male. However, a vegetative soul and a sensitive soul in combination may give shape to an animal but not to a human being. To give existence to a human being an intellective soul is also needed and this is not supplied by man or woman but comes from outside. I believe that Aristotle was unconsciously prompted by the notion that although the nous does not issue literally from the male, it comes via the male into a new human being. The divine principle comes from the side of the man and is utterly different from physical matter. We find here the oppositions of man and woman, of intellect and body, of divine and human, and of immortal and perishable. These dualistic tendencies must, without any doubt, be attributed to the teaching and influence of Plato.

26. The question of the first principles

a. Form and matter, the great 'archai' of Aristotle

Aristotle is rightly considered as the philosopher of coming to be, of the Many, of concrete things, as an empiricist and a researcher that is. However, this should not lead us to believe that, as a philosopher of being, as an ontologist or a metaphysician, he is without importance. On the contrary! More often than not he starts from reality as it presents itself to us, that is, from our observation of this reality. In doing this he assumes that observation and reality agree with each other; he objects to the viewpoint of the Sophists that observation is subjective, with the consequence that reality is subjective too. This conformity of observation and reality obtains only in principle; in practice people may make stupid errors and reach misleading conclusions as a result of faulty inductions from reality.

We order manifold and confused reality by means of concepts. We catalogue our observations with the help of such concepts. But then these concepts must be the right ones. Hence Aristotle devotes much attention to the way we form our judgments, especially to the method according to which we make the right judgments. Judgments are right when they tally with the reality observed. The instrument he developed to this end is logic; he is the founder of this primary department of all philosophy. With him we shall not find a dualism of intellect and reality nor the nominalism that goes with it. By means of this logic it is also possible to argue in the reverse direction, from the general to the particular - in other words, to operate deductively. Perhaps general induction is, in principle, the more obvious road, but in order to follow it consistently one would have to know all particular instances. Yet since our knowledge of reality is always fragmentary we are forced to start from the general.

Although Aristotle disavowed Plato's doctrine of Forms, nevertheless, for him too general concepts are highly important. Especially in physics we need well defined concepts. For what is physics other than a theory of movements? Since everything is a process of becoming and disappearing again, there is general movement, for movement is a word for the transition from one condition into another. In order to observe with some result the nearly interminable field of movements, it is necessary to catalogue their causes. There are four of them : matter, form, effective cause, and the objective. Mainly Aristotle uses only two of them : form and matter.

Matter is passive and formless, it is still potency; when forms operate upon it potency changes into actuality; then a substance comes into being, a shape. In a genial way Aristotle presents a solution here of an age-old problem that in Parmenides had ended in a complete impasse and that had not been brought much further by Plato, the problem of becoming. Since the Greeks were convinced that there is no 'creatio ex nihilo', that is, that something always comes from something else, and never from nothing, Parmenides came to the conclusion that there is no becoming at all, only being. Aristotle, for that matter, does not say either that something can come from nothing; but according to him, something that is (exists) may come from something that is not yet that later something but may become it. Now since the principles of form and matter are complementary, there is basically no question of dualism here.

b. What is Being?

In whole books of the 'Metaphysics' Aristotle argues as though substances, that is concrete objects and beings, are related to each other as substances. All of them are 'ousiai', a word that is a form of 'being'. The mutual relationship of factual beings and things rests on the fact that they are all 'beings'. There is, therefore, a general correspondence, an analogy, between existing things; their conformity is of a logical character (it may be discovered by the ordering mind). It is not something metaphysical or ontological (it is not dependent on some separate and really existing principle or on an abstract form of being).

Nevertheless, in other books of the 'Metaphysics' it looks as if things are knowable as 'being' because they partake in 'Being' itself, in a general form of Being that is independent of objects and men. Graeser uses here the word 'focus-like' [387], as though there existed an all-embracing Being from which light falls through a lens that fragmentates it to each different object, or, in other words, as though the 'lines of being' ascend from the objects, and then come together in a focus; this focus then is Being. In that case the mutual conformity of existing things rests on an ontological or metaphysical factor, because Being is postulated as something transcendent.

In the fourth book of the 'Metaphysics' Aristotle criticizes certain natural philosophers : they believed that they were occupying themselves with the totality of nature and, therefore, with the totality of Being. It is true that physics is a form of wisdom, but it is not the only one; this is because nature itself is only one specific mode of existing. There even may be found a kind of philosopher who rises above the natural philosopher, since his enquiry is of a general character and refers to the 'primary substance' [388]. It is evident that Aristotle is establishing a hierarchy here, not only among the philosophers - for the metaphysician has precedence over the natural philosopher - but also among the principles. There is a 'primary substance', and it will be clear in advance that this is not matter. Physics is incapable of defining the nature of this first essence or substance, the unchangeable element in everything. It cannot solve, therefore, the problem of Being.

In order to find an answer to the question what Being is one has to go beyond physic; one then arrives at 'metaphysics', the 'doctrine of Being' [389]. "If there is not some other substance besides those which are naturally composed, physics will be the primary science. But if there is a substance which is immutable, the science which studies this will be prior to physics, and will be the primary philosophy, and universal in this sense, that it is primary. And it will be the province of this science to study Being qua Being, what it is and what the attributes are which belong to it qua Being" [390]. For "it is obviously the province of a speculative science to discover whether a thing is eternal and immutable and separable (once again 'choriston') from matter". It is true that some branches of mathematics also study the immutable but, nevertheless, mathematics is not this prior science" [391]. Very clearly and consciously Aristotle creates in this way a distance between the world of concrete things and Being; with respect to quality the differences between them are considerable : movable-immovable, perishable-eternal. He stresses this by using the key-word 'choriston' : he keeps Being apart, he gives it a status of his own.

Aristotle does not make things easier for us because his system is probably not wholly consistent. On the one hand we have, in large stretches of his work, the two complementary primary principles of form and matter; the immaterial form represents the metaphysical element. From this point of view every concrete and individual object or living being is an authentic substance; in order to understand it there is no need to appeal to a general, objective and universal substance. On the other hand we find also a doctrine of Being; this Being keeps itself apart from the concrete things of this world and contemplates the eternal and immutable [392]. In this doctrine there certainly is a universal, objective and separate first principle; with it we are very near Plato. It is, therefore, possible, to say the very least of it, that a dualistic element may be detected in Aristotle's philosophy. Whether this is really the case is a question I will attempt to answer in the final section.

27. The Unmoved Mover

a. The bipartition of the cosmos

Graeser says rightly that this so-called 'prior science' of Aristotle is partly ontology or metaphysics but partly also theology [393]. This will not surprise us for we have seen earlier hat Aristotle uses the word 'divine' for the nous that comes into man 'from outside'. But let us first of all see how the universe is composed according to this philosopher [394]. There is only one cosmos [395]; it is not created and cannot perish (in this way Aristotle postulates the eternity of the world) [396]. It is limited [397] and spherical [398]. The earth is spherical too and is situated in a fixed place in the middle of the cosmos [399]. The universe contains the four elements; these, however, are not eternal, they constantly interact. Since they permanently collide with each other, there is a continuous coming-to-be [400]. The things which originate and perish again cannot come from the immaterial; nor can they find their origin outside the cosmos, for outside it there is nothing. What we observe is, therefore, a continuous mixing of the elements [401].

In addition to the four well-known elements, earth, water, fire and air, there is yet a fifth element, that was introduced by Aristotle and was destined for a long and succesful career; it even has a place of its own in modern radio parlance, for it is the 'ether' [402]. This fifth element, the 'quinta essentia', lives on in our word 'quintessence'. To us the ether is the fifth element but to Aristotle it was really the first one; it is something apart ('kechorismenon') from everything around us [403]. The ether is immutable, it does not grow greater or smaller, it has no origin and no end; all its movements are circular [404]. When Aristotle states that this primary element knows no time and is timeless, then his thoughts go automatically to the gods. To the Olympian gods? No, not really to them, rather to the 'divine'. Since both Greeks and barbarians believe in this 'divine', he says, the ether too must have something divine about it. The argument is somewhat bizarre.

This means that Aristotle acknowledged two kinds of elements, the four well-known ones and then, in addition, the ether. These two kinds never commingle; they always remain apart from each other. Qualitatively they are very different too, for it is evident that the ether is something far more sublime than the common elements. Even if our thoughts have not yet drifted in the direction of dualism, they will do so inevitably as soon as we hear that the cosmos is divided into two parts, into two halves. The upper half is for the ether, the nether one for the four elements. The dividing line is the course of the moon. The 'sublunary' is our own transitory world but above it is the imperishable one. This truly dualistic bipartition of the cosmos - which lives on in our phrase 'this sublunary world', used in a pessimistic sense - was proper to the Pythagoreans. In this respect too Aristotle may have been influenced by Plato. The farther the ether is removed from the sublunary world, the more sublime is its nature, the more pure it is [405].

Not only the stars but also the highest sphere of the heavens and the courses of the planets are composed of this thin, luminary, 'ethereal' matter. This means that the 'superlunary' is made of another material than the sublunary. The spheres of the stars and of the planets are animated and complete circular courses. By doing this they approach the perfection of the divine principle [406] for although they move, they do this in a perfect way, and the source of their movements is in themselves [407]. The stars are fixed to the vault of heaven and are carried around with it [408]. Guthrie considers it probable that at the time that Aristotle was lecturing on what now are the contents of 'On Heaven' and 'On Philosophy', he had not yet developed his concept of the 'Unmoved Mover'; then the ether provisionally took the place of the divine principle [409].

b. The separation of god and world

Initially, Aristotle did not know one 'Unmoved Mover' but 56 of them. He seems to have been in doubt about their number for a very long time [410] but finally he decided on 56 [411]. These movers are not the celestial bodies themselves but the tracks along which they move, the starry vault included, the highest arch to which the stars are fixed. Aristotle calls them the unmoved substances and principles [412]. These statements perhaps cannot be easily combined with the postulate of the philosopher that there must be something that sets bodies in motion although it itself is immovable. When he then speaks of 'the prime principle' ('archê') upon which the sensible universe and the world of nature depend [413], we expect one principle and not 56.

The great number of movers results from the old problem of how the irregular movements of the planets can be explained, since every planet behaves in its own peculiar way; therefore, they cannot be attached to one common vault nor to the dome of the stars. Each of the 55 spheres below the highest arch has its own mover. All of them share in the qualities of the prime mover : he is eternal, unmoved and without extent (i.e. he is not material) [414]; therefore, he is divine. But when we have passed all those 55 movers we see that they really are of a lower order. For the highest sphere, the outer sphere of the cosmos, is moved by the prime mover; this finally is the real immovable mover, the prime and essential 'archê' [415]. It is incorporeal and immaterial. Aristotle speaks somewhat disparingly of the theology of his forefathers, but, he says, they were right in one thing : that the prime substance is divine [416].

Aristotle's god, therefore, is this prime mover. It deserves attention that the philosopher uses the neuter here, 'the prime moving', he is evidently not speaking of a personal god. His god is a true 'dieu des philosophes' for he (or it) is nothing but 'nous', nothing but mind, in the sense of intellect or ratio. This mind thinks only what is supremely divine and immutable. The conclusion is evident : this god only thinks himself, "its thinking is a thinking of thinking" [417]. He is a god who is wholly enclosed in himself and wholly directed onto himself. He knows no object outside him, he is no creator - no Greek god is this -, he is no providence and does not occupy himself with the world and with mankind. In essential respects he is different from the Olympian gods. Praying or sacrificing to such a god is absolutely useless and still less loving him, for he does not answer our love with love in return [418]. Here we encounter the most radical separation of god and world that is imaginable; in my opinion this is the most dualistic element in Aristotle's writings.

c. Anticipating the future

This is also an element that causes us to anticipate the future. In several passages of Volumes I and II I have argued that the distance between Greek gods and men was great and that it showed the tendency to become greater still. Aristotle's god has got so far from us that he has become an unrecognizable god. What do we comprehend of a god that only thinks himself? Does such a god interest us? Actually he is already a 'hidden god', a 'deus absconditus', for our gaze has to rise upward through 55 celestial spheres before we can detect him. He is hidden from our view by one sphere after another. This is not conducive to a deeply religious life, but, n'en déplaisent the philosophers, people are in need of such a life. Two of Aristotle's main elements, the division of the universe into celestial spheres, each of them with its own divinity, and the secrecy of the prime god, we shall find back in Gnosticism. The Gnosis will be a desperate attempt, religiously defined, to discover, breaking through all the obstacles, the god who has disappeared and to reappropriate him. At the end of this volume our thoughts go therefore to a future that, at the time of the death of Aristotle in 322 B.C., was not really so very far distant.

NOTES TO CHAPTER III

1) Based on Taylor, Plato, Ch. I.
2) Plato, Ep. VII 324D-E.
3) Plato, Ep. VII 325C-326B.
4) Taylor 5/6.
5) Copleston I 1, 158/159.
6) Ar., Phys. 209b 14-15.
7) Plato, Ep. VII 341C.
8) Plato, Ep. II 314A-B.
9) To prove that such a doctrine really existed is the aim of 1 Hans Joachim Krämer, Arete bei Platon und Aristoteles. Zum Wesen und Geschichte der platonischen Ontologie. Heidelberg, 1959; 2 Konrad Gaiser, Platons ungeschriebene Lehre. Studien zur systematischen und geschichtlichen Begründung der Wissenschaften in der

platonischen Schule. Stuttgart, 1963. The problem is discussed in Das Problem der ungeschriebenen Lehre Platons. Beiträge zum Verständnis der platonischen Prinzipienphilosophie. Herausgegeben von Jürgen Wippern. Wege der Forschung, Bd. CLXXXVI. Darmstadt, 1972.

10) Plato, Phaedr. 276D.
11) Plato, Ep. VII 341E.
12) Plato, Ep. VII 341D.
13) Plato, Ep. VII 341E. See also Graeser 126 : "Zumindenst die These einer radikalen Esoterik (what is meant is the existence of a 'secret doctrine' in the Academy, apart from the dialogues) lässt sich nicht aufrechterhalten".
14) See my article 'Is Plato zijn ware roeping misgelopen?' ('Did Plato miss his true vocation?'), in 'Hermeneus', 58, 1 (Febr. 1986), 11-18.
15) DL III 5-6.
16) Lamb, Plato II, 377 (Loeb Class.Libr.).
17) Plato, Eutyphr. 1B.
18) Plato, Lach. 183E.
19) Plato, Charm. 155C.
20) Plato himself appears twice, first as present during the process, Ap. 34A, and then as absent on account of illness during the last conversation in prison, Phaedo 59B. Perhaps Plato 'signed' his works in this way, just like Alfred Hitchcock 'signed' many of his movies by appearing in them in an insignificant role.
21) Plato, Ep. II 314C.
22) Guthrie IV 213.
23) Pétrement, Dualisme.
24) Popper, Open Society I, 173/174.
25) Plato, Prot. 322A-324C.
26) Plato, Gorg. 489A-B.
27) Plato, Gorg. 502E-503C.
28) Plato, Gorg. 513A.
29) Plato, Gorg. 510E-511A.
30) Plato, Gorg. 513C.
31) Plato, Gorg. 515E-516C.
32) Plato, Gorg. 516E-517A.
33) Plato, Gorg. 526B.
34) Plato, Gorg. 525D-526A.
35) Plato, Gorg. 526E.
36) Plato, Gorg. 521D.
37) Plato, Gorg. 485A-D.
38) Plato, Meno 86B-C.
39) Plato, Euthyd. 281B.
40) Plato, Euthyd. 295E.
41) Plato, Meno 99A-C.
42) Plato, Meno 99A.
43) Plato, Meno 99 C and B.
44) Plato, Meno 98A.
45) Plato, Menex. 247A.
46) Plato, Gorg. 499E.

47) Plato, Gorg. 470E.
48) Plato, Meno 73E.
49) Plato, Euthyd. 301A. Plato does not yet employ for partaking the well-known terms 'metexis, mimêsis' et alia, but says instead 'paresti'.
50) Plato, Meno 98A.
51) Plato, Meno 89C.
52) Plato, Meno 89C and 76A.
53) Plato, Meno 72C-D.
54) Plato, Meno 89D.
55) Plato, Meno 94E.
56) Plato, Meno 99E.
57) Plato, Meno 100A, quoted from Od. X 494.
58) Plato, Gorg. 493A.
59) Plato, Meno 81B.
60) Plato, Meno 81C.
61) Plato, Meno 81C-D.
62) Plato, Meno 82B-85C.
63) Plato, Meno 85C-E.
64) Plato, Gorg. 493A.
65) Plato, Gorg. 523A.
66) Plato, Gorg. 523A-524D.
67) Plato, Phaedo 72A.
68) Plato, Phaedo 74C-D.
69) Plato, Phaedo 75C-D.
70) Plato, Phaedo 77B.
71) Plato, Phaedo 79B.
72) Plato, Phaedo 79B.
73) Plato, Phaedo 80A.
74) Plato, Phaedo 80E.
75) Plato, Phaedo 80B.
76) Plato, Rep. 611C.
77) Plato, Phaedr. 250C.
78) Plato, Phaedo 79C.
79) Plato, Phaedo 83A.
80) Plato, Phaedo 79D.
81) Plato, Phaedo 65A.
82) Plato, Phaedo 65E-66A.
83) Plato, Phaedo 66C-D.
84) Plato, Phaedo 66D.
85) Plato, Phaedo 66E.
86) Plato, Crat. 403E.
87) Plato, Phaedo 62B.
88) Plato, Rep. 387D.
89) Plato, Rep. 386A-387A.
90) Plato, Phaedo 62A.
91) Plato, Phaedo 64A.
92) Plato, Phaedo 64E-65A.
93) Plato, Phaedo 65C, 67A and 82B.
94) Plato, Phaedo 82C.
95) Plato, Phaedo 83A-B.

96) Plato, Phaedo 96C-D.
97) Plato, Symp. 218B.
98) Plato, Phaedo 78C and 80B.
99) Plato, Rep. 431A.
100) Plato, Rep. 413B-D.
101) Plato, Phaedr. 253D-254E.
102) Plato, Rep. 436A.
103) Plato, Rep. 439D-E and 580E-581C.
104) Plato, Rep. 439E.
105) Plato, Rep. 441E and 443D.
106) Plato, Rep. 499D.
107) Plato, Rep. 442D.
108) Plato, Rep. 442A-B.
109) Plato, Phaedr. 255D-256A.
110) Plato, Rep. 248D-E.
111) Plato, Rep. 329C-E.
112) Plato, Rep. 403A-B.
113) Plato, Phaedr. 255D-256A.
114) Plato, Symp. 217A-219D.
115) Plato, Phaedo 113E-114B.
116) Plato, Rep. 614D-615B and 617E.
117) Plato, Phaedr. 248A-249D.
118) Plato, Phaedr. 248C-E.
119) Plato, Phaedr. 249D.
120) Plato, Crat. 385E-386A.
121) Plato, Crat. 389D.
122) Plato, Crat. 390D-E.
123) Plato, Crat. 397B-C.
124) Plato, Crat. 391E.
125) Plato, Crat. 411B.
126) Plato, Crat. 440B.
127) Plato, Crat. 440C.
128) Plato, Crat. 423E.
129) Plato, Crat. 439C.
130) Plato, Phaedo 100D.
131) Plato, Phaedo 100C-D.
132) Plato, Phaedo 103B.
133) Plato, Rep. 596B.
134) Plato, Rep. 527D-E.
135) Plato, Phaedo 77A.
136) Plato, Rep. 476A and 507B.
137) Plato, Rep. 505A.
138) Plato, Rep. 508E.
139) Plato, Rep. 509B.
140) Plato, Rep. 509B.
141) Plato, Phaedo 109D-E.
142) Plato, Symp. 210A.
143) Plato, Symp. 219A-211E.
144) Plato, Rep. 476C-E.
145) Plato, Rep. 477A-B.
146) Plato, Rep. 477D-480A.
147) Plato, Rep. 586A.

148) White's bibliography 'Plato on Knowledge and Reality' mentions two articles : 1 D.W. Hamlyn, Communion of Forms, in Philosophical Quarterly 5 (1955), and 2 J.H. Lesher, Gnosis and Epistêmê in Socrates' Dream in the Theaetetus. Journal of Hellenic Studies 89 (1969), 72-78. Both essays refer to only a very small part of Plato's work.
149) White 195, n. 51.
150) Hugo Perls, Lexicon der Platonischen Begriffe. Bern/München (1974). Moline combats the notion that Plato might have differentiated his terminology in a conscious way.
151) White 195.
152) Plato, Laws 942C; Lyons 177.
153) Lyons 178. We do not find in Lyons an analytical inquiry into the use of 'gnosis' by Plato. Moline 187 n. 1 calls Lyons' study 'of great linguistic interest' but 'philosophically perverse' (sic). Moline says that if we were to interpret philosophical texts according to the method of Lyons, no philosopher would ever be able to bring forth anything new. Sometimes the philosopher is allowed to take liberties with words in order to present new ideas; it may even be his duty to do this. In the case that he uses words with a certain latitude of meaning, this does not diminish their philosophical significance. This is what Moline says but I don't think that Lyons would deny this. Lyons tries to make out how Plato begins to differentiate common words for 'knowledge'. Although I am writing a study of oppositions I must admit that I don't understand Moline's distinction between 'of linguistic interest' and 'philosophically perverse'.
154) Plato, Charm. 169E.
155) Plato, Crat. 440A-B.
156) Plato, Soph. 248E.
157) Plato, Rep. 484C.
158) Plato, Rep. 477A and 478C.
159) Contrary to this in Rep. 508E Plato mixes the terms epistêmê and gnosis.
160) Plato, Phaedr. 247C.
161) Plato, Phaedr. 247D.
162) Plato, Phaedr. 248B-C.
163) Plato, Rep. 514A-517A.
164) Plato, Rep. 509D-511E; see in Copleston I.1, 176-180 the crystal-clear exposition of this.
165) Plato, Rep. 434D.
166) Plato, Rep. 434B and 443B.
167) Plato, Rep. 471C.
168) Plato, Rep. 473D.
169) Plato, Rep. 473A.
170) Plato, Rep. 592B.
171) Bogner 70.
172) Vol. II, Ch. IV, Section 4.
173) Vol. I, Ch. 1, Section 5.
174) Plato, Rep. 347A-E.
175) Plato, Crat. 392D.

176) Plato, Rep. 388A.
177) Plato, Meno 71E.
178) Plato, Laws 781C.
179) Plato, Laws 781B and D.
180) Plato, Rep. 484D, 456B-C, 478B-C, 466C-D, 471D.
181) Plato, Rep. 457D.
182) Plato, Rep. 457C.
183) Plato, Rep. 459E.
184) Plato, Rep. 460E-461C.
185) Plato, Rep. 460D.
186) Plato, Rep. 460C.
187) Plato, Rep. 462B-C.
188) Plato, Rep. 464D.
189) Plato, Rep. 412D.
190) Plato, Rep. 415C.
191) Plato, Rep. 423C-D.
192) Plato, Rep. 540A.
193) Plato, Rep. 502B.
194) Plato, Rep. 429A.
195) Plato, Rep. 493E.
196) Plato, Rep. 499E-500A.
197) Plato, Rep. 493A-C.
198) Plato, Rep. 496C.
199) Plato, Rep. 487A-B.
200) Plato, Rep. 399E.
201) Plato, Rep. 501A.
202) Plato, Rep. 514A.
203) Plato, Rep. 410A.
204) Plato, Rep. 519D-E.
205) Mt. 13:28.
206) Plato, Rep. 500E.
207) Plato, Rep. 500D.
208) Plato, Rep. 487A and 503C.
209) Plato, Rep. 503B, 490D and 496C.
210) Plato, Rep. 499B.
211) Plato, Rep. 490E.
212) Plato, Rep. 496D-E.
213) Plato, Parm. 127B-C.
214) Plato, Parm. 130E.
215) Plato, Parm. 130B.
216) Plato, Parm. 130C-D.
217) Plato, Parm. 131A-E.
218) Plato, Parm. 132D.
219) Plato, Parm. 133A.
220) Plato, Parm. 133C-D.
221) Plato, Parm. 134A-B.
222) Plato, Parm. 135A-B.
223) Plato, Parm. 135C.
224) Plato, Parm. 136A.
225) Plato, Parm. 136D.
226) Plato, Parm. 160B.

227) Plato, Parm. 166B.
228) Plato, Parm. 166C.
229) Plato, Rep. 597B.
230) Plato, Parm. 130E.
231) Plato, Laws 710C.
232) Plato, Laws 710D.
233) Plato, Laws 875C.
234) Plato, Laws 713D.
235) Plato, Laws 631B-632D.
236) Plato, Laws 875E.
237) Plato, Laws 722C-723D.
238) Stalley 137.
239) Plato, Laws 955D and 958C.
240) Plato, Laws 853D.
241) Plato, Laws 807B.
242) Plato, Laws 822B.
243) Plato, Laws 875A.
244) See for his passage Laws 875B-D which, in my opinion, proves this very clearly.
245) Plato, Laws 704D-705B.
246) Guthrie V 341/342.
247) Plato, Laws 741E-742A; 743D.
248) Plato, Laws 846D and 919D.
249) Plato, Laws 743C-D.
250) Plato, Laws 733B.
251) Plato, Laws 733C.
252) Plato, Laws 733E.
253) Plato, Laws 756B.
254) Plato, Laws 753B-D.
255) Plato, Laws 754D.
256) Plato, Laws 770A-771A; 772B-D.
257) Plato, Laws 755B.
258) Plato, Laws 961B.
259) Plato, Laws 755C.
260) Plato, Laws 760A.
261) Plato, Laws 739B-D; see also 807B.
262) Plato, Laws 806E-807A.
263) Plato, Laws 814C.
264) Plato, Laws 804D.
265) Plato, Laws 814C.
266) Plato, Laws 780A.
267) Plato, Laws 807D.
268) Plato, Laws 807E.
269) Plato, Laws797A-B.
270) Plato, Laws 773B-774B.
271) Plato, Laws 783A.
272) Plato, Laws 784B.
273) Plato, Laws 783D.
274) Plato, Laws 783E-784D.
275) Plato, Laws 794B-C.
276) Plato, Laws 846E.

277) Plato. Laws 918D-E.
278) Plato, Laws 918C-D.
279) Plato, Laws 776C-778A.
280) Plato, Laws 746A-C.
281) Plato, Laws 803B-C.
282) Plato, Laws 803C.
283) Plato, Laws 804B.
284) Plato, Laws 875A.
285) Plato, Laws 950D-951A.
286) Plato, Laws 966E.
287) Plato, Tim. 28C-29B.
288) Plato, Tim. 29D-E.
289) Plato, Tim. 29B.
290) Plato, Tim. 28B.
291) Plato, Tim. 30C-31B.
292) Plato, Tim. 31A-34A.
293) Plato, Tim. 27D-28A.
294) Plato, Tim. 30B.
295) Plato, Tim. 30B-C.
296) Plato, Tim. 34C.
297) Plato, Tim. 35A.
298) Plato, Tim. 41D.
299) Plato, Tim. 41D-E. I remember that when I was a little boy of four or five years old, my mother, looking at the starry sky, used to tell me that in the stars lived the souls of children who were yet to be born. Still she had hardly ever heard of Plato, let alone read him.
300) Plato, Tim. 42A-C.
301) Plato, Tim. 41C-42D.
302) Plato, Tim. 44B-C.
303) Plato, Tim. 69C.
304) Plato, Tim. 69D-70E.
305) Plato, Laws 869E.
306) Plato, Laws 897B-898E.
307) Plato, Tim. 47E-48A.
308) Plato, Tim. 48A.
309) Plato, Politic. 268D.
310) The whole relation Politic. 269C-273E.
311) Plato, Politic. 272E.
312) Plato, Politic. 269D-E.
313) Plato, Politic. 270A.
314) Plato, Politic. 269E.
315) Plato, Politic. 273D.
316) Plato, Tim. 36B-C.
317) Plato, Tim. 37B.
318) Guthrie V 441/442.
319) Plato, Tim. 41A.
320) Plato, Politic. 271D, a passage in which it is not clear whether or not there is a difference between god and gods.
321) In my opinion one may not, with Guthrie, infer from Ar., Met. 442b22 that Ar. says this of Plato. It is true that Ar. says there that mind (nous) is one, but knowledge is two, plane three, and

cube four, to be read in this way : 1-2-3-4 (a kind of Platonic 'tetraktys'). The number 1 stands apart here and is the source of all numbers, while 2, 3 and 4 represent the three dimensions. According to Ar. the numbers are identical to the Forms. The point is that with nous = 1 not the divine Nous is meant but the human mind, just as knowledge means human knowledge. "The concrete world is in some cases known by mind, in others by knowledge, etc.". This passage does not force us to the equation : the Nous (or the Demiurge) is the One.
322) Plato, Tim. 28A.
323) De Vogel, Was Plato a dualist?
324) De Vogel 4.
325) De Vogel 4, immediately in the beginning.
326) De Vogel 6 and 9.
327) De Vogel 5.
328) De Vogel 37/38.
329) The 'aoristos duas', a term that Plato himself does not employ anywhere. Ar. says he did, Met. 1081a15-16 and De Vogel 45.
330) Plato, Phil. 24A-25A.
331) Ar., Met. 987b20-22.
332) Simpl. in Phys.Ar. 247.30-248.15.
333) Plato, Phil. 23C.
334) Vol. I, Ch. I, Sections 12 and 15.
335) Sext.Emp. X 261.9; for Al.Pol. see DL VIII,25. Al. is supposed here to have found this in a Pythagorean book of the 2nd cent. B.C. But how was a turnabout like this possible? DL writes somewhat hesitantingly, for his literal words are : "Al. says that ...".
336) Sext.Emp., Ad Math. X 270.27b.
337) De Vogel 55.
338) De Vogel 55/56.
339) Ar., Met. 1086a31-b7.
340) DL V 1.127.
341) Ar., De Gen.An. 727b8-9 and 728a32-34.
342) Ar., De Gen.An. 728a18-20.
343) Ar., De Gen.An. 766a22-24.
344) Ar., De Gen.An. 728a18.
345) Ar., De Gen.An. 783b27-784a12.
346) The archaic fear of menstruating is not alien to this learned researcher either : "If a woman looks into a highly polished mirror during the menstrual period, the surface of the mirror becomes clouded with a blood-red colour (and if the mirror is a new one the stain is not easy to remove, but if it is an old one there is less difficulty)", Ar., On Dreams 459b28-33.
347) Ar., De Gen.An. 727a28-29.
348) Ar., De Gen.An. 716a5-7 and 738b21.
349) Ar., De Gen.An. 716a21-24.
350) Ar., De Gen.An. 716a15-18.
351) Ar., De Gen.An. 716a18-19.
352) Ar., Pol. 1254b13-16; in Greek the literal words are 'better' and 'worse'.
353) Ar., Pol. 1258a37.

354) Ar., Pol. 1260a21-23 and 30, from Soph. Ajas 293.
255) Ar., NE 1161a22-25.
356) Ar., NE 1134a25-31.
357) Ar., NE 1134b16-18.
358) Vol. II, Ch. III, Section 3j.
359) Ar., Pol. 1252a26-35.
360) Ar., Pol. 1252b1-6.
361) Ar., Pol. 1253b18-23.
362) Ar., Pol. 1255a30-32.
363) Ar., Pol. 1253b31-33.
364) Ar., Pol. 1255a16-26.
365) Ar., Pol. 1254a16-26.
366) Ar., Pol. 1254b27-31.
367) Ar., De An. 413a21-33.
368) Ar., De An. 413b20sqq.
369) Ar., De An. 414a29-415a13.
370) Ar., De An. 429a10-27.
371) Ar., De An. 429b22-23.
372) Ar., De An. 429b18-21.
373) However, he uses 'eidos' = Form or Idea, just as Plato often says 'eidos' instead of 'Idea'.
374) Ar., De An. 429a11-12.
375) Ar., De An. 429b16-23.
376) Ar., De An. 428b10-12.
377) Ar., De An. 430a17-24.
378) Ar., De An. 736b13-29.
379) Moraux 293, note 2.
380) Berti 103; in this essay Berti, with regard to Ar., repeatedly uses the term : 'l'accusation que ...', viz, that Ar. was a dualist.
381) De Vogel in her afterword to Berti.
382) Berti 97.
383) Berti 103.
384) Berti ib.
385) Berti ib.
386) Ar., De An. 738b26-27.
387) Graeser 232.
388) Ar., Met. 1005a31-1005b2.
389) The term 'metaphysics' was used for the first time by Nicholas Damascus, a scholar in the 1st cent. B.C.; it is, therefore, not from Ar. himself. Nicholas probably derived it from an older contemporary, Andronicus, who arranged the writings of Ar. in a certain sequence. Therein the ontology of the philosoper came after the physics = 'meta ta phusika".
390) Ar., Met. 1026a27-32.
391) Ar., Met. 1026a8-12.
392) Graeser 232 : "Was er zu guter Letzt unter 'Metaphysik' verstanden wollte, bleibt ungesagt".
393) Graeser 230.
394) See Guthrie's clystar-clear descriptions in 1) his introduction to Ar., De Caelo, 'Aristotle's World-System', in the Loeb Class. edition ('On the Heavens'), 2) in his Hist.Gr.Phil. V 267 sqq.

395) Ar., De Caelo 276a18-279b3 and Met. 1047a32-38.
396) Ar., De Caelo 279b4-283b23.
397) Ar., De Caelo 284b6-286a1.
398) Ar., De Caelo 286b10-287a31.
399) Ar., De Caelo 287a31-287b14 and 296a24-298b20.
400) Ar., De Caelo 286a22-36.
401) Ar., De Caelo 305a14-34. The Greek doctrine of the elements has its origin with Empedocles and lasted until Lavoisier, ca. 1790. That the elements may pass into each other is a tenet that Ar. probably had from Plato who gives a theory of it in the 'Timaeus'. I still remember vividly that our teacher in primary school told us that, in very heavy fires, spouting was of no use. For, he said, in that case water will burn, and as a consequence the fire would become still worse. He believed, therefore, that water could turn into fire. What else is this than the old doctrine that the elements could turn into one another?
402) This fifth element is not the same as 'air', but is thought of as a thin diaphanous substance of very light weight. Ar. postulated it because of his theory of movement, De Caelo 286b11-269b17.
403) Ar., De Caelo 269b15.
404) Ar., De Caelo 269a10-12 and 269b18-270a35.
405) Ar., De Caelo 269b13-17 and Met. 340b6-11.
406) Ar., De Caelo 286a10-14.
407) Ar., De Caelo 285a29-30; Guthrie V 253/254.
408) Ar., De Caelo 291a27-28.
409) Guthrie V 263/264.
410) In Phys. 258b11, 259a6-8 he does not mention a number.
411) The sum in arithmetic in Met. 1074a1-14; to the 55 one must add the prime mover.
412) Ar., Met. 1074a15-9.
413) Ar., Met. 1072b14-15.
414) Ar., Met. 1073a29-1073b1.
415) Ar., Met. 1074a37-39.
416) Ar., Met. 1074a39-1074b14.
417) Ar., Met. 1074b25-35.
418) Ar., MM 1208b29-33.

BIBLIOGRAPHY

I ORIGINAL SOURCES

Of the works mentioned below there exist, of course, many editions. I cite only those that I used myself - hoping that they will also be useful to the general reader. Most of the time these editions are those of the Loeb Classical Library, with their parallel texts in Greek and in English. With some exceptions I have cited, throughout this volume, the Loeb Classical translations. However, I have tried to modernize the most archaically sounding of them somewhat.

A COLLECTIONS

DIOGENES LAERTIUS
  Lives of Eminent Philosophers. Loeb Classical Library 184 and 185 (Cited as DL).

TRAGICORUM graecorum fragmenta. Rec. Aug. Nauck. Lipsiae, 1889.

VORSOKRATIKER, Die Fragmente der -- griechisch und deutsch. Herausgegeben von Hermann Diels. Sechste verbesserte Auflage herausgegeben von Walther Kranz. Teil II. Berlin, 1952 (cited as DK).

B INDIVIDUAL AUTHORS

AESCHINES
  The Speeches of --. Loeb Classical Library 106 (cited as Aeschin.). Translated by C.D.Adams.

AESCHYLUS
  Loeb Classical Library 145 and 146 (cited as Aesch.). Translation by H. Weird Smyth.

  Agamemnon (Ag.)
  Eumenides (Eum.)
  Prometheus bound (Prom.)
  Seven against Thebes (Hepta).

ANTIPHON
  Ant., fragments in DK.

ARCHELAUS, fragments in DK.

ARISTOPHANES
Loeb Classical Library 178, 179, 180 (cited as Aristoph.). Translated by Benjamin Bickely Rogers.

The Birds
The Clouds
Ekklesiazousai (Ekkl.)
The Frogs (Batr.)
The Knights (Hipp.)
Lysistrata (Lys.)
Thesmophoriazousai (Thesm.).

ARISTOTLE
Loeb Classical Library, 23 vol. (cited as Ar.).

De Anima (On the Soul, De An.)
De Caelo (On the Heavens)
On Dreams
Eudemian Ethics (EE)
De Generatione Animalium (De Gen.An.)
Metaphysics (Met.)
Magna Moralia (MM)
Nicomachean Ethics (NE)
Physics (Phys.)
Poetica (Poet.)
Politeia (Pol.).

ATHENAEUS
The Deipnosophists (cited as Ath.). Loeb Classical Library 235 (Vol. IV). Translated by Charles Burton Gulick.

AULUS GELLIUS
Attic Nights (Noctes Atticae). Loeb Classical Library 212 (Vol. III). Translated by John C.Rolfe.

CRITIAS
Krit., fragments in DK.

DIODORUS SICULUS
Library of History. Loeb Classical Library 279 (Vol. I, cited as Diod. Sic.). Translated by C.H.Oldfather.

EURIPIDES
Loeb Classical Library 9, 10, 11, 12 (cited as Eur.). Translated by A.S. Way.

Andromache (Andr.)
The Bacchanals (Bacch.)
The Children of Heracles (Herakleidai)
Cyclops (Kykl.)
The Daughters of Troy (Troiades)

EURIPIDES (continued)
 Hecuba (Hek.)
 Helen (Hel.)
 Hippolytus (Hipp.)
 Ion
 Iphigeneia in Aulis (Iph.Aul.)
 Iphigeneia in Tauris (Iph.Taur.)
 The Madness of Heracles (Her.Main.)
 Medea (Med.)
 Orestes (Or.)
 The Phoenician Maidens (Phoin.)
 Suppliants (Hik.).

GORGIAS
 Gorg., fragments in DK.

HERODOTUS
 Historiai. Loeb Classical Library 117 (Vol. I, cited as Her.). Translated by A.D.Godley.

HOMER
 The Iliad (cited as Il.). Translated by E.V.Rieu. Penguin Classics L14. 1950.
 The Odyssey (cited as Od.). Translated by E.V.Rieu. Penguin Classics L1. 1958 (1946[1]).

PLATO
 Loeb Classical Library, twelve vol.

 Apology (Ap.)
 Charmides (Charm.)
 Cratylus (Krat.)
 Critias
 Crito
 Euthydemus (Euth.)
 Eutyphron (Eutyphr.)
 Gorgias (Gorg.)
 Hippias Major (Hipp.Maj.)
 Hippias Minor (Hipp.Min.)
 Laches (Lach.)
 Laws
 Letters (Ep.)
 Lysis (Lys.)
 Menexenus (Menex.)
 Meno
 Parmenides (Parm.)
 Phaedo
 Phaedrus (Phaedr.)
 Philebus (Phil.)
 Protagoras (Prot.)
 The Republic (Pol.)

PLATO (continued)
The Statesman (Politic.)
The Sophist (Soph.)
Theaetetus (Theait.)
Timaeus (Tim.).

PROTAGORAS
Prot., fragments in DK.

PSEUDO-ARISTOTLE
De Melisso, Xenophane, Gorgia (cited as MXG). Immanuel Bekker, Aristotelis Opera graece. Vol. II, Berolini, 1831.

SEXTUS EMPIRICUS (cited as Sext.Emp.)
Adversus Logicos (Adv.Log.)
Adversus Mathematicos (Adv.Math.)
Adversus Physicos (Adv.Phys.).

SIMPLICIUS (cited as Simpl.)
In Aristotelis Categorias Commentarium (in cat.Ar.). Ed. H.Kalbfleisch. Berolini, 1907
In Aristotelis Physica Commentaria (in Phys.Ar.). Ed. H.Diels. Berolini, 1895.

SOPHOCLES
Loeb Classical Library 20 and 21 (cited as Soph.). Translated by F.Storr.

Antigone (Ant.)
King Oedipus (Oed.Rex)
Oedipus in Colonus (Oid.Kol.)
Trachiniae (Trach.)

XENOPHON
Memorabilia. Loeb Classical Library 168 (Vol. IV, cited as Xen.,Mem.). Translated by E.C.Marchant.

II SECONDARY WORKS

A WORKS OF REFERENCE

Lexicon der Alten Welt. Zürich und Stuttgart (1965) (cited as Lex.d. Alt.Welt).

Paulys Real-Encyclopädie der classischen Altertumswissenschaft. Neue Bearbeitung von Georg Wissowa. Stuttgart (cited as PW).

B MONOGRAPHS

AUGER, Danièle, Le théâtre d'Aristophane. Le mythe, l'utopie et les femmes. Cahiers de Fontenay nr. 17. Aristophane, les femmes et la cité. Déc. 1979.

BERTI, Enrico, Aristote était-il un penseur dualiste? Thêta Phi II no. 2 (Oct. 1973), 73-111.

BOGNER, Hans, Der tragische Gegensatz. Seine Entdeckung und Gestaltung in der frühgriechischen Tragödie. Heidelberg, 1947.

BULLOUGH, Vern L. (with the assistance of Bonnie Bullough), The Subordinate Sex. A History of Atitudes towards Women. Chicago/London (1973).

COPLESTON s.J., Frederick, A History of Philosophy. Vol. I, Part I and II. New York, 1962 (1946^1).

DAWE, R.D, Some Reflections on ate and hamartia. Series : Harvard Studies in Classical Philology 72 (1967).

DECHARME, Paul, Euripide et l'esprit de son théâtre. Paris, 1893 (impression anastatique Bruxelles 1966).

DRACHMANN, A.B., Atheism in Antiquity. Chicago, 1977 (Atheisme i det antike hedenskab. København, 1919).

EHRENBERG, Victor, Man, State and Deity. London, 1974.

ELLIS-FERMOR, Una, The Frontiers of Drama. London, 1927.

FRESCO, M.F., Sokrates. Zijn wijsgerige betekenis. Assen, 1983.

FRITZ, Kurt von, Tragische Schuld und poetische Gerechtigkeit in der griechischen Tragödie. In : Antike und Moderne Tragödie. Berlin, 1962.

GAGARIN, Michel, Aeschylean Drama. Berkeley (Cal.) (1976).

GRAESER, Andreas, Die Philosophie der Antike 2. Sophistik und Sokratik, Plato und Aristoteles. Geschichte der Philosophie, herausgegeben von Wolfgang Röd. Bd. II. München (1983).

GREENE, W.C., Moira. Fate, God and Evil in Greek Thought. Harper Torch Book. New York, 1963 (1944^1).

GRIFFITH, Mark, The Authenticity of 'Prometheus Bound'. London, 1977.

GRUBE, G.M.A., Zeus in Aeschylus. American Journal of Philosophy 91 (1970). Also as : Zeus bei Aischylos. Wege zu Aischylos II. Herausgegeben von Hildebrecht Hommel. Darmstadt, 1974.

GUTHRIE, W.K.C., A History of Greek Philosophy. Cambridge, Vol. III (1969). Volume IV (1975), Volume V (1978), Vol. VI (1981).

HEINIMANN, Felix, Nomos und Physis. Herkunft und Bedeutung einer Antithese im griechischen Denken des 5. Jahrhunderts. Schweizerische Beiträge zur Altertumswissenschaft. Heft 1. Basel, 1965.

HENDERSON, Jeffrey, 1. Lysistrata. The Play and its Themes. In : Aristophanes, Essays in Interpretation. Ed. Jeffrey Henderson. Cambridge (Mass.) (1980);
2. The Maculate Muse. Obscene Language in Attic Comedy. New Haven and London, 1975.

LLOYD-JONES, Hugh, 1. The Suppliants of Aeschylus. The New Date and Old Problems. L'Antiquité Classique 33 (1904), also in Wege zu Aisch. (see under Grube);
2. Zeus in Aeschylus. Journal of Hellenic Studies 76 (1956). Also as : Zeus bei Aischylos. In Wege (see under 1).

LORAUX, Nicole, Les enfants d'Athèna. Idées athéniennes sur la citoyenneté et la division des sexes. Série : Textes à l'appui. · Paris, 1981.

LYONS, John, 1. Introduction to theoretical linguistics. Cambridge, 1968;
2. Semantics. Cambridge, 1977;
3. Structural Semantics. An analysis of part of the vocabulary of Plato. Oxford, 1963.

MAIR, Lucy, Marriage. London, 1971 (I used the Dutch translation by Enny and Lodewijk Brunt : Het Huwelijk. Meppel, 1974).

MOLINE, Jon, Plato's Theory of Understanding. Madison (Wisc.), 1981.

MORAUX, P., A propos de nous thuratên chez Aristote. In : Récueil offert à Mgr. A.Mansion. Louvain, 1955.

NEBEL, Gerhard, Weltangst und Götterzorn. Eine Deutung der griechischen Tragödie. Stuttgart (1951).

NILSSON, Martin P., Geschichte der griechischen Religion. I. Band Die Religion der Griechen bis auf die griechische Weltherrschaft. Handbuch der Altertumswissenschaft V 2.1. München, 1967.

OPSTELTEN, J.C., Sophocles en het Griekse pessimisme. Leiden, 1945.

PETREMENT, Simone, Le dualisme chez Platon, les Gnostiques et les Manichéens. Bibliothèque de philosophie contemporaine. Paris, 1947.

POMEROY, Sarah B., Goddesses, Whores, Wives and Slaves. New York (1975).

POPPER, K.R., The Open Society and its Enemies. Vol. I. London (1965^5, revised edition (1945^1).

RAPHAEL, D.D., The Paradox of Tragedy. The Mahlon Powell Lectures 1959. London (1960).

ROSELLINI, Michèle, Lysistrata : une mise en scène de la féminité. Cahiers de Fontenay nr. 17 (see under Auger).

ROSSET, Clément, La philosophie tragique. Paris, 1960.

SAID, Suzanne, 1. L'assemblée des femmes : les femmes, l'économie et la politique. Cahiers de Fontenay nr. 17 (see under Auger).
2. La faute tragique. Textes à l'appui. Paris, 1978.

SEGAL, Charles, Tragedy and Civilization. An Interpretation of Sophocles. Cambridge (Mass.)/London, 1981.

STALLEY, R.F., An Introduction to Plato's Laws. Oxford, 1983.

TAYLOR, A.E., Plato. The Man and his work. London (1960^7, 1926^1).

TRILLING, Lionel, Sincerity and Authenticity. Cambridge (Mass.), 1972.

UNTERSTEINER, Mario, 1. Le origini della tragedia. Serie : Il pensiere greco. Vol. 16. Milano, 1942;
2. The Sophists (translated from the Italian by Kathleen Freeman). Oxford, 1954.

VERRALL, A.W., Euripides the Rationalist. A Study in the History of Art and Religion. Cambridge, 1913.

VOGEL, Cornelia de, Was Plato a Dualist? In : Thêta Phi (see under Berti).

WALDOCK, A.J.A., Sophocles the Dramatist. Cambridge, 1960.

WEBER, Alfred, Das Tragische und die Geschichte. Hamburg, 1943.

WHITE, Nicholas R., Plato on Knowledge and Reality. Indianapolis (1976).

WHITMAN, Cedric H., Aristophanes and the Comic Hero. Martin Classical Lectures. Vol. XIX. Cambridge (Mass.), 1964.

WINNINGTON-INGRAM, R.P., Sophocles. An Interpretation. Cambridge, 1980.

ZAWADKA, Irene, Die Echtheit des 'Gefesselten Prometheus'. Geschichte und gegenwärtiger Stand der Forschung. 1966. In 'Wege zu Aischylos', ed. Hildebrecht Hommel. II, 333-351.

GENERAL INDEX

Abdera, 86
Abisai, 58
Academy (of Plato), 120, 121, 127, 132, 155, 182, 183, 202
Achaeans, 57
Achilles, 6, 7, 10
Acropolis of Athens, 52, 53
Admetus, 82
Adrastus, 42
Aegean Sea, 59
Aegisthus, 5, 8, 33, 34, 35, 42
Aeolians, 58
Aeropage, 9
Aeschines, 116
Aeschylus, 1, 3, 8-9, 13, 25-32, 32-35, 45, 54, 64, 66, 69, 71, 78, 79, 80, 123
Aethra, 45
Agamemnon, 6, 8, 33, 34, 46, 64, 68, 82
Agathon, 49
Agave, 21, 22, 35
agnosticism, agnostic, 24, 69, 88
Ajax, 6, 24
Akademos, 120
Albee, Edward, 11
Alcestis, 82
Alcibiades, 103, 106, 134, 138
Alexander, Alexandrus see Paris
Alexander the Great, 183
Alexander Polyhistor, 179, 209
Allen, Woody, 36
Ammonius, 100
Amphitryon (father of Heracles), 2
Amyntas III, 182
Anaxagoras, 55, 91, 101
Anaximander, 91
Anaximenes, 91
Andromache, 6, 7, 10
Andronicus, 210
Andros, 182
anthropology, anthropological, 89, 90, 101, 125
Antigone, 3, 4, 10, 35, 42, 65, 72, 73
Antiphon (philosopher), 104, 116
Antiphon (half-brother of Plato), 156
Antippe, 41
Antisthenes, 100
Aphrodite, 16, 17, 18, 19, 20, 21, 41, 47, 77
Apollo, 9, 18, 19, 20, 32, 44, 108, 183
Archelaus (king), 55
Archelaus (philosopher), 101, 116
Archytas, 120
Argeia, 42
Argos, Argive, 3, 9, 14, 34, 35, 42, 45, 76
Aristides, 127
Aristodemus, 12
Aristophanes, 12, 37, 47-54, 56, 76, 81, 82, 84, 105, 106, 115, 123, 152
Aristotle, 62-64, 64, 67, 71, 72, 82, 83, 96, 100, 106, 110, 112, 113, 116, 117, 120, 121, 178, 181, 182-201 passim, 201, 208, 209, 210, 211
Artemis, 5, 9, 19
Artemisium (battle of), 54
Asclepius, 24
Asia Minor, 57, 58, 183
Assus, 183
astronomy, 120
Astyanax, 6
Atarneus, 183
atheism, atheistic, atheists, 12, 13, 20, 69, 70, 86, 88, 90, 91, 106, 142
Athena, 16, 18, 19, 24, 33, 52
Athenaeus, 79

Athenian(s), 18, 40, 44, 45, 47, 50, 52, 57, 61, 65, 67, 68, 81, 85, 89, 105, 110, 119, 124, 126, 137, 149, 154, 162, 166, 171, 182
Athens, 3, 9, 14, 15, 19, 40, 41, 51, 53, 55, 56, 85, 87, 89, 104, 105, 106, 119, 120, 126, 127, 152, 154, 162, 182, 183
Atreus, 4, 5
Atrides, 1, 4, 15, 37, 65, 68
Attica, Attic, 1, 3, 54
Auger, D., 50, 81
Aulis, 5, 9
Aulus Gellius, 43, 80

Bacchant(s), 23
Bacchus see Dionysus
Balkans, 57
barbarian(s), 8, 10, 46, 58, 187, 188, 198
Bayreuth, 57
Beethoven, Ludwig von, 55
Beowulf, 58
Berti, E., 192, 193, 210
Björnbo, 115
Blumenthal, von, 81
Boeotia, 2
Bogner, H., 150, 205
Bullough, V. and B., 80

Cadmeia, 2
Cadmus, 2
Calchas, 5, 6
Callias, 87, 99
Callicles, 102-103, 126, 127, 128, 131
Canaan, 57
Cassandra, 6, 7, 8, 34
Cassola, Carlo, 80
Castor, 5
Cephalus, 137, 156
Chalcidice, 182
Chalcis, 183
Charmides, 123
China, Chinese, 55, 57, 58
Christ, 29
Christian(s), 29
Chryseis, 34
Clazomenae, 156
Clisthenes, 150
Clytaemnestra, 5, 8, 18, 33, 34, 35, 42, 64, 74

Colonus, 3, 54
Copleston, F., 115, 116, 201, 205
Cordelia, 40
Corinth(ian), 3, 44, 72, 97
Corpus Hippocraticum, 45
Corsica(n), 76
cosmos, 23, 59, 167, 168, 169, 170, 171, 172, 174, 178, 180, 198, 199
Couperus, Louis, 160
Cratylus, 97, 99
Creon, 2, 3, 4, 14, 15, 35, 43, 44
Crete, 41, 57
Creusa (daughter of Creon), 44
Creusa (daughter of Erechtheus), 19, 20, 44
Crimea, 9
Critias, 89-90, 106, 113, 124
Crito, 107
Cronus, 27
Cyclades, 87
Cypris see Aphrodite

Darius I, 82
David, 58, 59
Dawe, R.D., 82
Decharme, P., 16, 22, 76, 77
deism, 174
Delphi (oracle of), 9, 10, 19, 28, 65, 110
Demeter, 88
Demiurge, 168-173, 174, 175, 178, 180, 209
democracy, democratic, 14, 50, 52, 106, 125, 126, 149, 150, 161, 162, 186
Democritus, 94
Demosthenes, 183
Diagoras, 91
Dietrich, A., 81
Diodorus Siculus, 79
Diogenes Laertius, 184, 202, 209
Diomedes, 6
Dion, 119, 120
Dionysius I, 119, 120
Dionysius II, 120
Dionysus(-cult), 2, 20, 30, 56, 57, 60, 61, 62, 70, 88
Dioscuri, 5
Diotima, 143
Dolon, 5, 6
Dorian(s), 58

Drachmann, A.B., 76, 88, 90, 115
dualism, dualistic, 23, 24, 40, 61, 62, 68, 69, 73, 71-75, 77, 93, 98, 100, 104, 107, 109, 111, 113, 114, 124, 125, 130, 131, 133, 134, 135, 139, 141, 144, 147, 148, 149, 152, 153, 155, 157, 158, 161, 165, 166, 172, 173-180, 180-181, 181-182, 184, 188, 189, 190-192, 192, 194, 195, 197, 199, 201, 210
Dutch, 80, 84, 99, 160

Eeden, Frederik van, 99
Egypt(ian), 7, 16, 57, 79, 88, 119
Ehrenberg, V., 79
Eisenstein, Sergej, 55
Eleates, Eleatic School, 87, 91, 92, 94, 124, 160
Electra, 8, 9, 35, 42, 45, 73, 76
Eleusis, 54
Elis, 4, 87
Ellis-Fermor, U., 69, 83
Empedocles, 92, 211
Enlightenment, 90, 174
Epimetheus, 31
Er (myth of), 138
Erechtheus, 19
Erinyes, 9, 64, 68
Eros, 134, 137, 138, 143
esoteric, 109
Eteocles, 3, 4, 32, 35, 42
ether, 198, 199
ethics, 95, 96, 101, 103
Etna, 66
Euboea, 183
Euripides, 1, 2, 3, 5, 6-8, 9-10, 12-24 passim, 24, 25, 41, 43-46, 49, 50, 54, 55, 56, 64, 68, 76, 77, 80, 81, 82, 91
Europe(an), 85, 120
Eurydice, 4, 35
Eurystheus, 18
Eutyphron, 111

Farnell, L.R., 79
Festugière, A.J., 79
Flake, Otto, 83
Fontenelle, B., 67, 82
Fresco, M.F., 106, 107, 116, 117
Fritz, K. von, 71, 72, 74, 83, 115

Furies see Erinyes
Fyfe, W.Hamilton, 83

Gagarin, M., 34, 78, 79
Gela, 54
German, 80, 131
Germanic, 58
Gigon, O., 115
Gnostic(ism), gnosis, 23, 24, 68, 74-75, 98, 107, 109, 110, 134, 145, 146, 147, 201
Goethe, J.W., 29, 63
Golden Fleece, 44
Goliath, 59
Gorgias, 86-87, 92-95, 99, 116, 127
Graeser, A., 89, 93, 100, 115, 116, 198, 202, 210
Greene, W.C., 25, 77, 78
Griffith, M., 78
Grube, G.M.A., 79
Guthrie, W.K.C., 95, 100, 107, 115, 116, 117, 118, 174, 175, 199, 207, 208, 210, 211

Haemon, 4, 35, 42, 43
Hamlyn, D.W., 205
Hecabe, 5, 6, 7, 13, 14, 16, 17, 19, 46
Hector, 6, 7, 10
Hegel, F.W., 125
Heinimann, F., 100, 102, 116
Helen, 5, 7, 9, 10, 16, 17, 18, 19, 35, 46
Helios, 16
Henderson, J., 81
Hephaestus, 88
Hera, 2, 16, 17, 18, 20, 27, 60
Heracles, 2, 6, 15, 17, 18, 35, 45, 66, 82
Heraclitus, 91, 97, 124, 140, 141, 146, 160, 161
Hermes, 19, 28
Hermione, 9, 10, 81
Hermodorus, 178
Hermogenes, 99, 100
Herodotus, 76
Hieron I, 54
Hesiod(ic), 30, 31
Hett, W.S., 190
Hildebrand, 58

Hippias, 87, 111, 114
Hippodamia, 4
Hippolyte see Antippe
Hippolytus, 19, 41, 47
Hitchcock, Alfred, 202
Hoffmannsthal, Hugo von, 83
Hogarth Press, 82
Holst, Henriette Roland, 44
Homer(ic), 17, 29, 30, 63, 71, 130, 134
Hyksos, 57

Iliad, 5, 59, 63, 82
Inachus, 27
incest(uous), 38-43, 80
India(n), 57, 58
Indo-European, 61
Io, 27, 29
Iocaste, 2, 3, 15, 35, 40, 45
Ion, 20
Ionian(s), 58, 59, 70, 91, 92, 98
Iphigeneia, 5, 8, 14, 15, 33, 34, 35, 46, 64
Iran, 57
Iris, 18
Ismene, 3, 35
Israel, 57, 62, 174
Italian, Italy, 80, 86, 119, 120, 130
Iulia, 87

Jahve, 30, 174
Jason, 35, 43, 44, 80

Kaiser, K., 201
Keos, 87
Kitto, H.D.F., 30
Krämer, H.J., 201
Ku Klux Klan, 163
Kubrick, Stanley, 55

Laius, 2, 3, 35
Lamb, W.R.M., 123, 202
Lavoisier, A.-L., 211
Lear, King, 40
Leda, 5
Lemnos, 6
Leontini, 86
Lesbos, 183
Lesher, J.H., 205
Lloyd-Jones, H., 30, 78, 79
Loraux, N., 46, 81

Lucas, F.W., 67, 82
Lyceum, 183
Lycus (king of Thebes), 2
Lyons, J., 146, 205
Lysistrata, 48, 52-53

Macaria, 45
Macbeth, 33, 76
Macedonia(n), 55, 182, 183, 187
Maenad(s), 21, 22
Magna Mater, 60
Mair, L., 80
Malle, Louis, 38
Mansfeld, J., 177
Marathon (battle of), 52, 54
Marx, Karl, 125
Massari, Léa, 38
mathematics, -icians, 120, 148, 149
Medea, 10, 35, 43, 44, 67
Mediterranean Sea, 60, 61
Megara (city), 119
Megara (wife of Heracles), 2
Meletus, 123
Melos, 91
Menelaus, 5, 6, 7, 8, 9, 10, 13, 33, 35, 46, 76
Menoeceus, 14
Merimée, Prosper, 76
Middle Ages, 55, 184
Minos, 41
Mitchell, Margaret, 115
Mnesilochus, 49, 50
Moira, 23
Moline, J., 205
Molossus, 10
monism, 174, 175
monotheistic, 143
Moraux, P., 192, 210
Muse, 109
Mussert, A., 80
Musset, Alfred de, 70
Mycenae(an), 2, 4, 8, 64
Mytilene, 183

Nebel, G., 61, 64, 65, 66, 68, 70, 82, 83
neohumanism, 10, 60
Neoptolemus, 6, 10
Nestle, W., 18, 30, 76, 77, 79
Netherlands, the, 38, 44
New Testament, 30

Nibelungen (see also : Ring), 58
Nicholas Damascus, 210
Nicias, 111
Nietzsche, F., 66, 83, 103
nihilism, 24
Nile, 88
Nilsson, M.P., 15, 22, 23, 24, 45, 76, 77, 78, 79
nominalism, 94, 98-100, 195
nomos-physis, 98, 100-104, 126
North-Africa, 119

Oceanides, 28
Oceanus, 26, 28
Odysseus, 6, 24
Odyssey, 63
Oedipus, 2, 3, 4, 17, 25, 35, 37, 40, 41, 63, 65, 68, 69, 72, 73, 75
Old Testament, 30
Olympian gods, 13, 14, 16, 17, 18, 22, 23, 24, 31, 32, 66, 98, 101, 142, 174, 198, 200
Olympian religion, 14, 21, 24, 32, 69-71, 89, 91, 98, 113
Olympic Games, 4, 85
Olympus, 28
Opstelten, J.C., 24, 78
Orestes, 8, 9, 10, 17, 32, 35, 42, 45, 64, 74, 76
Orphic, 131, 134

Paris, 5, 6, 7, 16, 19, 46
Parmenides, 87, 91, 92, 93, 97, 109, 124, 141, 144, 156-161, 175, 177, 195
Pascal, Blaise, 174
Peleus, 10
Pella, 55, 183
Peloponnese, -sian, 87, 105
Pelops, 4
Pentheus, 2, 21, 35
Pericles, 12, 55, 86, 127, 154
Perls, H., 145, 205
Persia(n)(s), 15, 75, 86
Pêtrement, S., 124, 202
Phaedra, 19, 41, 65, 67
phenomenalism, 95, 97
Pherae, 82
Philippus II, 183
Philolaus, 130
Philoctetes, 6

Phocis, 8
Phoebus see Apollo
Phrygia(n), 60
physis see nomos-physis
Piraeus, 89
Plataeae, battle of, 54
Plato, Platonic, 30, 70, 79, 84, 87, 88, 93, 94, 95, 97, 98, 99, 100, 102, 103, 106, 107, 108, 111, 112, 113, 114, 115, 116, 117, 118, 119-182 passim, 183, 184, 189, 191, 194, 195, 197, 199, 201, 202, 203, 204, 205, 206, 207, 208, 209, 210, 211
Plutarch, 15, 76
Pollux, 5
Polydorus, 7
Polymestor, 7, 46
Polynices, 3, 4, 17, 35, 42, 43, 45, 64
Polyxena, 7, 14, 15
Pomeroy, S., 34, 43, 45, 79
Popper, K., 125, 133
Poseidon, 88
Praxagora, 50, 52
Priam, 5, 6, 7
Prodicus, 87, 88-89, 115
Prometheus, 10, 26-32, 66, 69, 71, 78, 79
Protagoras, 55, 85, 86, 88, 95-97, 97, 101, 102, 116, 125, 126, 140
Ptolemaeus, 80
Pylades, 8, 9, 42, 80
Pythagorean(s), 79, 111, 120, 124, 130, 131, 134, 150, 179, 199, 209
Pythia, 19

Racine, Jean, 19, 55
Raphael, D.D., 74, 82, 83
Reformation, 55
Reinhardt, K., 79
relativism, 92, 94, 95, 98, 140
Renaissance, 10
Rhesus, 5, 6
rhetoric, 85, 86, 92, 94, 111
Richards, I.A., 69
Ring des Nibelungen, 55, 62
Roman(s), 29
Romanticism, 29
Rosellini, M., 53, 81
Rosset, C., 65, 66. 67, 82, 83

Rossini, Gioacchino, 8

Said, S., 51, 52, 72, 81, 83
Salamis (battle of), 15, 52, 54, 55
satyr, 46
Scamander, 18
Schmid, 79
Schwinge, E.R., 81
Sea League, 54
Segal, Ch., 35, 79
Semele, 60
Sextus Empiricus, 115, 116, 179, 209
sexuality, 37, 137, 164, 184, 185
Shakespeare, William, 55
Shelley, Percy B., 29
Sicily, 54, 86, 119, 120, 130, 132
Siegfried, 80
Sieglinde, 80
Siegmund, 80
Simplicius, 100, 116, 209
Sisyphus, 90
Socrates, 55, 56, 70, 85, 87, 91, 95, 97, 98, 99, 100, 102, 103, 104-114, 116, 117, 119, 121, 122, 123, 124, 126, 127, 128, 130, 131, 132, 134, 136, 137, 138, 140, 141, 143, 156-161, 181
Solon, 84
Sophist(s), Sophism, 24, 70, 84-104 passim, 105, 106, 109, 110, 114, 112, 120, 124, 125, 139, 140, 159, 188, 194
Sophocles, 1, 2, 3, 4, 6, 8, 18, 24-25, 25, 31, 35, 39, 39-41, 42, 43, 54-55, 56, 68, 76, 78, 79, 80, 123, 186
Sparta(n)(s), Spartiate, 5, 7, 16, 52, 151
Stagira (Stagiros), 182
Stalley, R.F., 162, 207
Stein, Gertrud, 100
Stesichorus, 7, 76
Stesilaus, 123
Stobaeus, 79
Storr, F., 25
Strauss, Richard, 83
Syracuse, 54, 119, 120, 155, 161

Tantalus, 4
Tarent, 120
Tartarus, 28, 127, 138
Tauris, 5, 9
Taylor, A.E., 120, 201
Tertullian, 29
Thales, 70, 191
Thaltybius, 23
Thebes, Thebans, 1, 2, 3, 14, 18, 21, 32, 41, 42
theism, theistic, 174, 175
Themistocles, 15
Theophrastus, 183
theorem of Pythagoras, 131
Theseus, 3, 14, 41, 45, 69
Thoas, 9
Thrace, 5, 7, 14
Thucydides, 12
Thurii, 86, 102
Thyestes, 4, 5, 8
Tiresias, 4, 14, 22, 130
Titan(s), 26, 28, 29, 30, 31, 66, 69, 70
Trilling, L., 36, 79
Troy, Trojan(s), 1, 4, 5, 6, 7, 8, 14, 16, 17, 18, 19, 33, 34, 35, 46, 57, 68
Tyndareus, 5

Untersteiner, M., 59, 60, 61, 82, 93, 95, 96, 97, 115, 116
Uranus, 27

Verdi, Giuseppe, 55
Verrall, A.W., 13, 21, 76, 77
Vogel, C. de, 174, 176-180, 192, 209

Wagner, Richard, 55, 61, 80
Waldock, A.J.A., 42, 80
Warsaw, 103
Weber, A., 55, 57, 58, 59, 61, 62, 82
Wellmann, E., 115
White, N., 145, 205
Whitman, C., 49, 81
Wilamowitz-Moellendorf, U. von, 79
Winnington-Ingram, R.P., 77
Witlam, R., 80
Woolf, Leonard and Virginia, 82

Xanthippe, 105

Xeniades, 97
Xenophon, 76, 106, 108, 115, 116, 117
Xerxes I, 15, 65, 71, 86

Zawadka, I., 26, 78
Zemelo, 60